translation
Jeremy Scott
editorial coordination
Giovanna Crespi
graphic design
Tassinari/Vetta (CODEsign)
page layout
Paola Forini
editing
Gail Swerling
photo research
Sonia Servida
cover design
CODEsign
technical coordination
Mario Farè
quality control
Giancarlo Berti

Distributed by Phaidon Press
ISBN 1-904313-34-5

www.phaidon.com

www.electaweb.it

First published in English 2005

Printed in Hong Kong

Electaarchitecture

RAILWAY STATIONS

from the gare de l'est to penn station

alessia ferrarini

aix-en-provence
arnhem
berlin
florence
frankfurt-am-main
kyoto
lyons
london
new york
paris
singapore
seville
zurich

the railway station: an urban monument to progress

alessia ferrarini

This discussion of various train stations built over the last one hundred and fifty years aims to chart a history of the "paradigm shifts" in railway architecture,[1] selecting and analyzing examples that played a key role in defining what would then become important models of reference for such buildings.

For many years, railway stations were the "monuments" around which large modern cities developed, structures that reflected the nature and embodied the characteristic features of their urban location. Marcel Proust, in fact, saw train stations as containing the very "spirit" of the city, just as they were identified with its name on a large platform signpost. These buildings reveal the essence of the city because, to a certain extent, they are the mirror of it; their size and structure reflecting many characteristics of urban existence and life. But, at the same time, train stations are also an expression of the architectural and artistic trends of the period in which they are built; indeed, sometimes, they become the most significant expression of such trends. For example, when—towards the middle of the nineteenth century—railway architecture was taking form, important technological innovations in the use of cast iron and glass meant that the wide, arching roofs of train sheds became the most spectacular feature of the new stations—the very symbol of their role as functional environments.

In the late nineteenth and early twentieth century, the "representative" role of the station was performed by a large building which fronted that functional structure. In Beaux-Arts or eclectic style, this station building proper was characteristically made up of atmospheric spaces on a vast scale. In the period after the First World War, this palatial notion of stations gave way to designs that focused on essential geometrical forms that were stripped of adornment. And in our own age, there has been a tendency for stations to be envisaged as multi-level "machines," large-scale junctions through which flow various forms of traffic (a notion that was already prefigured in the visionary projects and designs of Sant'Elia). However, from the extant stations of the nineteenth century to the new stations that are still under construction, the history of this architecture can be read as a sort of palimpsest, with traces of more recent periods overlaying those of the past. Borrowing a notion from Walter Benjamin,[2] one might argue that the history of railway architecture is not a linear but a stratified history, not a continuous narrative but one in which interruption and overlapping can be seen. Within this vast accumulation of material I have tried to draw up a history, charting the ways in which the railway station has been envisaged as an emblem of the city itself. What emerges is a stratified narrative that affords glimpses of the essence of the urban reality such architecture is intended to serve. In effect, the railway station is an urban monument to progress; a gateway to the city, it is also a machine in its own right, the place where traffic is *in actu*.

Tradition and innovation

Discussing early railway architecture in England and France, Alan Colquhoun[3] claims that the station was the most "subversive" tangible expression of the Industrial Revolution; more so even than factories, because while they were isolated in peripheral areas, the station was the first industrial structure to be raised in the very heart of the city. What is more, these buildings were home to a "new type of machinery," which was no longer a static implement of production but a dynamic instrument for public use. This originality of function and location meant that the station was a "new" type of architecture that was highly symbolic. It brought the machine—the train—right into the center of the city and, at the same time, was designed to receive from the city the people who were about to employ this new mode of transport. Hence, the station was a place of transit, where two very different types of traffic—trains and people—interacted and co-existed. This specific feature of the building, as a space within which man and machine came into contact with each other, would have a great influence on the canons employed in this very special—and heterogeneous—type of architecture. From its earliest days, in fact, the station was made up of two conjoined parts[4] that were wildly out of proportion with each other. On the one hand there was the train shed—that is, the industrial space of the station—and on

Crown Street Station, Liverpool 1829–30

King's Cross Station, London 1851–52

Euston Station, London 1835–39

Hauptbahnhof, Frankfurt 1879–88

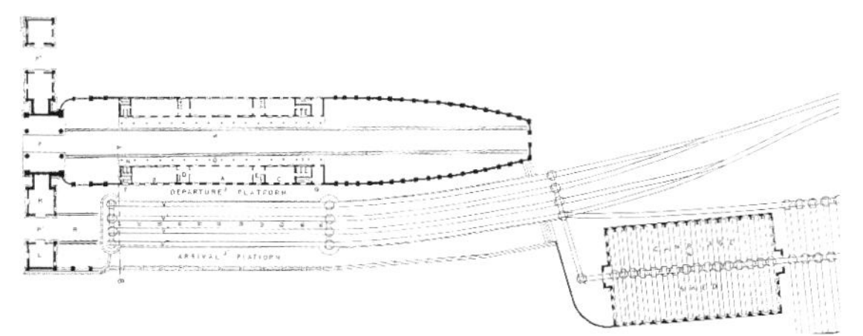

the other, the station building proper, designed to receive travelers. This latter was a "filter" between the urban fabric of the city and the railway; its cosmetic ornamentalism was intended to disguise the "technological" and machine-inspired nature of the train shed beyond it.
The first railway station in the world was the Crown Street Station in Liverpool which was built in 1829–30—with the assistance of the railway engineer George Stephenson—and set the benchmark for future developments in this type of architecture. Made up of two distinct but conjoined parts—a wooden vault over the tracks and a building rather similar to the post inns of the day—it has been defined by Meeks[5] as a "precursor" precisely because this dual nature reflects what would be the essential feature of all the great railway stations of the nineteenth century. The physical interface between city and train shed would be provided by the façade and body of the structure designed to receive passengers; turned towards the city itself, this latter building—in both its size and structure—obeyed the design and aesthetic canons applied in traditional urban architecture. The station building, therefore, was a sort of limit or boundary between the space of the railway and the traditional urban fabric; the former was on a vast, open scale, the latter more circumscribed and closely defined.
As Alan Colquhoun points out, it was this reception structure, conceived of as a sort of propylaeum, that stimulated the imagination of nineteenth-century architects. Built between 1835 and 1839 by Philip Hardwock and Robert Stephenson, Euston Station in London[6] is a typical example of the use of ornament to disguise the industrial character of stations. Approached by a monumental Greek portal which emphasized the role of the station as a gateway to the city, the building illustrates a point which Benjamin took up from Giedion when he observed that "the nineteenth century covered every new creation with the mask of history... New means of construction were being created, but they caused a certain amount of fear, and were endlessly disguised behind stage-sets of stone... These historically inspired masks are indissolubly linked with the image of the nineteenth century and their existence cannot be ignored."[7] In railway stations, it was the façade that performed this role of the "historically inspired mask";[8] reiterating the academic notions of an architecture of the past, it echoed the private villa, the town hall and the basilica, incorporating such features as the triumphal arch and the bell-tower. The impact of the new railway upon the urban fabric was mediated by a station building that was presented in familiar terms.[9]

However, once under the glass-and-iron vault of the train shed, the traveler was overwhelmed by the novelty and power of the vast space in which he found himself—a disturbing locus in which the machine seemed to predominate. It was this industrial character which made the station an alien presence in the urban fabric. The preserve of engineers alone, the enormous train sheds were structures in which the most daring and innovative techniques could be tried out; originally in wood, they were then constructed in glass and iron—materials which made it possible to cover much vaster areas and thus raise imposing edifices within the heart of the city.

As Walter Benjamin notes in his "Constructions in Iron,"[10] the introduction and spread of this material introduced a new art of building, with structural statics being conceived on a much mightier scale than had been the case in Greek or medieval architecture. The new system for building vaults over railway tracks initiated a "reign of new forms"; architecture in iron and glass brought with it a new organization of space. According to Meyer,[11] the use of iron to create weight-bearing structures and glass as a roofing material undermined consolidated architectural values and brought about a revolution that had three distinct effects: the values of force and mass were turned upside down (calculation of statics made it possible to establish the minimum quantity of materials required for a structure; forces could be calculated rationally—that is, divided into those of traction and compression—and the end result was a solid structure apparently without mass); the notion of the delimitation of space was undercut (the wall mass was reduced to thin surfaces delimiting space); the values of light and shade were reversed (before the advent of electric light, the glass roofs of these vast spaces provided more uniform illumination, which was free of the contrasts traditionally associated with artifical lighting). By placing an almost immaterial barrier between the enclosed space and the elements outside, iron-and-glass architecture proposed a new sort of space, a new sort of light and shade. These innovative features had a great impact upon those who experienced them; the train shed became part of the collective imagination of the nineteenth century, with writers and painters identifying this new space as expressing the very essence of the railway station.

The architecture of such structures was caught between innovation and tradition, academic historicism and modernism. These were the themes around which the architectural debate regarding stations developed, in an attempt to find a language of architectural form that would adequately reflect the specific character of this new type of building. A new art of design was required, which did not resort solely to models drawn from tradition.

Between 1830 and 1860, it was France and England that were most involved in this attempt to define the formal and functional aspects of railway buildings.[12] Both countries carried out important research to establish what should be the typical models for the stations of the future; however, there were substantial differences between English and French ideas regarding not only the architecture of such structures but also the type of relation that should be established between them and the city as a whole. In France, the stations of the 1850s and 60s were conceived of as "urban monuments," designed to emphasize the core importance of the city center with respect to outlying areas and suburbs. In London, on the other hand, such buildings were more utilitarian than monumental. Furthermore, though the difference in architectural treatment and materials between the train shed and the station building proper implied a distinction of roles between engineer and architect, in France these two figures tended to collaborate more closely, producing designs that reveal "an order, hierarchy and symmetry that are lacking in the English plans, which are arranged empirically."[13] French architects and engineers of the 1850s and 60s worked extensively on the difficult task of reconciling the two parts of the station so that they formed one harmonious whole. One of the first "canonical" solutions to this problem was François Duquesney's Gare de l'Est (1847–52). The façade here is designed on different levels. The lower level—a colonnade—marks the entrance to the internal space of the atrium for arrivals and departures, while above it, the fronton and thermal window reflect the form of the actual train shed extending over tracks and platforms; the same insistence upon the form of the train shed beyond can be seen in the façade of the Gare du Nord—designed by Jacques-Ignace Hittorff (1861–64)—where pairs of Ionic pilasters flank a large arched window at the very center of the imposing neoclassical elevation. In both of these stations, the glass of the gallery roofing allows abundant light to flow into the atrium building itself, transforming it into a covered thoroughfare.

In England, on the other hand, the need to reconcile art and technology was much less pressing. The sole example of a major station similar in inspiration to those in Paris is Lewis Cubbitt's King's Cross (1851–52), where Alan Colquhoun has identified various analogies with the Gare de l'Est: Cubbitt, too, uses two thermal windows in the façade that reflect the form of the train sheds beyond. According to a critic of the day, though the Gare de l'Est remained a superior design, King's Cross was "thoroughly convincing... Thanks to the high level of ornamentation, it becomes an object of architectural art, perfectly suited to its purpose without excessive imitation of any particular style."[14] If the Gare de l'Est is more uniform, more "elegant" in its resort to greater decoration, the monumental aspect of King's Cross is due entirely to the proportions and solidity of the structure.

Their successful synthesis of functional organization and architectural expression made the French railway stations of the period important models for many of the terminal stations built in the next few years throughout Europe (for example, the Italian stations of Turin and the old Termini in Rome). However, with the one exception of King's Cross, no English architect seems to have felt the need to bestow that degree of monumentality upon railway stations, or to reflect the form of the train sheds in the design of the main façade. In fact, the typical London station hid that shed between a large hotel. This is the case, for example, with Paddington, Cannon Street, Charing Cross and St. Pancras; the latter (built 1868–76) marks the high point of this trend to combine station and hotel. In effect, these designs reveal "the refusal of England to grant the railway station the status of a representational public building or to consider it as possessing architectural unity."[15] At St. Pancras both the hotel itself and the station train shed were tours de force, but they belonged to totally distinct worlds. Built in iron and glass, the train shed[16] comprised one single pointed-arch vault with a span of 234 feet and a length of 690; it was the most famous such structure of the period and would remain unsurpassed until 1889, when the three-hinge trussed-arch covering was built over the Palais des Machines in Paris. However, while the St. Pancras train shed was a feat of modern technology, the Midland Terminal Grand Hotel in front of it was an enormous "Gothic extravaganza."

Though, for functional and technical reasons, the architecture of railway stations would radically change over the next few years, French architects and engineers remained true to their explicit, open use of iron and glass in the stations they designed for the countries of Eastern Europe. Gustav Eiffel's Budapest Station (built in the 1860s) was one of the last examples of this aesthetic employment of iron: the entire end façade is in that material, with only the flanking pilasters in stone. Another very significant example of how the iron-and-glass roofing of the train shed might be used to identify a station as such was the Alexanderplatz Bahnhof in Berlin (1880–85). Here, the entire

Gare d'Orsay, Paris 1897–1900

Pennsylvania Station, New York 1906–10

Central Station, Helsinki 1904–19

structure was enveloped in iron and glass, anticipating a trend that would be developed in the station design of our own day, when the characteristic aesthetic feature of the historic iron-and-glass gallery would be transformed into a massive "technological" covering over the entire station, enclosing all the different functional environments associated with it. The importance of the Alexanderplatz development in station design was such that it was echoed in other stations of the day—for example, the Frankfurt Bahnhof or the Lehrter Bahnhof (Berlin).

The heyday of the nineteenth-century station

With the advent of the Second Industrial Revolution, the years around 1870 saw the next stage in the development of station design and construction. The existence of multiple tracks and the need for enormous side atria to take passenger flow—for example, in the stations of Frankfurt (1879–88) and Leipzig (1907–15)[17]—resulted in great increases in the overall size and ground area of such structures. The massive façades of the late-nineteenth-century stations are, however, still in a neoclassical or neo-baroque idiom.

The new buildings were imposing stone presences within the urban fabric, veritable parts of a city (given that they occupied the area of entire neighborhoods). One of the most famous of the day, the Frankfurt station, was designed by Hermann Eggert and Johann Wilhelm Schwedler and included all the characteristic innovations of this period in the layout of its interior and in the design of its façade. The—by then, usual—concourse running across the head of the platforms to link them together, was replaced by an ample "midway" that not only provided access to the trains but was also a covered street lined with shops and services for passengers.[18] Side entrances meant the tunnel could be entered without passing through the station building at the head of the platforms. As for the main elevation, this was constructed of a combination of volumes above which the tops of the central three arches of the train shed were visible. Inside, the atrium extended up through two floors and was reached by entrances in a long wall surmounted by a central thermal window which provided illumination; from there, passengers filtered through to the platforms under the iron-and-glass vault by passing down to the underpass which linked them. The station was bound on either side by buildings designed to house offices. Designed by Ulisse Stacchini, Milan Station (1905–31) is a late example of this type of layout. Like a "grotesque brontosaurus," the end building hides the five-arched train shed of glass and iron. The "monstrous" but fascinating façade is as imposing as an Egyptian monument and emphasizes the gigantic scale of the spaces within. The station building proper comprises a sort of large *porte cochère* within a central pronaos, beyond which is an intermediate space occupied by atrium and ticket offices. Two large monumental staircases lead up to the end concourse linking the platforms. The station of Milan is, in effect, one monumental act of homage to the eclecticism and the iron-and-glass engineering of the nineteenth century.[19]

The station becomes a city

With the change from steam-powered to electric-powered trains at the end of the nineteenth century, the huge train shed lost its *raison d'être*. The sinking of tracks beneath ground level—and the subsequent availability of vast surface areas—were the features that would have a decisive effect on changing models of railway station design. In the large stations of America (Grand Central Terminal and Pennsylvania Station in New York) and Europe (Gare d'Orsay in Paris), the train-as-machine is absorbed as part of the building, through a sort of mimesis; it is, in effect, hidden, only becoming visible within the station itself. The structure can be said to have metabolized its mechanistic appearance, transforming itself into a multi-level apparatus that is disguised behind/beneath "romantic" traces.

The layout of the various internal spaces—the grandiosely-decorated atria; the transversal underpasses; the magnificent restaurants—all project the notion of rail travel as a sort of cruise-on-wheels. The most typical feature of innovative late-nineteenth-century stations was the space which was designed to be symbolic of the structure as a whole: a massive concourse of entrance atrium and ticket office which was conceived of as an urban promenade, an attractive public meeting-place. There was now a paradigm shift away from linear structures characterized by transparency to gigantic and majestic structures occupying sizable areas. "The meaning of the station retreats from the phenomenon of contact between people and machinery, which no longer holds the imagination."[20] This shift away from the industrial space of glass-and-iron vault to a more massive, extensive structure can perhaps be seen in Manet's 1873 painting *Le Chemin de Fer*: the station is now an integral part of the urban fabric and thus is almost absent from the picture; its position is denoted solely by the smoking train, a mere reminder of the industrial space that is about to receive it.

According to Carroll Meeks,[21] the prototype of this new station model was the Gare d'Orsay by Victor Laloux

(1897–1900), constructed to provide a more central station for the Orleans line bringing people to the 1900 Great Exhibition. Thanks to the advent of electrification, the station could now spread above the tracks and platforms, with the vestibule, waiting rooms and main atrium all laid out as part of one single space at street level (linked to the platforms below by stairs).
With the disappearance of the overarching train shed[22]—a change which first occurs in the United States—the concourse becomes a more interior space,[23] and the form and size of the nineteenth-century iron-and-glass roofing changes.[24] The station and the city gradually tend to reflect each other more thoroughly. The concourse becomes a permeable space, a large transit area that absorbs and redistributes the flow of passengers towards the trains; it functions like a sort of self-regulatory traffic junction. Within Pennsylvania Station (New York) a series of monumental spaces—waiting rooms and concourse—mark out the rhythm of the gradual approach to the trains themselves. The different spaces are heterogeneous in design: the massive walls of the waiting rooms evoke the monumental atmosphere of Roman ruins, while the concourse, with its weight-bearing structure of reticular supports and its roofing in steel and glass, echoes the design of nineteenth-century train sheds and functions as a sort of physical and visual go-between, linking the station building proper with the tracks and platforms below. One of the most significant products of this new "multi-level" approach to station design was undoubtedly New York's Grand Central Terminal, on which work was completed in 1913. In the words of Matthew Kennedy, this structure offers a "brilliant solution to the functional problems posed by a complex metropolitan train station," as well as serving as "a key catalyst in an exceptional scheme of great technological daring,"[25] whose impact on the surrounding urban fabric would result in the radical transformation of a good part of Central Manhattan.
The train and subway tracks are organized at seven different underground levels, with express trains above, subway tracks further below. The ample suburban and express concourses were laid out again at two different levels, thus transforming the building into a number of superimposed stations—a model that heralds the imaginative designs of Sant'Elia. In fact, it was Antonio Sant'Elia himself who, at the beginning of the twentieth century, took to its extreme that notion of the station-as-machine which one can already find in the works of Zola and the Impressionists. In 1913 he presented his "utopian" vision of a train station: a machine of various levels, all intercommunicating by means of moving staircases and elevators, with neon lighting and extensive advertising hoardings. The train station had become a body of interconnecting walkways, one massive mechanism of transit; and the Grand Central Terminal was both an example of and model for such a conception.
The same tendency towards the gigantic can also be found in European station design. At the end of the nineteenth/beginning of the twentieth century, there was a renewed taste for asymmetrical Romantic structures. Among the most significant examples are Helsinki Central, built by Eliel Saarinen between 1904 and 1919, and the Stuttgart Station (1911–28) by the architects Bonatz and Scholer. Both of these structures are made up of a body of components that identify the various functions and define the visual fulcrum of the design. The façade echoes those of late-nineteenth century German stations—for example, in Lucerne and Leipzig—within which jutting volumes mark the presence of imposing atria entered through massive archways. To the right stands a tower which, visually, serves to link the structure with the surrounding urban fabric. Every detail reveals the use of a composite architectural language which is both new and antiquated, atmospheric and functional.[26]
The long and troubled history of the building of Stuttgart Station would finally come to an end in the period 1922–28, with the addition of a station hotel and post office, and there is no doubt that the Helsinki Central and Leipzig were both sources of inspiration for Bonatz. Starting from this premise, Ulrich Krings argues that "the station of Stuttgart represents the last link in the long chain of historical development within a certain type of station design."[27] This building marks a further advance upon previous models because of the coordination of its own functional requirements with the urban-planning and design requirements of the area within which it is sited. Passing under the low cantilever roofs, the passengers enter a monumental atrium aligned asymmetrically. Alongside it are two halls of different size which, from the outside, look like isolated volumes and thus stand as identifying features of the circumambient urban fabric. The carefully calculated asymmetry and this composition of a whole made up of apparently distinct elements would be further explored by the designers of Italian train stations in the 1920s–40s. Hence, both in terms of type and of approach to questions of urban planning, the Stuttgart station opened up the way to a number of innovations. In size and structure, it has the appearance of a large urban neighborhood, within which the modulation of the heterogeneous components reflects differences of function.

New models for station design

Electrification and the advent of reinforced concrete brought about a great change in the architecture of European railway stations. The period of the 1920s to 1940s saw an important phase in the development of Italian railway buildings, with the emergence of a new architectural language of great interest and quality. The large overarching train shed was replaced by individual cantilever roofs; stations were conceived in terms of horizontal structures within which formal and functional unity was now greater thanks to the suppression of the sharp distinctions between the area allocated for machines and that designed for passengers.
An important role in all this was played by Angiolo Mazzoni, the Architect-in-Chief for the Italian State Railway Company, who headed an office set up in 1921 to supervise all the construction work commissioned by the State Railway Company—in particular, the design and building of new stations. The projects for Siena, Montecatini Terme, Trento and Reggio Calabria marked fundamental steps in the development of a typically Italian railway architecture, and are also important as marking a break with the inheritance of the nineteenth century. The poetics adopted by Mazzoni can be identified by certain characteristic features: concentration on the relation between solid and open spaces, between solid walls and glass; the use of jutting cantilever roofs to emphasize horizontal planes; the presence of pure geometrical forms—such as the parallelepiped and the cylinder; the careful calibration of the relation between tall and low bodies (think, for example, of the clock-tower that is the defining visual feature of the Montecatini Terme station).
The project that was, however, the veritable manifesto of this phase in the development of station design was undoubtedly the work on the Florence station of Santa Maria Novella which began in 1932—that is, just one year after the completion of Ulisse Stacchini's Milan Central Station. Designed by the Gruppo Toscano headed by Giovanni Michelucci, the station would at the time be hailed internationally as a masterpiece of modern architecture.
Another fundamental work, which case marks the end of this phase of development in Italian railway architecture, was the design of the Rome Station, built between 1948 and 1950 by a group of architects under Eugenio Montuori. As Francesco Dal Co comments, "the exceptional quality of the architectural concept behind this project; the extraordinary inventiveness in the undulant roof of the projecting body of the passenger building; the mastery of structural design and the impeccable execution—all serve to breathe new life into the tradition exemplified by Santa Maria Novella."[28]

Estación de Atocha, Madrid 1984–92

Hauptbahnhof, Stuttgart 1911–28

Station Building, Siena 1931–35

Traffic junctions

In the decades after the Second World War, other forms of transport—the car and the plane—took over from the train. However by the 1980s there was a renewed interest in rail travel, which led to the production of projects either for the redevelopment of existing stations or the building of new ones (to serve areas of urban expansion or airports). This interest in stations as significant urban locations resulted in some of the most famous architects of the moment working on projects that, while revealing substantial differences, all exemplify a common view of the railway station: from being the traditional point of arrival and departure, the station becomes a junction, an interchange of different means of transport, which might also serve to meet a variety of other needs. Located as they are within contemporary cities, the large historic terminals have become important resources in their own right, with the potential to attract profitable commercial activities. As mentioned, work in this period involved either the construction of new stations or the redevelopment of old, and among the more significant examples of either one might list: the Atocha station project, redesigned by Rafael Moneo; Santiago Calatrava's projects for the stations of Stadelhofen and Lyon-Satolas; Nicholas Grimshaw's work on Waterloo Station; the Cruz and Ortiz project for the station of Santa Justa; and the work on the Lille-Europe station produced by Jean-Marie Duthilleul and Étienne Tricaud in collaboration with the Agence d'Étude des Gares of the SNCF.

If the redevelopment of Atocha or the design for the Seville station of Santa Justa favor an approach that is not overtly "technological"—that is, without the "emphasis on the structure of the station that one sees in nineteenth-century designs"[29]—there are other projects (for example, the works of Santiago Calatrava or Nicholas Grimshaw's redevelopment of Waterloo) in which the study of structural details and the proposal of innovative technical solutions is the key to the whole project. In redevelopment schemes certain basic decisions have to be taken. Should the fabric of the whole station be maintained intact? Should the new project be divided according to specific functions, so it remains in keeping with the scale and character of the place? Having answered these questions, Moneo's work on the Atocha station aimed to reestablish a dialogue between the city and the old railway building, while maintaining the symbolic and monumental character of the latter. Partly dismantled as a result of being decommissioned, the original nineteenth-century structure was transformed into an urban piazza, a sort of public garden with shops and restaurants.

This tendency to focus on the secondary (commercial) uses of the space is now the usual tactic followed in the redevelopment of existing stations.

Nicholas Grimshaw's project for Waterloo develops a new approach, making the railway station into a sort of openwork machine in which all structural and technological features are on view. The functional distinctions between the station building proper and the train shed cease to exist, with a curved covering in glass enveloping the entire station like a shell, becoming both façade and structure. Given its particular layout and the service areas it requires—shops and restaurants but also customs offices and distinct arrivals and departures areas (it is from here that the trains for the Channel Tunnel leave)—the station has something of the nature of an airport. The distinctive features are the walkways and vertical links between the different levels. Given this necessity to separate arrivals and departures, the flow of passengers is more directly channeled into designated areas; the mechanized systems linking the different levels are located in clearly visible positions within the areas that passengers have to pass through.

In his stations designs, Santiago Calatrava also makes a very refined use of the possibilities offered by technology. The idea of the train shed as a place for the celebration of mechanical movement is reinterpreted in a very surprising and original fashion, with "sculptural" structural frameworks and daring individual details being the hallmark of the Spanish architect's work. The Zurich Stadelhofen Bahnhof, the first of Calatrava's railway projects, would subsequently be seen as a manifesto of his entire architecture, while later projects—the Lisbon Orient Station, the Liege station (still under construction) and the competition designs for the high-speed train station in Florence—offer further developments upon this idea of a new type of railway architecture, which reinterprets the traditional models for such designs and highlights the bare bones of the structure.

For all their differences of context, project specifications and proposed solutions, these designs have one basic idea in common: the stations are envisaged as junctions of different kinds of traffic, and thus become the fulcrum for the reorganization of the surrounding area itself. The Lille station is a perfect example of the effects this station-as-junction has "on an urban scale." The station becomes the fulcrum of an entire system, the "coordinator of a number of functions that serve the collectivity as a whole."[30] The core of the construction is a great concourse—270 meters long, 8 meters wide—which not only serves as a sort of belvedere looking out over the city but also functions as the interchange between the surrounding area and a dense network of transport systems. In effect, the projects of the 1980s marked a transformation in the very conception of the railway station, with the ideas they introduced being developed further in designs produced at the end of the century. The station had become a junction within a territorial system of mixed traffic flow.

The station as a mall

The advent of high-speed train travel—first in France, then in the rest of Europe—reawakened interest in this means of transport and led to a further redefinition of railway architecture. The new stations, often underground, are in effect urban galleries, whose ample spaces are open to a through traffic of pedestrians. They are conceived of as a place one passes through; waiting-rooms are replaced by shopping areas or by zones in which waiting is nothing more than a brief pause. One of the leading figures in the BRT studio of architects, which in recent years has been in the forefront of developments in this field, Hadi Teherani sees the contemporary station as an "airport" for trains—a place in which architects can try out new types of structures and "meet the challenge posed by the very resistance of materials."[31]

In Italy, the introduction of the high-speed trains opened up a new chapter in the history of railway architecture. Among the numerous projects that have resulted, those that stand out include designs for three new stations: Porta Susa in Turin, by the AREP Group; the Florence high-speed station, by Foster and Arup; and Naples Afragola, by Zaha Hadid. All of these projects exemplify one basic idea: envisaged as a junction between various systems of traffic flow and transport, the station is also an attractive part of the urban fabric, richly equipped with shopping and other facilities.

Designed by AREP and Silvio D'Ascia in collaboration with Agostino Magnaghi, the Turin Porta Susa station comprises an internal space conceived of as a series of intercommunicating links (covered walkways, escalators, elevators) that connect both inside and outside (that is, the main hall, the city and the old station) and the various underground levels. In effect, the station has become a street, a shopping mall and a traffic interchange. However, from the outside this complexity is masked by a covering of glass and metal, in which architecture becomes a statement of structure.

Similar features are to be seen in the Foster and Arup design for the new Florence station. Both the width and height of the glassed-in volumes of the nineteenth-century station are changed, with the very form and nature of the traditional train sheds being reinterpreted.[32] An arched covering identifies the station as such. Beneath it, the upper level is occupied by two porticoed walkways (to be given over to shopping malls). These link the inside and outside, and also provide a viewing platform down onto the pedestrian traffic of the lower levels. Wells of light fall down through the different levels to the train tracks and platforms themselves.

A common feature of these designs is the disappearance of the façade as such. There is no proscenium introducing us to the world of the railway, but—in most cases—a transparent shell around the structure. This aesthetic change reflects a change in the station's relation to the city as a whole: in the first stations, passengers' initial contact with the railway was the façade of the building within the urban fabric, but nowadays—particularly in the large metropolitan areas—most passengers arrive by means of urban transport that enter the building underground. In effect, a passenger's first experience of the station is its interior; there is no perception of the exterior. This means that the notion of a monumental structure which poses itself in relation to the city now gives way to a different image of the station, as a junction of underground traffic flow. The building tends to becomes less visible—almost imperceptible; the light structure[33] that emerges from the ground is the sole visual and physical interface between interior and exterior. This tendency is taken to its logical extreme in the design for the extension to the Stuttgart station[34] drawn up by Ingenhoven, Overdiek and Partners. The new underground structure created alongside the Bonatz station links the old city center and the areas of the extension. A park—the green lung of the district—occupies the ground over the underground station, which is covered by a concrete roof of only a few millimeters in thickness (designed by the architects in collaboration with Frei Otto). Inside, the mushroom-headed pillars are topped by eye-shaped skylights that rise above ground rather like spy-glasses. It is these which not only establish a visual connection between the park and the station, but also provide the natural light that illuminates the interior beneath.[35]

One can see a similar principle at work in the project for the rebuilding of the London Bridge Station drawn up by T.P. Bennet and Wilkinson Eyre. This envisages the total demolition of the old station and the construction of a new underground concourse connected via escalators to the platforms situated above them. This new concourse will function as a traffic interchange and as a shopping mall, while the station's visual appearance within the urban fabric will be defined by an office block to be built above it.

Project for the Gare TGV Liège-Guillemins, Liege 1996–

Project for the extension of the Main Station, Stuttgart 1997–

Project for the high-speed train station of Porta Susa, Turin 2002–

Project for the London Bridge Station, London 1998–

From the point of view of form, the most recent designs are significant expressions of a clear shift—or even a total break—with the traditional concepts of railway architecture. It is true that the station and city still remain symbolic reflections of each other; but while the European and American stations of the end of the nineteenth/beginning of the twentieth century remained autonomous parts of an urban fabric to which they were anchored, contemporary stations attempt to metabolize the very congestion and density of the modern urban environment—and it is this very process of assimilation that can be said to "restore" them to the city. As the station gradually loses its connotation of a "frontier" area, its predominant characteristics become disembodied architectural form and flexibility of layout.

Designed by the Un Studio, the Arnhem Central Station (under construction) is perhaps the most powerful expression of this new concept of railway stations. The pivot of the composition is a large fluid space, an air-conditioned concourse which is the very symbol of movement and flux. As an area intended to establish a relation between city and station, this hall is designed to meet the shared needs of both,[36] providing direct access not only to various means of transport (trains, buses, taxis, private cars and bicycles) but also to offices. Inspired by the notion of "deep planning," the railway station becomes a locus of flux, borrowing its main characteristic therefore from the modern city itself.[37] The result is a hybrid organization of space, with the station functioning as a traffic interchange, as a multi-functional structure comprising various levels, and as an open public space. The project for the Arnhem station provides a sort of ideal outline of all the various models of movement exemplified in the designs of the contemporary train station, with the interaction of the different levels of the infrastructure working to create effective interaction between the various systems that feed into the station.

The embodiment of a complex of dynamic relations, the contemporary railway station once more identifies itself with the urban reality around it; once again, it reflects the personality of the city as such. The examples illustrated in this book (Stratford Regional Station in London, the Gare d'Aix-en-Provence TGV, the Cologne/Bonn Airport Railway Station, the Changi Railway Station and the Lehrter Bahnhof) all reveal this celebration of the station as an important fulcrum of urban activity. The ability of railway design to generate new architectural languages and propose new solutions to the problems posed by such spaces reveals its capacity to adapt to the changing circumstances of the contemporary world.

Notes

1 For a clearer picture of the more significant stages in the development of railway architecture, I have divided the presentation into three phases: the emergence of this type of architecture as such (1830–70); the period that runs up until the 1930s; a third phase from after the Second World War to 1970s. A fourth phase would cover the present period of late modernist or post-modernist works. Obviously, this division is designed solely to serve my own specific purposes and does not necessarily reflect the changes in railway architecture that were often a response to specific locations or contexts. The phases I describe might also overlap at times.

2 W. Benjamin, *On the Concept of History*, Suhrkamp Verlag, Frankfurt-am-Main 1997.

3 A. Colquhoun, "The 19th Century Terminal Station in France and England as Cultural Artifact," *Casabella*, 624, June 1995, pp. 68–71.

4 A. Colquhoun, *op. cit.*, pp. 68–71.

5 C. Meeks, *The Railroad Station. An Architectural History*, Yale University Press, New Haven 1956.

6 This is the first example of a station specifically designed so that arrivals and departures use opposite platforms, thus facilitating the flow of trains. The departures side is obviously more fully equipped, with ticket office, baggage deposit and waiting rooms. The large entrance propylaea celebrate the role of the station as a gateway to the city. C. Meeks, *op. cit.*, p. 29.

7 Reference is to the Italian edition: W. Benjamin, *Opere complete, vol. IX. I "passages" di Parigi*, edited by E. Ganni, Einaudi, Turin 2000, p. 455. See also S. Giedion, *Bauen in Frankreich eisen*, esienboten, Leipzig, Berlin 1928, pp. 1–2.

8 This encounter with the train shed was a rather traumatic experience for the early travelers, who saw themselves enveloped in a new and disturbing world; Schivelbusch describes the trauma as a "visual" one. The glass roofing meant that there was a new relationship between interior and exterior. Natural light flooded into the vast space, creating different effects of illumination, producing a "monstrous" space whose appearance changed according to the time of day. These effects are powerfully described in Zola's *La Bête Humaine*. See also S. Kern *The Culture of Time and Space, 1880–1918*, Harvard University Press, New York 1983 and W. Schivelbusch, *Geschichte der Eisenbahnreise*, Carl Hanser Verlag, Munich-Vienna, 1977. The station building proper tended to regulate the shift between the urban environment and the train shed. Very quickly, the latter ceased to be a traumatic space and was celebrated as the very emblem of railway architecture, ultimately being assimilated as part of the design of late-nineteenth-century stations.

9 Upon entering a station, the traveler had the impression of being in a familiar space, similar to other public buildings of the preindustrial city.

10 W. Benjamin, *Opere complete..., op. cit.*

11 In W. Schivelbusch, *op. cit.*, pp. 48–49. Reference is to the Italian edition, *Storia dei viaggi in ferrovia*, Einaudi, Turin 1988.

12 This was a time of great developments in railway architecture and in train traffic, with new ideas and types of design thus being put forward. In the 1830s the modest-sized stations were generally laid out in one of two ways: with buildings only on a single side of the tracks or on both sides (these "twinned" buildings, for arrivals and departures respectively, were linked by the iron-and-glass roofing over the tracks). With the increase in train traffic during the 1840s, the structure and form of the stations gradually changed. The number of tracks and platforms increased, making it necessary to provide a structure linking them; this resulted in the creation of the terminal station, with a single concourse joining the exit/entrance end of all the platforms; from the middle of the nineteenth century onwards, such stations would become a key presence in the urban fabric of the great cities of Europe. See C. Meeks, *op. cit.* and W. Schivelbusch, *op. cit.*

13 A. Colquhoun, *op. cit.*, p. 70. In France there was a more systematic and theoretical approach, with the standards to be adopted by the railway being the object of studies that looked at various aspects of technology, function and traffic distribution. See, for example, A. Perdonnet, *Traité élémentaire des Chemins de Fer*, Langlois et Leclercq, Paris 1855–56.

14 In C. Meeks, *op. cit.*, p. 65.

15 A. Colquhoun, *op. cit.*, p. 70.

16 The structural design adopted reveals the high level of technological innovation. Engineering at this point stimulated a step forward in the aesthetic ideas being promulgated. At St. Pancras, the distinction between wall and roofing was abolished, creating a fluid and very atmospheric space.

17 In the Leipzig station the tracks are raised above the level of the square outside; they are linked to the entrance by means of two monumental staircases.

18 A solution that was also adopted in Leipzig and Washington, C. Meeks, *op. cit.*, p. 114.

19 The eclecticism of the main station building, often overburdened with decorative features, concealed the modern and functional heart of the station itself. "It is precisely in the ambiguity of this last great flourish of the nineteenth century that one can see all its greatness... The last expression of all that the century would produce ... was a monument in stone to an iron-based technology." L.V. Ferretti, "La tipologia della stazioni ferroviarie tra XIX e XX secolo," in the collection of essays *La stazione e la città. Riferimenti storici e proposte per Roma*, Gangemi, Rome 1990, pp. 55–57.

20 A. Colquhoun, *op. cit.*, p. 70.

21 C. Meeks, *op. cit.*, p. 112. The Gare d'Orsay would become a model that influenced many other stations. That in Copenhagen (rebuilt 1906–11) took up its layout: the tracks are located beneath the terminal station, which runs across them like a bridge.

22 The iron-and-glass train shed disappeared in the United States around the beginning of the twentieth century, being substituted by the so-called "bush-sheds" (named after their inventor), which offered cover for individual platforms and cost less to build and maintain. Again it was the USA which saw the beginning of electrification and the introduction of electric light, which by 1930 was widespread and relatively cheap. In Europe, where technology had yet to develop to the same extent, the engineers of the day were still largely in favor of the use of natural light within stations. See W. Schivelbusch, *op. cit.*, p. 54 and Hefele, *Das Fabrik-Oberlicht*, Berlin, 1931.

23 The modifications in the internal layout of train stations during the second half of the nineteenth century reveal a certain simplification of the relation between city and railway. There was now a direct link from the atrium to the platforms; waiting rooms ceased to function as "locks" governing passenger flow from city to train and were moved to the sides of the building. At the same time, the atrium—now a concourse—became the hub of the entire station, the area through which passenger traffic was funneled and redistributed. This new layout was the direct result of an acceleration in the links between city and station. Previously, a period in the waiting room interrupted the flow of traffic, making the encounter with the new space of the train shed less traumatic. But now the uninterrupted flow of passengers through the concourse directly into the train shed resulted in the complete assimilation of the space of the railway within the urban space around it. In effect, the removal of the transversal tunnel linking the heads of platforms took place in the large multi-level American stations at the beginning of the twentieth century, while in Europe—see, for example, Germany—there was a tendency to preserve the tunnel as the route from the atrium to the (often raised) platforms.

24 Around 1890, in both St. Louis and Chicago, architects built large station halls that were richly decorated yet echoed the form of train sheds. In the Union Station, for example, the train concourse recalls the form of the glass-and-iron covered space, even if shifted from its usual position to stand at right angles to the platforms. Its barrel vaulting raises above the entrance to the station, and from the outside is the most dominant feature of the building.

25 M. Kennedy, "Terminal City: architecure and railways in New York," *Casabella*, 624, June 1995, pp. 67–68.

26 See F. Dal Co, "La Stazione di Helsinki: Eliel Saarinen, 1904–1919 / Rafael Moneo, 1995," *Casabella*, 646, June 1997, pp. 13–14.

27 U. Krings, *Bahnhofsarchitektur—Desutsche Grosstadtbahnhöfer des Historismus*, Munich 1985, pp. 54 et seq. See also F. Werner, "The Myth of the Atemporal," *Lotus*, 59, 1988.

28 F. Dal Co, "Le stazioni italiane e la sfida al progresso," *Casabella*, 710, April 2003, p. 7.

29 The station of Santa Justa is not imposing in appearance; of a flattened, elongated, rather aerodynamic form, it seems to be turned within itself. Built in brick, this is an example of silent architecture, an architecture "in repose." See J-J. Lahuerta, "The New Station of Seville. An Underground Movement," *Lotus*, 70, 1991, pp. 6–22.

30 See M. Canonico, "L'Agence d'étude des gares. I progetti per le stazioni del TGV," in *ArQ 13*, monograph issue on *La stazione ferroviaria. Verso un nuovo modello d'uso*, December 1994, pp. 110–17.

31 D. Meyhöfer, "Bothe, Richter, Teherani ... in acht Jaren von Null auf Hündert," *BDZ*, 1, 2000, p. 109.

32 However, in nineteenth-century terminal stations the tracks were at ground level; here, they are 25 metres below ground. This notion of reemploying the ideal image of the old train shed reveals the designers' intention of creating a space that, within this kind of architecture, is rich in significance. As one can read in the presentation of the project: "The large stations of the past were made up of vast volumes, mostly enclosed by glass. In spite of the enormous changes in both construction and railway technology since the nineteenth century, the width and height of such spaces remain indispensable features of contemporary stations, and the project presented herein aims to respect this fact." In "Concorso di progettazione per la nuova stazione alta velocità di Firenze," supplement included with *Casabella*, 709, March 2003.

33 The use of glass and steel, of apparently light-weight roofing, and of innovative details of construction technology are all features of these new railway stations.

34 The building had to be extended to meet the need of high-speed lines. The plan envisages the construction of an underground rail network and a through station, so that it will be possible for departing trains to reach high speed very quickly. The existing tracks will be decommissioned and the old station turned into an open public facility with shops and restaurants.

35 The architects' aim is to develop the solutions that best exploit the character of the place and make it possible to eliminate the more mechanical equipment and installations. Stations thus become important opportunities for trying out innovative technology and alternative "zero-energy" systems.

36 "This required the evaluation of the different 'times' of a city (times of production, consumption, etc.) within the space of a single day. Temporal considerations are thus closely bound up with the program behind the design. The individual strata of infrastructures are designed and tried out individually before being interconnected in a system of relations that thence set the parameters, the frame of reference." In *Less Aesthetic more Ethics*, catalogue of the VII Biennale di Architettura di Venezia, Marsilio, Venice 2000, pp. 382–84.

37 "The contemporary city is a 'city of flux,' an open and dynamic structure of interchanges and junctions... Facility of access is defined by the distance between such nodes in terms of time. To organize the structure of this city one has to incorporate notions of duration and time within both architecture and planning." In *Less Aesthetic more Ethics*, *op. cit.*, p. 382.

1 françois duquesney

gare de l'est

paris, france 1847–52

project
François-Alexandre Duquesney
with
Pierre Cabanel de Sermet
client
Compagnie des Chemins de Fer de Strasbourg
location
Paris, France
chronology
1847–50: building of the station designed by Duquesney
1924–31: building of extensions designed by Bertaud

With the expansion of railways in the 1840s, stations were required that could meet the needs of growing rail traffic, providing easy transfer between the increased number of platforms contained under the wide glass roof of a single-span train shed. The solution adopted was that of the terminal station, with the train shed in iron and steel ending in a structure that served to link the various platforms together. A feature of all great European cities from the middle of the nineteenth century onwards, such terminal stations comprised an end building which functioned as a sort of "lock," a space of mediation between railway and urban fabric, a junction of urban and rail traffic. This dual type of architecture "on the one hand had a classical-inspired atrium in brick and stone, which was part of the city, and on the other, an iron-and-glass train shed which was an entirely functional expression of the 'industrial' world of the railway" (W. Schivelbusch, *Storia dei viaggi in ferrovia*, Einaudi, Turin 1988, p. 188).
The difference in materials and architectural treatment between the train shed and the station building proper implied a distinction of roles between architect and engineer. France, however, was the country in which these two figures collaborated most closely together, producing designs that were characterized by qualities of "order, symmetry and a respect for a hierarchy of functions." One of the first canonical models for the terminal station was François Duquesney's Gare de l'Est, whose successful synthesis of functional organization and overall architectural design meant that the building was soon being taken as a model for numerous such stations built throughout Europe in the period soon afterwards (for example, the Italian stations of Turin and Roma Termini).
With its façade colonnade, semicircular glass window—the external manifestation of the actual form of the train shed—and its four corner pavilions in neo-Renaissance style, Gare de l'Est was undoubtedly one of the station designs that was most extensively copied. Its renown was in part helped by the publication of an engraving of its elevations—together with an enthusiastic comment on its construction—in Auguste Perdonnet's important *Traité Elémentaire des Chemins de Fer*. Various contemporary historians and critics praised the architectural design of the station. *L'Illustration*, for example, in the issue of July 21, 1849, commented "It would not be excessive to define such a construction as monumental; there is no railway station that bears comparison with the Gare de l'Est."
The front elevation of the building is composed of different levels. At ground level there is a large colonnade atrium that stretches the entire width of the façade; this marks the internal area reserved for the use of arriving and departing passengers. Above that, there is a central fronton and a thermal window that echoes the form of the train shed within. According to Fergusson, the high degree of ornamentation in the Gare de l'Est makes it an authentic work of architectural art, perfectly adapted to the role it is to play without excessive borrowings from other kinds of building.
But let us look at the history of the construction of this station and the urban-planning schemes that were associated with it (these involved, among other things, the laying-out of three new streets: Rue d'Alsace, Rue de Metz and Rue de Nancy). Initially named Gare de Strasbourg after the line it was to serve, the station design was commissioned from François Duquesney by the Compagnie des Chemins

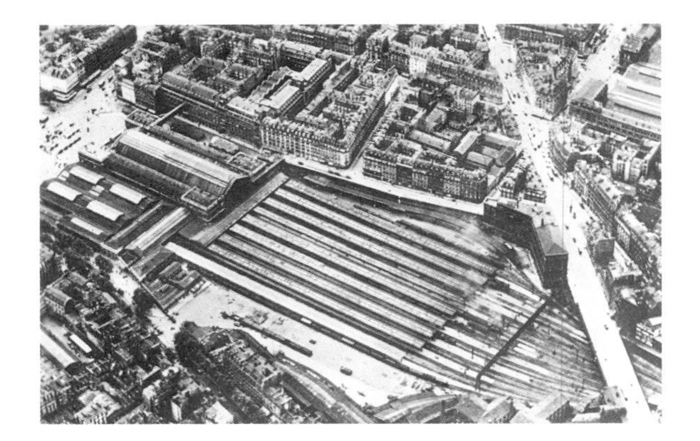

de Fer de Strasbourg. The idea of turning to an architect was taken after an initial project drawn up by the company's engineers was judged to be too "spare"; the major French railway companies envisaged their main stations as large structures which would not only meet the predicted needs of growing rail traffic, but also stand as "monumental" celebrations of this new means of transport. Initially, Duquesney's designs were criticized by the Conseil Général des Ponts et Chaussées for ornamental excess and a certain stylistic eclecticism in the exterior, which some did not hesitate to define as simply in "bad taste." However, in spite of these reservations, the Conseil Général did give its final approval, stating that the "work was in keeping with the era and with the mixture of styles that was characteristic of present-day architecture and could be noted in most buildings of recent construction" (*Gare de l'Est*, 1931, p. 11). During the building phase, however, some of the ornamental features of the façade were considered too "bold" and were eliminated from the design.

In effect, Duquesney's design is organized around the train shed. Linked by arcaded galleries, the four corner pavilions mark out the extent of the station, while the characteristic feature of the atrium is a rounded vault upon a reticular arch. To the west, the station was bounded by Passage Lafayette, to the east by Rue de Metz, which ran into the then Rue de Nancy. Further small guard pavilions were constructed at the corners of the forecourt in front of the building. When completed, the Gare de Strasbourg met with a very enthusiastic reception from society in general; indeed, it soon became a tourist attraction in its own right and was reproduced in numerous prints. Perdonnet, for example, praised both the general proportions and the decorative features, the more distinctive of which include the large clock above the trabeation of the atrium colonnade; this was flanked by two half-reclining figures symbolizing the Seine and the Rhine. Perdonnet also singled out the rather original capitals of the peristyle, which he described as "most successful" (*Gare de l'Est*, 1931, p. 12); each of them is adorned with sculpted representations of the various crops cultivated in the different areas through which the Strasbourg line ran. That city itself is represented, at the summit of the fronton of the train shed, by a symbolic figure seated "in a curule chair." Inside, the hall of the station, the work of the master iron engineer Jacquemant was described as "a prodigy of lightness and elegance."

However, while there was general praise for the architecture of the station, the technical and functional appraisal of the finished building was much harsher. The *Journal des chemins de fer*, whose contributors included the most renowned engineers of the day, was very severe in its judgment of the horseshoe layout of the buildings around the tracks, which not only inhibited extension of the tracks beyond the limit marked by the building intended to serve suburban traffic, but also meant that those suburban lines themselves had no area of extension. In the journal's view, the Gare de l'Est was much more interesting from the formal and aesthetic point of view than from the technical and the functional.

The area that has the greatest impact is undoubtedly the train shed; the use of rounded vaults here was an exception in France (where generally such galleries were truss constructions—see, for example, Gare du Nord II and Gare Saint-Lazare) and employed the groundbreaking new technology developed by Polonceau. The original station had two platforms—one for arriving, one for departing passengers—as well as facilities for the loading of postal wagons and public coaches. At the end of the train shed, there was originally a system of rotating turntables on which the locomotives could be turned around (in 1850, to avoid the need for such complex maneuvers, these turntables were eliminated, and thus the locomotives themselves could not pull in under the train shed). Between 1855 and 1877, after the Mulhouse line was added—the service had been acquired by the Compagnie des Chemins de Fer de l'Est in 1854—various modifications were made in the area between the side of the atrium and Pont Lafayette: in line with the buildings which ran alongside the train shed, giving onto Rue de Metz and Rue d'Alsace, new structures were raised for the arriving and departing trains of this second line. From that point onwards, the Gare de l'Est became home to two distinct stations, serving the Strasbourg and Mulhouse lines with their own independent facilities. This "reorganized" station would remain unchanged until 1877, when the central track was converted to increase the number of platforms within the train shed.

A further sizable increase in the number of tracks took place in the years 1888–91, when fourteen new tracks and platforms were constructed—together with a new addition to the station building; this latter was aligned perpendicular to the departures section of the old station and ran as far as Rue du Faubourg Saint-Martin. In the same period, the internal layout of the station was changed: the English model of organizing the departures section of the station was adopted, and it was no longer obligatory for passengers to pass through the waiting rooms before gaining access to

Bird's-eye view of the station and the rail tracks. As a result of the 1931 extension project, the station became a "double" structure.

their train. In fact, as early as 1854 August Perdonnet, a board member of the Compagnie de Strasbourg, had criticized this obligation imposed by the French company, praising the English system which allowed much freer access to the platforms. In his *Traité élémentaire*, he had waxed lyrical over "those magnificent platforms, along which flow crowds of travelers; those doors always open to the public; those numerous tracks with their locomotives, which come to a halt as if by magic, like something restrained by an irresistible force."

The continuing increase in the volume of passenger traffic led to further extensions: the covered hall was reduced in width and cleared of platforms, thus becoming a *salle des pas-perdus* (a throughway and concourse); the body of the building perpendicular to the hall (by then used for arrivals) was demolished; existing platforms were extended to handle longer trains; and two new sets of tracks and platforms were added to the right. For the first time all sixteen platforms were used interchangeably for arrival and departures. New structures destined to house the baggage deposits were built in Rue de Metz and Rue de Nancy, with the area of the two roads being incorporated into the station.

The most sizable work, which would actually double the volume of the station, came in 1931. A first proposal for extensions had been put forward by the Head Engineer of the Compagnie des Chemins de Fer de l'Est in 1911. The preliminary plan then drawn up, and adopted by the Board of Directors in March 1912, was substantially the same as that which was put into effect some twenty years later. The proposal envisaged an increase in the number of tracks, a widening of platforms, the development of the built-up areas—such as the hall—which had become "squashed," and extension of the facilities provided for arriving and departing passengers. The façade was extended around 45 meters up to the limit of Rue du Faubourg Saint-Martin, with the new terminal building housing only the facilities associated with departing trains—ticket offices and areas of registering luggage; the services for arriving passengers were to be at a lower level (reached by new staircases from the Rue du Faubourg Saint-Martin and Rue d'Alsace). Administration offices would be constructed to the right side of the building, along the rerouted Rue du Faubourg Saint-Martin, while a central conveyor belt would carry postal packages (fed in through trap-doors) to a sorting room in the arrivals section.

The time necessary to assess and approve the plan dragged on to the outbreak of the First World War, when obviously nothing was done, and after the end of hostilities priority was given to the reconstruction of areas destroyed by bombing. It was not until 1924 that the final plans were put forward. These envisaged the addition of a further ten to the twenty existing platforms and the construction of three large bridges: the Pont Philippe de Girard (1924–29) which was 108 meters long and 41 wide; the Pont Lafayette (1927–28), a reinforced concrete structure designed by the engineer Caquot; and the Pont de l'Aqueduc (1928–30), a 114-meter-high structure in metal girders.

Work began on the new right wing of the station in 1927–28, with the construction of the vestibule and the arrivals hall; this latter was located underground, on one of the four levels of the extended new station building. Facilities for departing passengers on the first floor were laid out to either side of the central atrium (suburban lines to one side, intercity lines to the other) and a vestibule at the same level served to link together the various areas; vertical links down to the underground arrival hall were located between the terminal gallery and the large central space of the station. In May 1930 work began on the replacement of the old tracks and platforms to produce the thirty envisaged for the extended station; and the final phase of work ended in December 1931, with the layout of the ticket office for the intercity lines in the main atrium. The whole scheme involved the excavation, consolidation and resurfacing of an area of more than twelve hectares lying between Rue de Strasbourg and Rue Louis Blanc, with work carried out by some 350 different contractors (along with consulting agencies and architectural and engineering studios). The large number of executive plans and drawings created; the extensive use of reinforced concrete; the ready solutions that had to be found to unexpected problems (for example, those posed by the foundations); the experimental use of new machinery and equipment—all these made the extended Gare de l'Est not only an important scheme of urban planning but also a large-scale technical undertaking, which brought into play innovative technology and new modern techniques of construction.

Bibliography

M. Bouche-Leclercq, "Transformation et Agrandissement de la Gare de L'Est à Paris," *Revue Générale des Chemins de Fer*, January 1931, pp. 3–32.

La Gare de l'Est, *Compagnie des Chemins de Fer de l'Est*, Paris 1931.

P. Cognasson, *Gare de l'Est: porte ouverte sur l'Europe*, La Vie du Rail et des Trasports, Paris 1993.

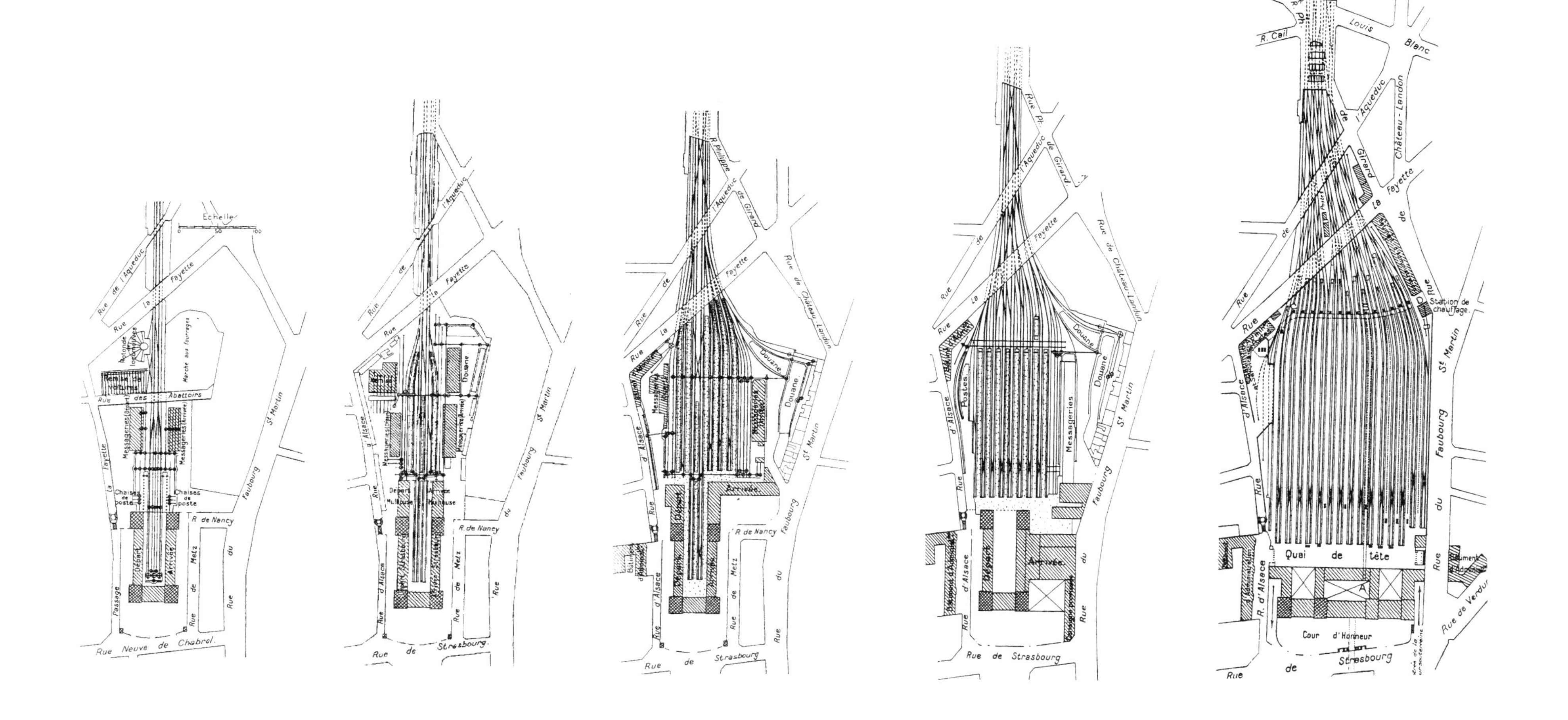

The Strasbourg *embarcadère* at the time the station was opened: to the right side of the train shed is the departures area, to the left that for arrivals.

The development of the station during its various extensions. From left to right: 1855, 1877, 1900, 1931.

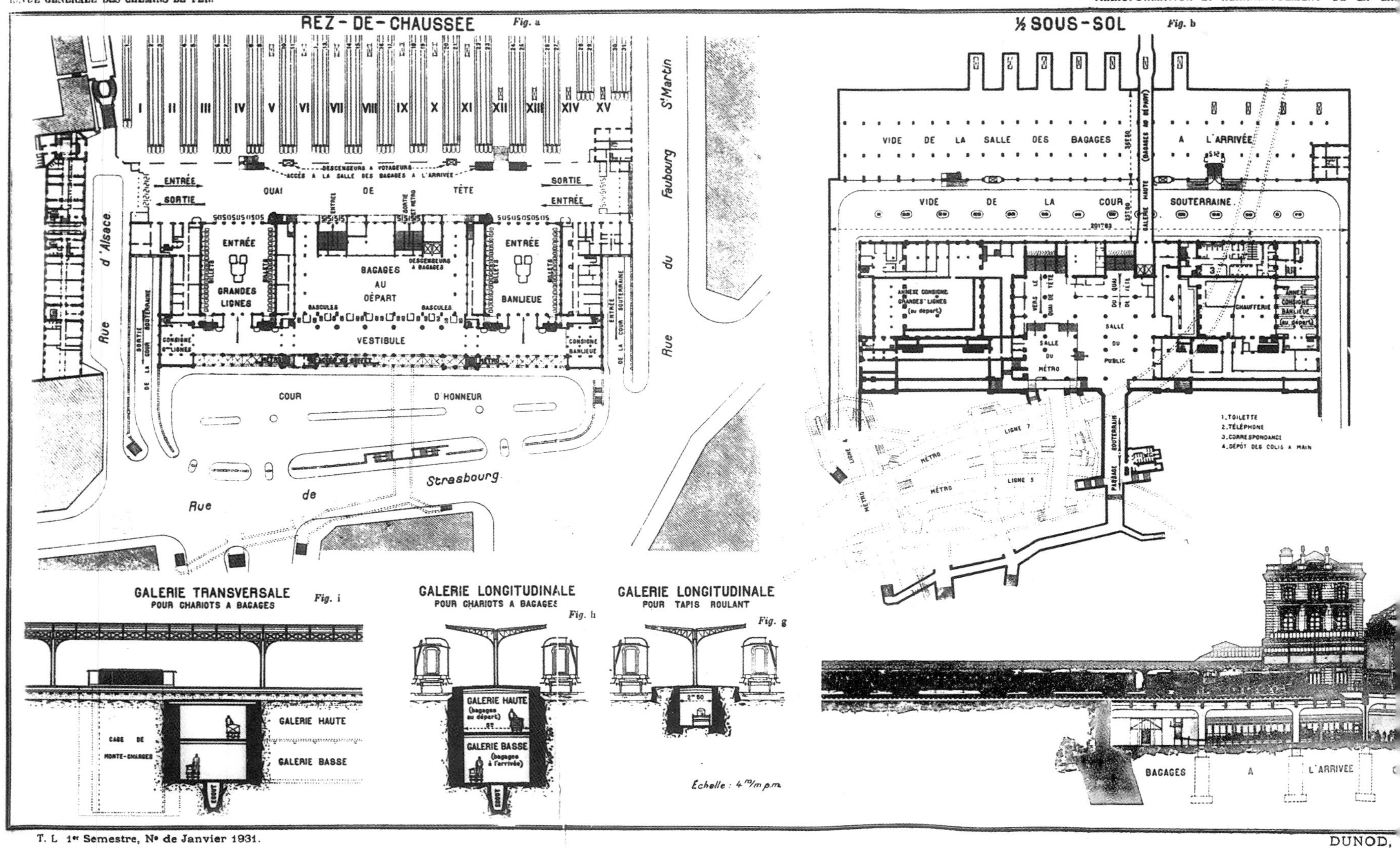

REZ-DE-CHAUSSEE Fig. a
½ SOUS-SOL Fig. b
ENTRÉE
SORTIE
QUAI DE TÊTE
BAGAGES AU DÉPART
ENTRÉE GRANDES LIGNES
ENTRÉE BANLIEUE
VESTIBULE
COUR D'HONNEUR
Rue d'Alsace
Rue du Faubourg St Martin
Rue de Strasbourg
VIDE DE LA SALLE DES BAGAGES A L'ARRIVÉE
VIDE DE LA COUR SOUTERRAINE
SALLE DU PUBLIC
SALLE DU MÉTRO
CHAUFFERIE
MÉTRO
LIGNE 7
LIGNE 5
LIGNE 4
PASSAGE SOUTERRAIN
1. TOILETTE
2. TÉLÉPHONE
3. CORRESPONDANCE
4. DÉPÔT DES COLIS A MAIN
GALERIE TRANSVERSALE POUR CHARIOTS A BAGAGES Fig. i
GALERIE HAUTE
GALERIE BASSE
CAGE DE MONTE-CHARGES
GALERIE LONGITUDINALE POUR CHARIOTS A BAGAGES Fig. h
GALERIE HAUTE (bagages au départ)
GALERIE BASSE (bagages à l'arrivée)
GALERIE LONGITUDINALE POUR TAPIS ROULANT Fig. g
Échelle : 4 m/m p.m.
BAGAGES A L'ARRIVÉE

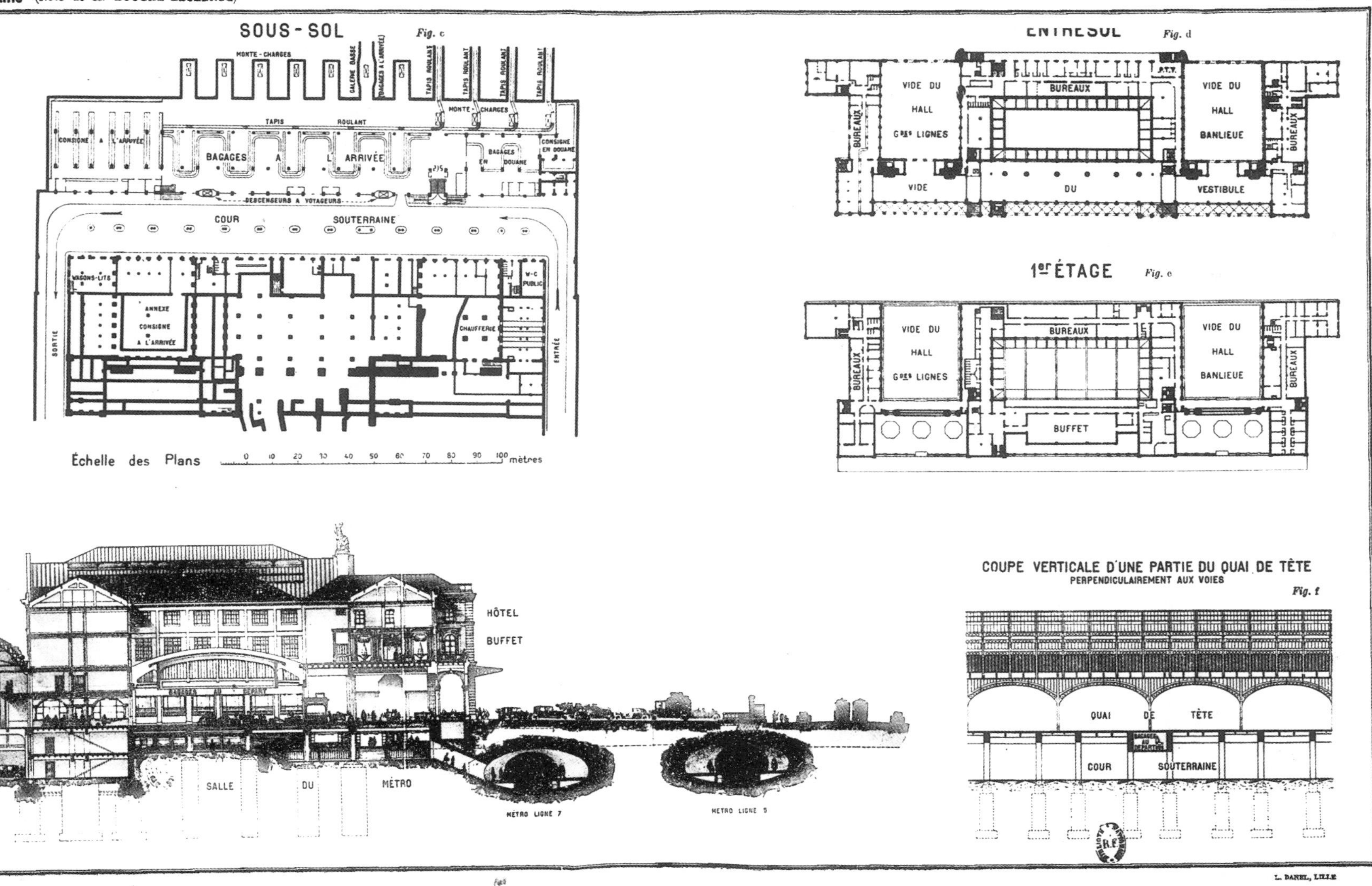
SOUS-SOL
Fig. c
BAGAGES A L'ARRIVÉE
COUR SOUTERRAINE
Échelle des Plans
ENTRESOL
Fig. d
VIDE DU HALL Gdes LIGNES
BUREAUX
VIDE DU HALL BANLIEUE
VIDE DU VESTIBULE
1er ÉTAGE
Fig. e
BUFFET
HÔTEL
BUFFET
SALLE DU MÉTRO
COUPE VERTICALE D'UNE PARTIE DU QUAI DE TÊTE
PERPENDICULAIREMENT AUX VOIES
Fig. f
QUAI DE TÊTE
COUR SOUTERRAINE

11 — PARIS - Gare de l'Est
B. F., PARIS

The main elevation after the work of 1888–91.

The station building seen from the train tracks after the first extension of the station in 1859; to the sides of the main train shed, note the small covered platforms for the Mulhouse trains.
The space which made the greatest impact was that of the original train shed, with a braced rounded vault.

Previous pages:
Plates from the presentation of the 1931 extension project.

2 reed & stern and warren & wetmore

grand central terminal

new york, united states 1903–13

project
Reed & Stern and Warren & Wetmore
location
New York, United States
chronology
1903: open competition for designs
1903–11: project
1911–13: construction

This station was designed and built in the years 1903–13 by the Associated Architects of Grand Central Terminal (a group which comprised two studios of architects: Reed & Stern and Warren & Wetmore). One of the United States' more important works of Beaux-Arts architecture, it was also one of the most technologically-advanced building projects of the early twentieth century. In the words of Matthew Kennedy, the terminal provides "a brilliant solution to the functional problems posed by a complex metropolitan railroad station," as well as being "the core of a city-planning scheme that was of exceptional technological daring and enormous impact on the surrounding urban fabric" (Kennedy 1995, p. 67). In effect, the new station resulted in a radical change of a large part of Central Manhattan.

The idea for a new Grand Central Terminal to replace the old Grand Central Depot of 1869 was largely inspired by the introduction of electrical train lines—a very important innovation that made it possible for tracks to be laid underground and thus allow alternative uses of the surface space. Not only was the existing station inadequate to handle this new technology, but there was also a pressing need to alleviate the severe traffic congestion problems within the urban area it occupied. Commissioned by Cornelius Vanderbilt—who saw the station as a symbol of his growing railway empire—the old Grand Central Depot had been designed by the architect John B. Snook and stood above Park Avenue (then called Fourth Avenue) at the junction with 42nd Street, marking a break in Manhattan's rigorously geometrical street grid of "arterial avenues (oriented north-south) and narrow, capillary streets (oriented east-west)" (Kennedy 1995, p. 67). From the point of view of city planning, the Depot soon revealed itself to be a cumbersome presence, increasing the traffic load in this particular area and thus causing congestion; its disruptive character within the surrounding urban fabric was then accentuated when the area occupied by railway tracks was extended. The construction of new streets in the area did little to solve the problem, and within the space of some twenty years the building was proving to be totally inadequate: not only was it an unsuitable neighbor for the so-called Vanderbilt Row projects on Fifth Avenue (between 42nd and 57th Street) which had been commissioned by various wealthy New York families, but it was also incapable of meeting the needs of increased rail traffic (in 1878 the New York Elevated Railway Company had built the "El" along the newly-completed Third Avenue, linking it up with the Grand Central Depot in 1880). By the end of the century, further extension work on the station itself and increases in the number of tracks—by then, more than 300 trains a day were flowing into the Depot—could do little more than offer a stop-gap solution, leading to even greater congestion in the area. What is more, as one writer put it, "the Park Avenue train yards were unsightly and dirty; crosstown traffic was hindered by the spray of smoke and ash that erupted onto the street from the trains traveling just below the street level" (Adams 1998, p. 43).

It was in this period that William J. Wilgus, Head Architect to the New York Central Railroad, anticipated one of the main features of the future GCT when he presented the company board with a project that envisaged sinking the tracks under to create a rail ring that would carry trains beneath the station. However, it was only at the end of 1902—after a tragic collision between two trains in the

entrance tunnel had caused the death of seventeen people—that the City Council approved a plan which obliged the rail company to introduce electrification, lower the level of the tracks and redevelop all the streets in the area (including this end stretch of Park Avenue).
Respecting the conditions laid down by this plan, Wilgus drew up his own design for the new building to occupy the site of the old Depot: a massive towered structure that would be fifteen floors high and house the station, a hotel, offices, restaurants and shops, with the train tracks all underground. The design also included a raised roadway around the station and a network of roads that would run above the tracks visible beneath and guarantee adequate traffic flow east-west and north-south. Within the station building itself, the external approaches became part of a well-organized system of vertical and horizontal links that connected the entrance level (flush with the street) to the underground levels dedicated to the various types of transport using the station. Together with elevators and stairs, ramps running down directly to the platforms guaranteed easy access to the covered area where the waiting trains were visible. In effect, there would be two distinct underground stations at different levels, one handling suburban rail traffic and the other national.
The visionary ideas put forward in this plan were at the basis of the subsequent building of the Grand Central Terminal, being encapsulated in the specifications Wilgus himself drew up for the design competition opened to various architects in 1903. Those invited to participate were Stanford White of the McKim, Mead & White studio, Daniel Burnham, Samuel Huckel Jr. and the Reed & Stern studio—the latter being the winner.
The project presented by these two architects envisaged the redevelopment of Park Avenue as once again a road running uninterruptedly north-south, which "passed not through the terminal but around it, on raised platforms; to the south it bridged crowded 42nd Street on a raised viaduct" (Kennedy 1995, p. 67). Above the track and platform area there would be a "Court of Honor" which, according to Kennedy, echoed the "bold elaboration of the park concept forwarded in the public petitions of 1902" and took up the famous Court of Honor that Daniel Burnham had created for the World's Colombian Exposition in Chicago in 1893. Along either side of the Court ran the two lanes of Park Lane that were to "divide" around the Terminal and then join again at the junction with 48th Street. In keeping with Wilgus's original idea—partly inspired by the desire to fully exploit the value of the Railroad Company's real estate at street level—all the tracks were below ground and could not be seen from outside the station.
However, the original Reed & Stern designs would be substantially revised when another group of architects was called in at the behest of the New York Central stockholders. In fact, William K. Vanderbilt, Chairman of the Board of Directors and a person of great influence, would involve his cousin Whitney Warren—a great enthusiast for the French architecture, who had studied at the École des Beaux-Arts in Paris—and his partner William Wetmore in the project. The two worked not only in New York City, where they would subsequently design most of the buildings around the Grand Central Terminal, but also elsewhere in the United States and abroad (their other projects include the stations of Detroit and Kansas City).
Combined under the ad hoc label of the Associated Architects of Grand Central Terminal, the two studios then embarked on a rather strained collaboration. Many of the ideas that had been put forward in the designs successfully submitted by Reed & Stern were ultimately modified, with the layout of the station being redrawn and various ideas being scrapped (for example, the Court of Honor and the twenty-three-floor hotel that was to have been built on an adjacent site). In 1904, the Associated Architects drew up a new design, whose keyfeature was a vast glass and iron roof which was to be visible from outside the building; this was inspired by the Grand Palais built for the 1900 Paris International Exhibition. The ultimate plans and designs, finally settled in 1907, made the GCT an imposing structure of massive walls, with the main elevation (the work of Warren) having three massive arches that evoke memories of triumphal arches and thus celebrate the station as a new city gateway. Actual building work, directed by Warren & Wetmore, would begin in 1911.
Kenneth Powell sees the main inspiration for the GCT as being Victor Laloux's Gare d'Orsay, built in Paris in 1900. One of the first in Europe to be designed for electric-powered trains, the layout of this station anticipates that main functional features of the New York terminal: the tracks and platforms are underground, linked to the large entrance atrium above by a system of staircases. Early designs for the Grand Central Terminal reveal a similar layout, with a "train room" incorporated in the "concourse" that looked out over the tracks and platforms visible from the waiting room. However, while the idea of a multi-level station may have come from the Gare d'Orsay, the ultimate layout of the GCT is very different. In the final designs, the tracks run under the "express concourse" and—the very opposite of what happens in the Paris station—it is possible to cross from one side of the Grand Central Terminal to the other without being aware of the presence of trains at all. There is no visual relation between the entrance level and the track level beneath.
A symbol of the new industrial and cultural power of the United States, the GCT is, in effect, a combination of the most modern building technologies and traditional materials. In keeping with the principles of Beaux-Arts architecture, the architects decided to conceal the weight-bearing structure behind a massive facing of Indiana limestone and Connecticut granite. Designed by Warren, the weighty arched façade giving onto 42nd Street has been described as "impressive both for its monumentality and its purity of form" (Powell 1996, p. 15); decorative motifs are used courageously but with restraint, culminating in the group *The Glory of Commerce* by the sculptor Jules Alexis Contan.
Inside, the station is organized like a multi-level machine. The subway and intercity train lines are divided between the seven underground levels; the former obviously occupying the lower levels. There are two ample concourses—the Express and Suburban—at two different levels, making the GCT into two superimposed stations.
The architects strove for designs that would reflect the pulsating energy of urban existence, with great care and attention being dedicated to the decoration and layout of the large spaces to be used by passengers and public alike. Wide galleries on three sides of the rectangular building formed raised piazzas overlooking the large entrance atrium, which thus becomes the hub of the building. The gigantic main concourse (470 × 160 feet) has been returned to its original splendor by recent restoration work that has confirmed its standing as a masterpiece of Beaux-Arts architecture. Inspired by Roman thermae, it has floral-motif wall decoration in Tennessee marble and a painted ceiling by Paul Helleu showing "the constellations of the autumn night sky (October–March); by accident the constellations were painted backwards" (Adams 1998, p. 44). This area houses the ticket office, the information desk and the luggage deposit, while to the far west end of the concourse—giving onto Vanderbilt Avenue and the taxi stand—there is a wide staircase. Exits are located along the south, east and west sides of the

The first version of the Grand Central Depot built by John B. Snook; and the building after the redevelopment of 1897–98.

building, while the ramps down to the underground levels are on the 42nd Street side of the station, between the ticket office and the waiting room. The most substantial modification made as a result of the 1995 refurbishment commissioned by the Metropolitan Transportation Authority was the addition of a staircase on the east side (this was included in the original plans, but never built) and the restoration of all the original painted surfaces.
A system of ramps that leads to the suburban concourse continues the downward movement of passengers as they flow in from the street. Within the terminal, the numerous corridors, the vertical links between the different levels and the very layout of the different "substations" (for suburban and intercity trains) all facilitate the movement of the thousands of people passing through the building.
The underground rail tracks and the street-level (or raised) road system running around the station make the GCT into a massive junction of different types of transport. In an article published in *L'Illustration* (September 24, 1927) Le Corbusier himself commented on another surprising aspect of the development of underground railways, with stations becoming a sort of "other" city that pulse with their own life: "Beneath the roots of the trees are two underground levels of train tracks and platforms, meaning that the pedestrian walking the streets of the city cannot see but only imagine this submerged city beneath him." As Adams claims, "this multi-level traffic system and the strange sense of disequilibrium it provokes was the essence of modern urbanism" (Adams 1998, p. 44).
Upon completion, the GCT became the core of an area of urban development simply known as "Terminal City." According to Adams, "the most important long-term urbanistic effect of Grand Central Terminal development was on the north side of the station along Park Avenue. Railway embankments were closed, the tracks were depressed further below ground, and the old train yard was covered." This scheme reflected the spirit with which Warren & Wetmore approached the project; for them "the new Grand Central Terminal [was] the heart of 'The Terminal City,' a specialized city-within-a-city" which covered a total of thirty blocks and would comprise "hotels and modern apartment houses, convention and exhibition halls, clubs and restaurants, and department stores" (Adams 1998, p. 44). The buildings subsequently constructed in this area—the Grand Central Palace (1909–11), the Grand Central Station Post Office (1913), the Biltmore Hotel (1911–13), the Hotel Chatman (1917) and the Racquet and Tennis Club (designed by McKim, Mead & White, 1918)—created a regular urban fabric of relatively uniform height (between twelve and twenty stories) that occupied the area between Park Avenue and 42nd and 57th Street. The buildings closest to the Terminal were linked to it directly by pedestrian underpasses, allowing residents direct access to trains and to the shopping facilities contained within the station.
The culminating point in the development of techniques for building above underground tracks came with the Park Lexington Building, between the Grand Central Palace and Park Avenue. As Kennedy comments, "the structure of the first buildings incorporated two levels of underground tracks, rising directly from their massive steel frameworks, but that system was abandoned because the superstructures were adversely affected by the vibrations caused by moving trains." In the Park Lexington Building, however, the support steel frameworks were entirely independent of the underground rail levels, with pilasters (placed between the tracks and the platforms) being sunk into a foundation ca. 56 feet below street level; it was this technique which would resolve the problem of the vibrations and thus make it possible to raise higher structures. Hence, not only was the Grand Central Terminal an important monument to rail travel, a technological and aesthetic marvel that marked a key step in the development of a new model of railway station, but the "Terminal City" area around it also provided sizable opportunities for the development of innovative construction techniques.

Bibliography

W.J. Wilgus, *"The Grand Central Terminal in Perspective," Transactions of the American Society of Civil Engineers*, 106, 1941, pp. 992–1024.
J. Marston Fitch, D.S. Waite, *Grand Central Terminal and Rockfeller Center: a Historic-critical Estimate of their Significance*, New York 1971.
D. Nevins (ed.), *Grand Central Terminal: City within the City*, Municipal Arts Society, New York 1982.
M. Kennedy, "'Terminal City': Architecture and Railways in New York," *Casabella*, June 1995, pp. 22–33.
K. Powell, *Grand Central Terminal: Warren and Wetmore*, Phaidon, London 1996.
N. Adams, "The Rebirth of the Grand Central Terminal, New York: The Electric Modern Restored," *Casabella*, 661, November 1998, pp. 43–47.

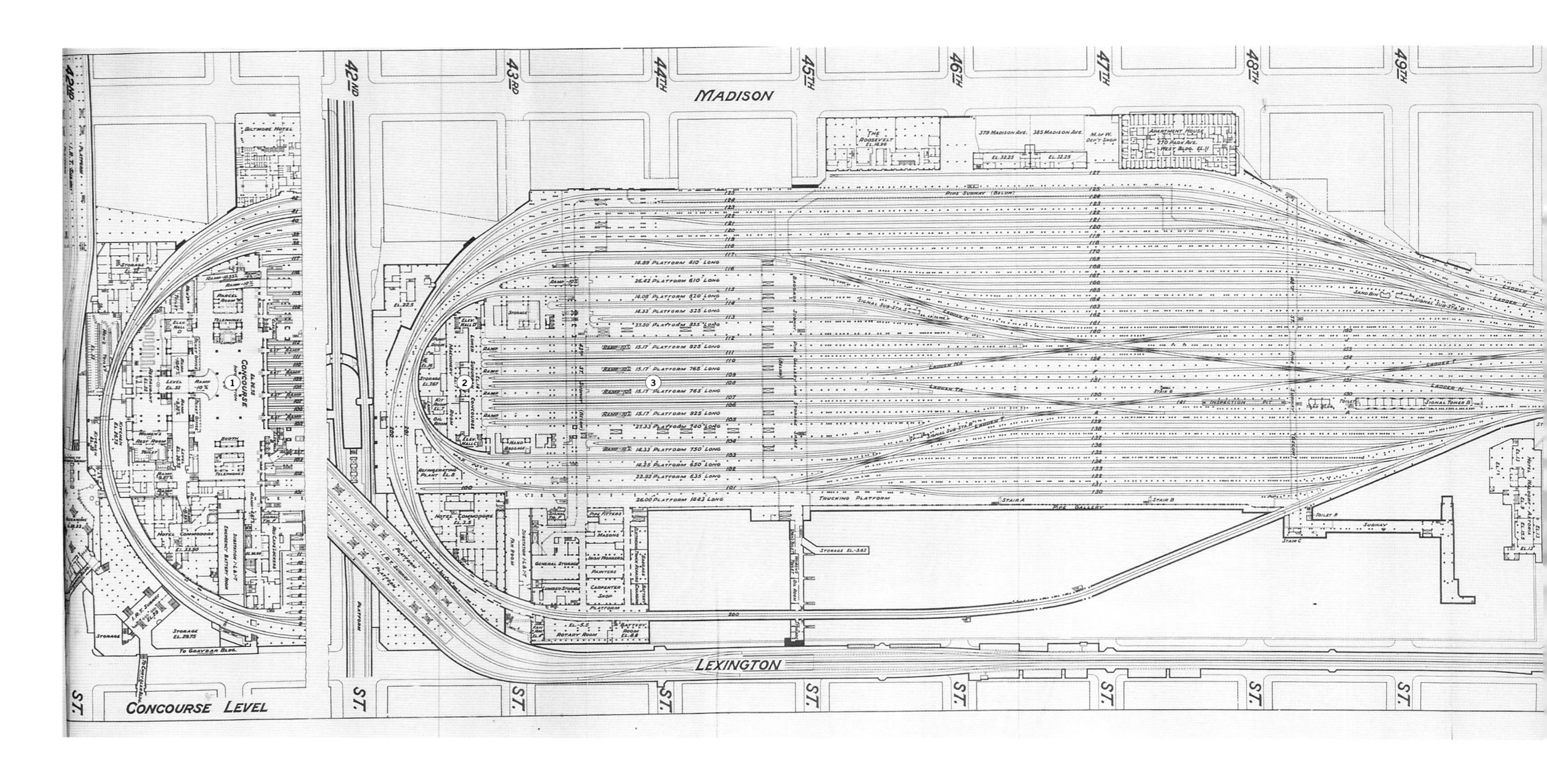
MADISON
LEXINGTON
CONCOURSE LEVEL
42ND
43RD
44TH
45TH
46TH
47TH
48TH
49TH
ST.
BILTMORE HOTEL
CONCOURSE
HOTEL COMMODORE
THE ROOSEVELT
APARTMENT HOUSE
TRUCKING PLATFORM
INSPECTION PIT
SIGNAL TOWER B
ROTARY ROOM
CARPENTER SHOP
PAINTERS
GENERAL STORAGE

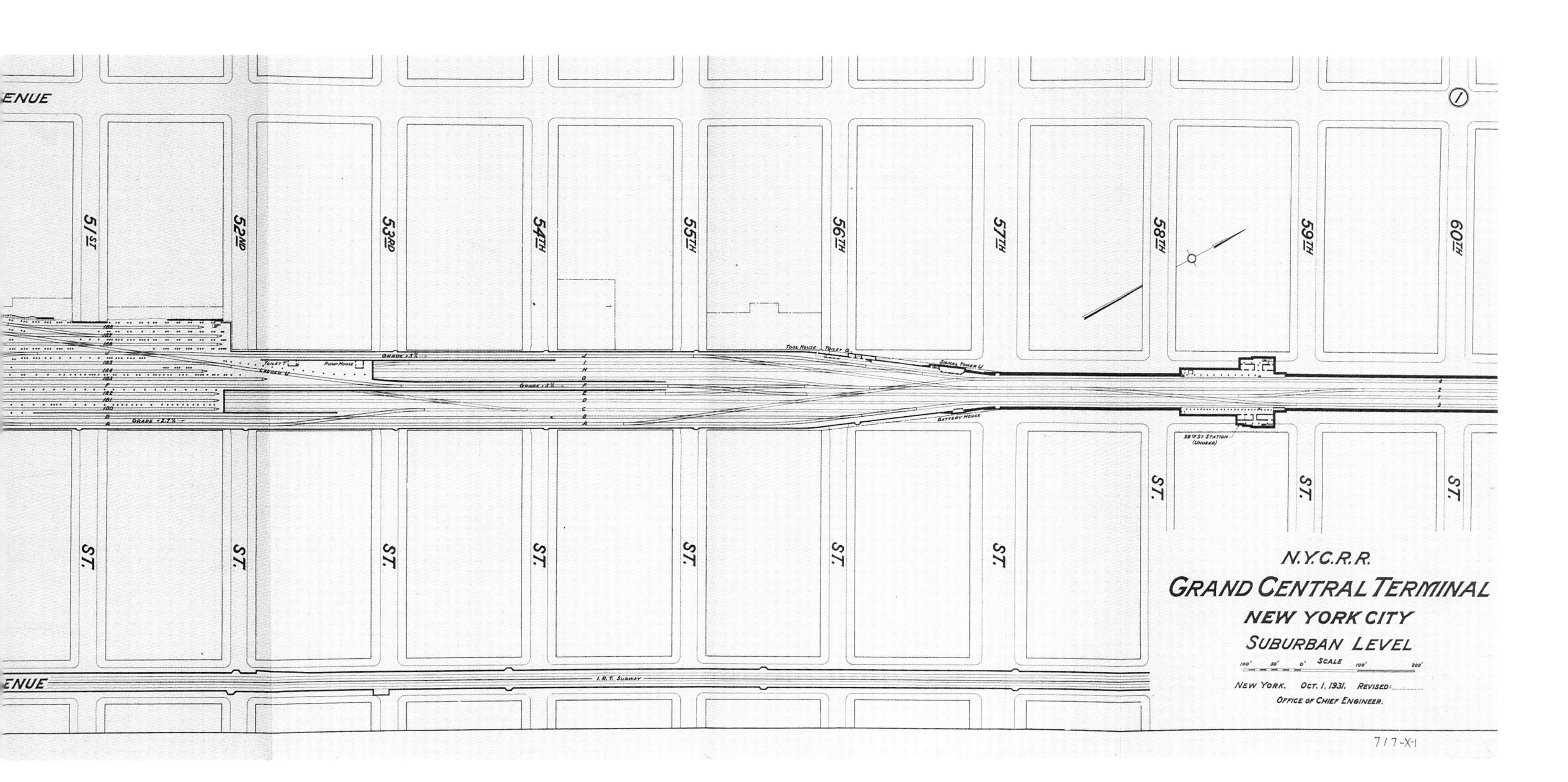

Plan of the underground level for subway trains.
Key: **1** suburban concourse **2** lower-level concourse **3** platforms

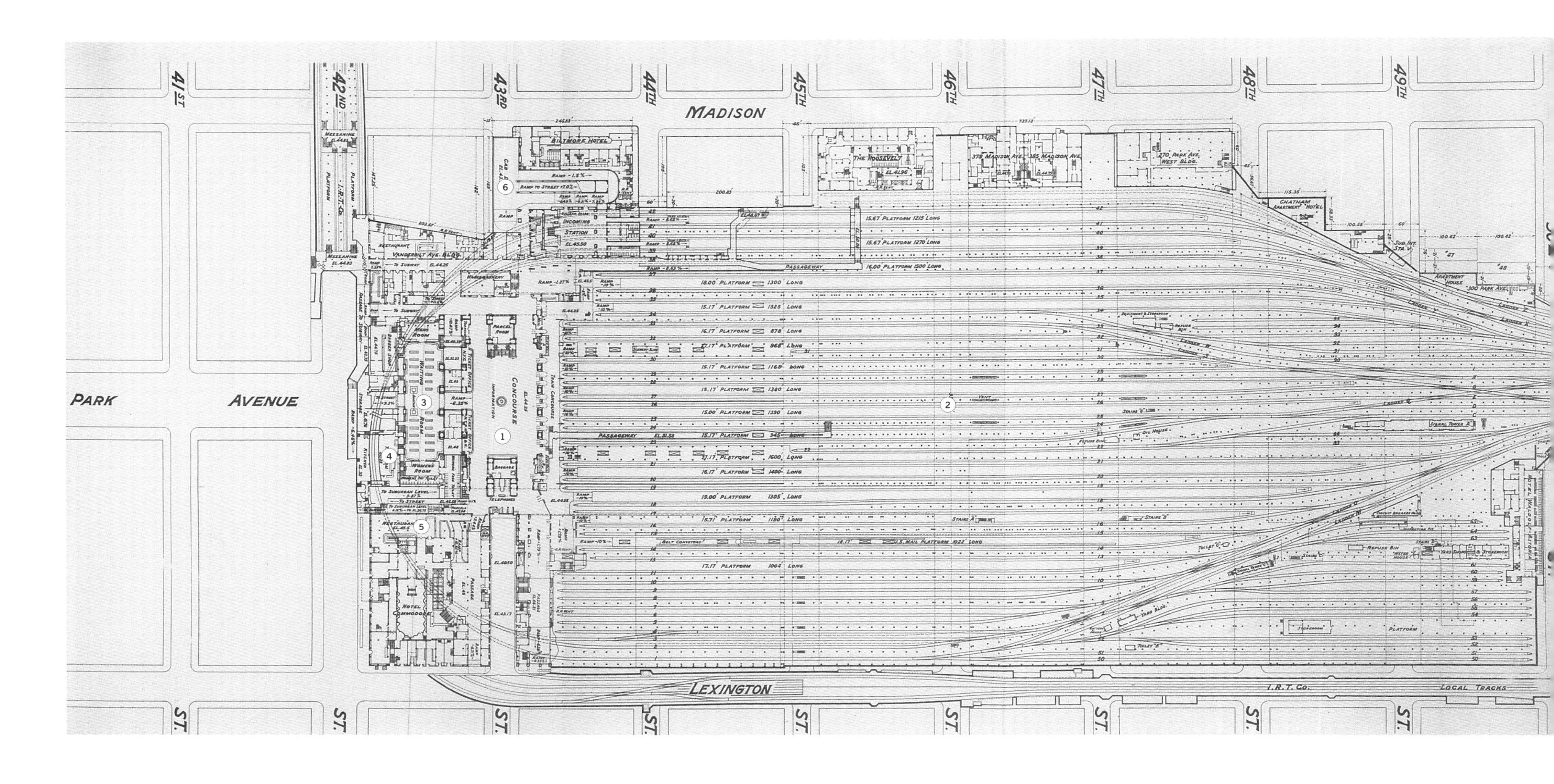
41ST
42ND
43RD
44TH
45TH
46TH
47TH
48TH
49TH
MADISON
PARK
AVENUE
LEXINGTON
BILTMORE HOTEL
THE ROOSEVELT
379 MADISON AVE.
385 MADISON AVE.
270 PARK AVE. WEST BLDG.
CHATHAM APARTMENT HOTEL
CONCOURSE
HOTEL COMMODORE
VANDERBILT AVE. BLDG.
PASSAGEWAY
I.R.T. CO.
LOCAL TRACKS
ST.
1
2
3
4
5
6

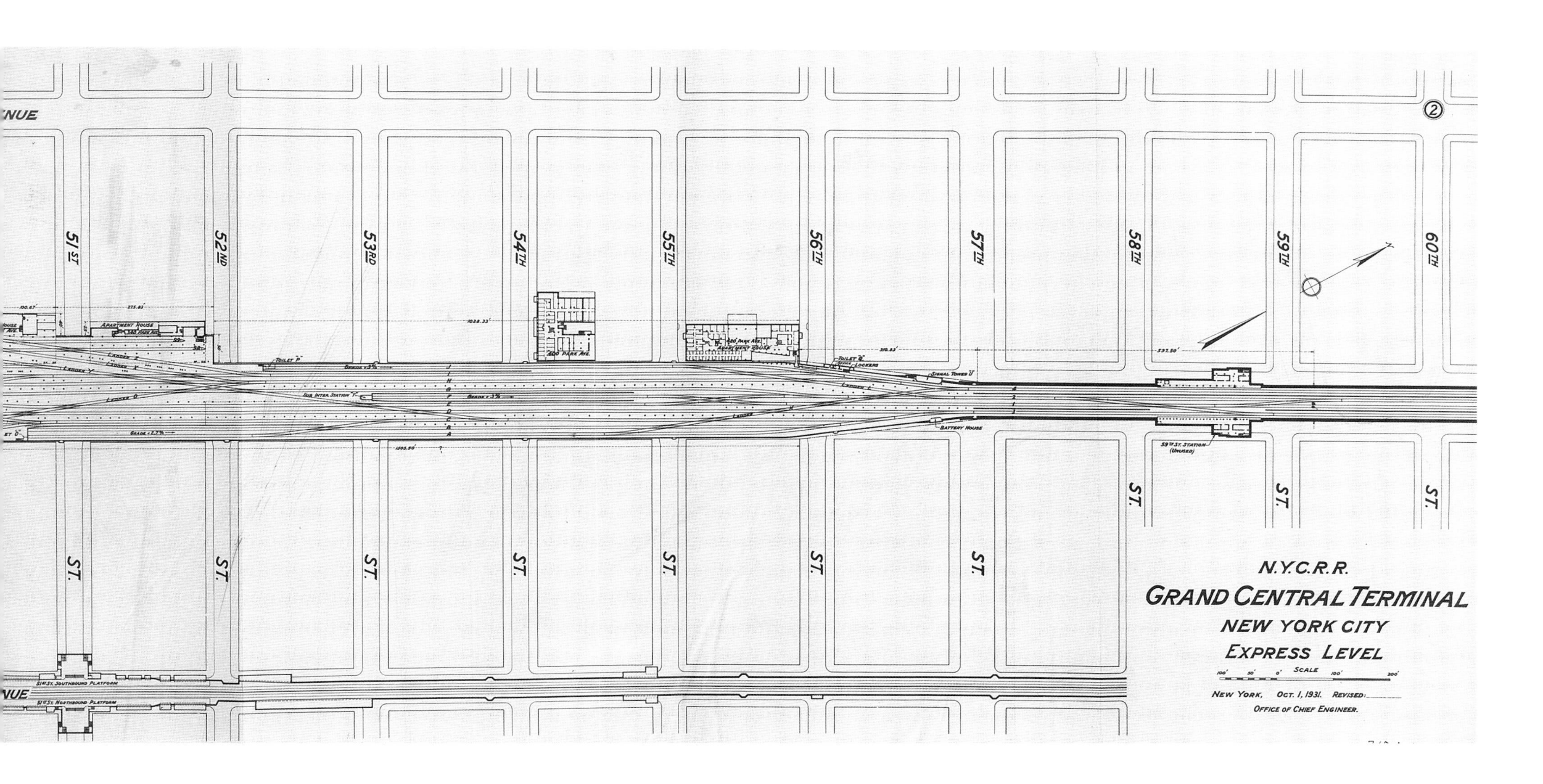

Plan of the underground level for intercity trains
Key: **1** express concourse **2** platforms **3** waiting room **4** tea room
5 restaurant **6** ramp up to street level.

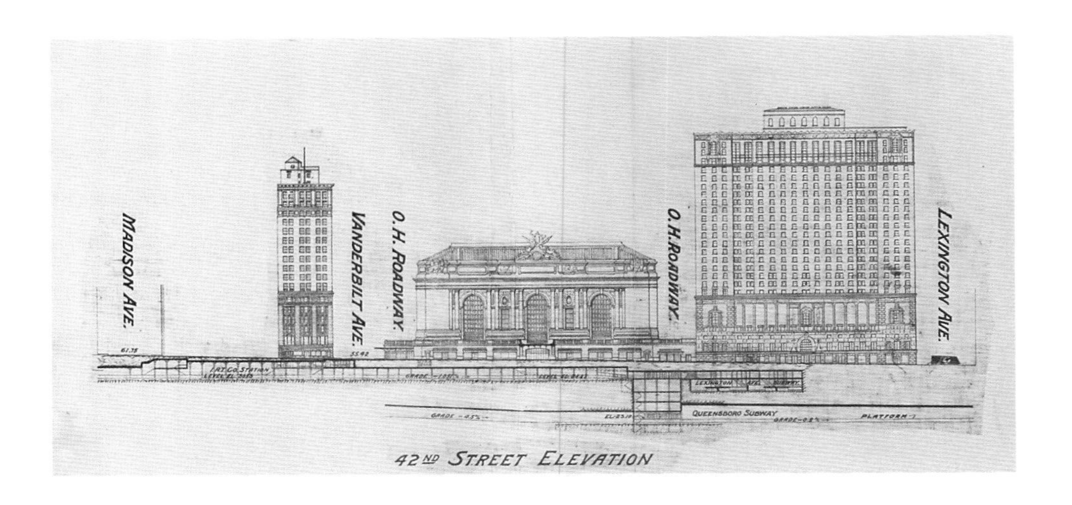
MADISON AVE.
VANDERBILT AVE.
O.H. ROADWAY.
O.H. ROADWAY.
LEXINGTON AVE.
QUEENSBORO SUBWAY
42ND STREET ELEVATION

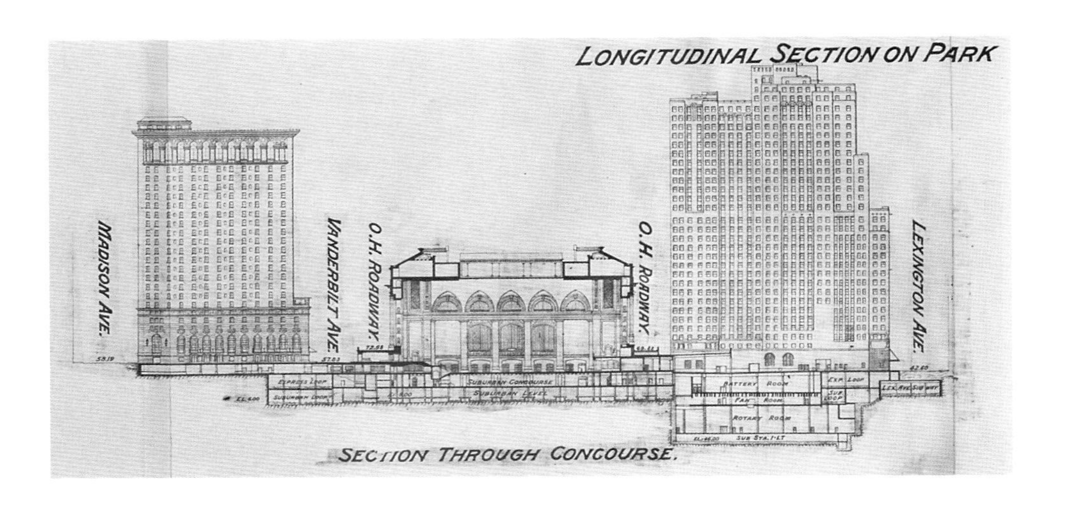
LONGITUDINAL SECTION ON PARK
MADISON AVE.
VANDERBILT AVE.
O.H. ROADWAY.
O.H. ROADWAY.
LEXINGTON AVE.
SUBURBAN CONCOURSE
SECTION THROUGH CONCOURSE.

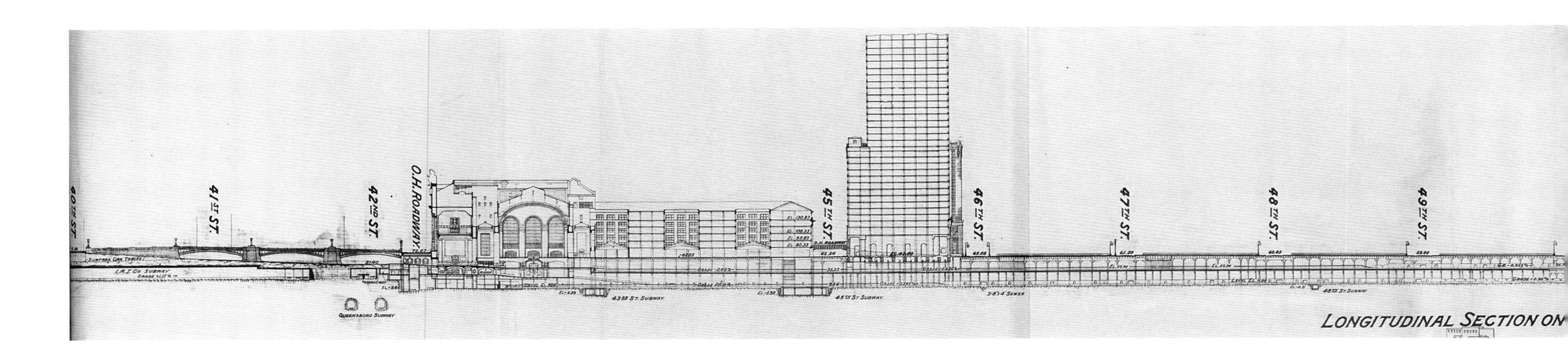
40TH ST.
41ST ST.
42ND ST.
O.H. ROADWAY.
45TH ST.
46TH ST.
47TH ST.
48TH ST.
49TH ST.
QUEENSBORO SUBWAY
43RD ST. SUBWAY
45TH ST. SUBWAY
48TH ST. SUBWAY
LONGITUDINAL SECTION ON

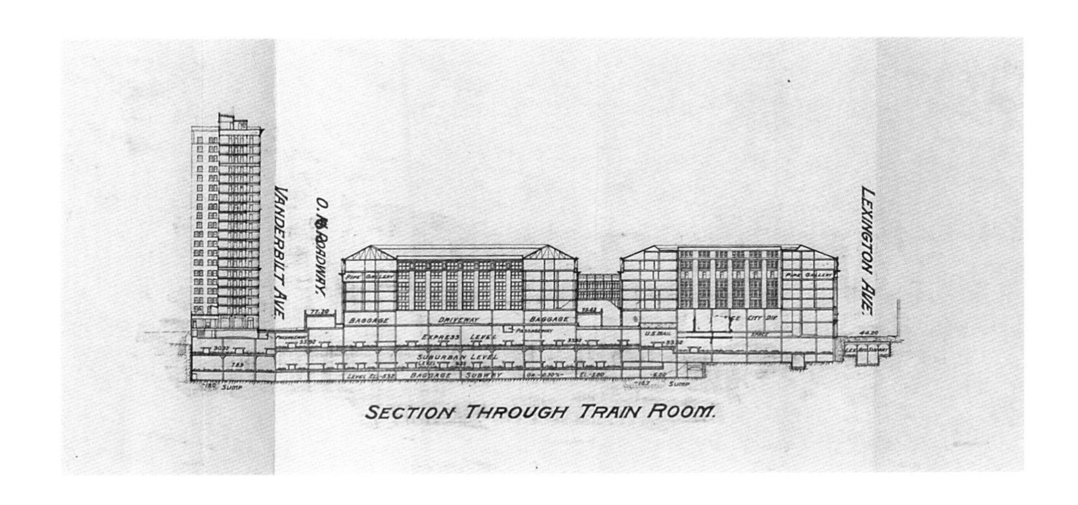

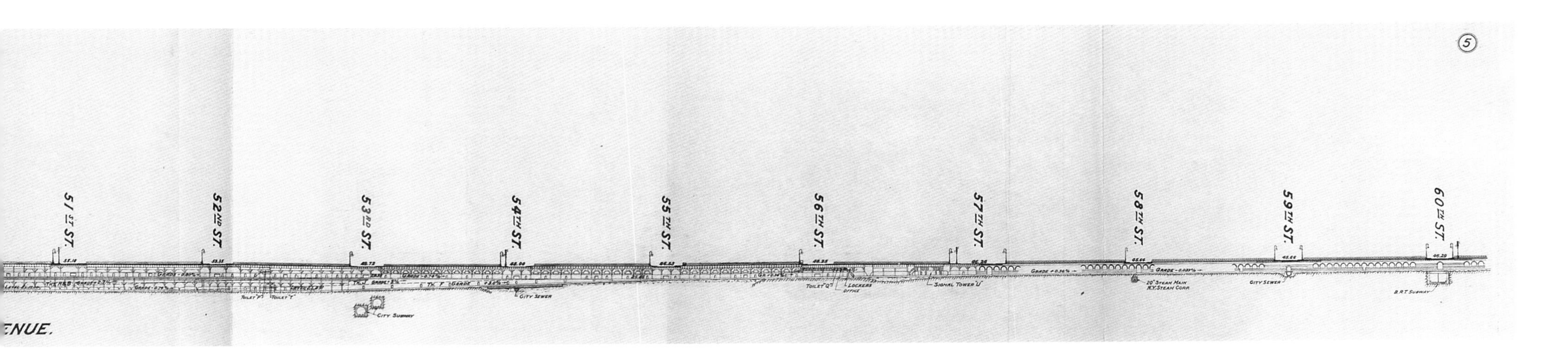

Elevation on 42nd Street, section through the concourse and longitudinal section.

Section through train room.

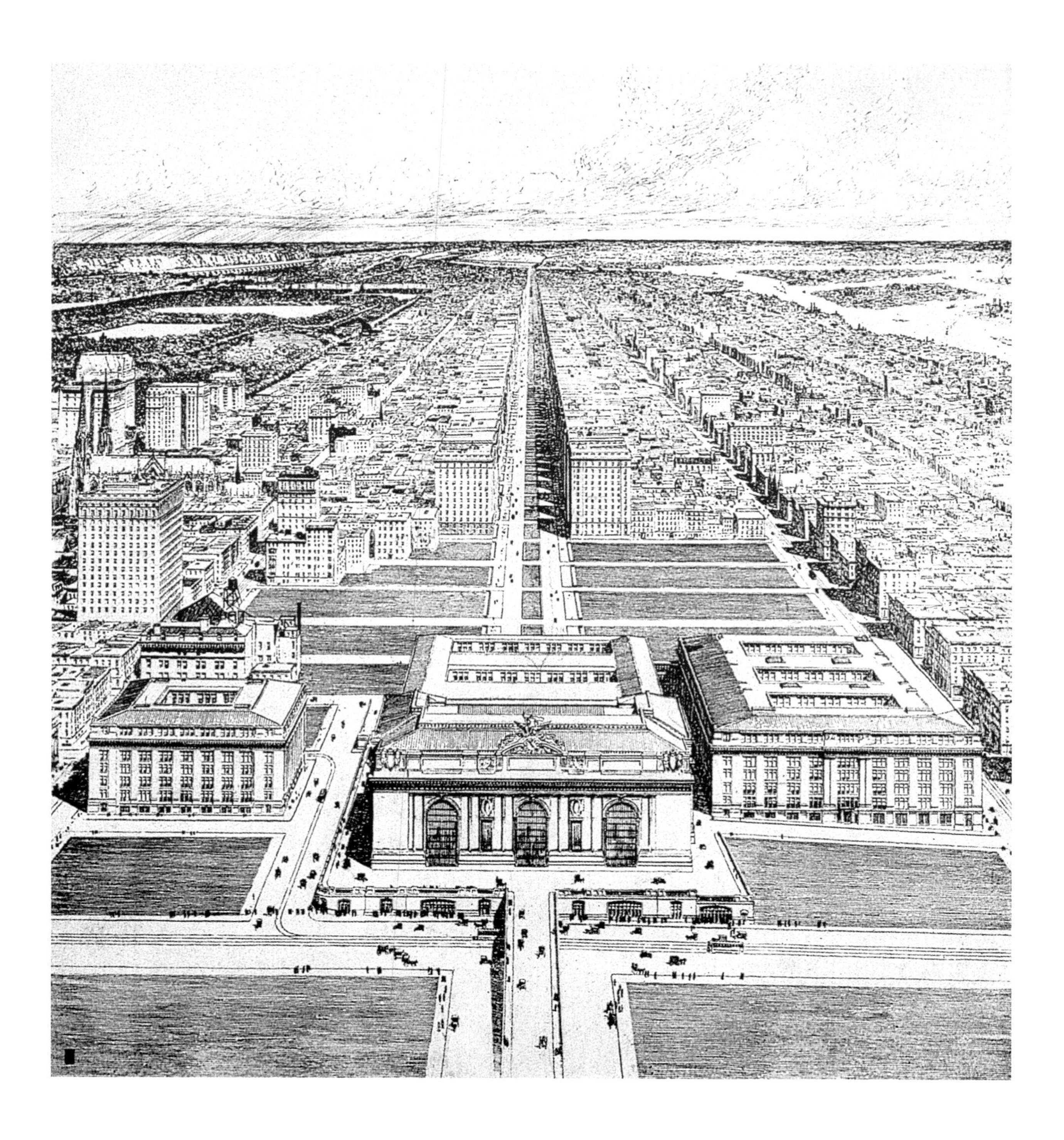

The Grand Central Terminal and Terminal City in a map produced
for the New York World's Fair of 1939.

A 1931 photograph showing the view from Park Avenue
to 40th Street and the road bridge; view of the New York Central Building
and Terminal City seen from Park Avenue.

The large entrance atrium, one of the largest public spaces in America, lit from above by the daylight falling through the lunettes.

The painting on the ceiling of the atrium shows a reverse view of the constellations as seen in an autumnal night sky (from October to March).
The main waiting room; recently restored, this was designed in Classical taste.

Between the ticket office and the waiting-room are the ramps down to the lower levels.
A view of the ramps leading to the suburban concourse.
The famous double windows on the eastern side of the building.

The main concourse after the 1995 restoration, with the double-glass windows once more visible and all the surfaces restored to their lighter colors.
Before in a dark blue-green, the ceiling can now be seen in its original cerulean blue.
The most important architectural modification was the addition of a staircase.
The curved canopies over the lunettes at the sides of the vault are cream-colored; the walls, once a dull brown, are once again tan-colored.

3 gruppo toscano

stazione di santa maria novella

florence, italy 1932–35

project
Gruppo Toscano
architects
Giovanni Michelucci (head architect),
Nello Baroni, Pier Niccolò Berardi,
Italo Gamberini, Sarre Guarnieri,
Leonardo Lusanna
client
Ferrovie dello Stato
location
Piazza Santa Maria Novella, Florence, Italy
chronology
1932: open competition for designs
1932–33: project
1933–35: construction

The twenty-year period 1920–40 was one that saw great development both in the scope and quality of the architecture of Italian railway stations. The wide overarching train shed was abolished in favor of individual cantilever roofs; and in buildings which developed horizontally rather than vertically, the sharp separation between the train area and that reserved to passengers was gradually suppressed, meaning that—in both form and layout—the resultant stations comprised a more unified single space.
The manifesto for this phase of development was undoubtedly the station of Santa Maria Novella in Florence, on the design of which the Gruppo Toscano, headed by Giovanni Michelucci, began work in 1932. The finished building would immediately receive international recognition as a masterpiece of modern architecture, and a close study of the history of the project—from the first plans drawn up by the Works Department of the Italian State Railways to the Gruppo Toscano designs finally employed when building work began in 1933—casts light on all the salient features of the approach to this particularly important question of modern design taken by early-twentieth-century Italian architecture.
Initially, plans had been commissioned from Angiolo Mazzoni, Head of the Works Department of the Italian State Railways, who presented three distinct proposals, all of which envisaged shifting the passenger structure of the station further back towards the actual tracks, thus creating a large trapezoidal public square between the front of the station and the apse of the church of Santa Maria Novella. But the very location of the building—in the heart of Florence and so close to the historical church—inevitably raised the question of the relation between the ancient urban structure and the modern building. Such comparisons led to the rejection of each of Mazzoni's schemes, with all their subsequent variants (for a more detailed discussion of this question, see U. Cao, "La Stazione di Santa Maria Novella a Firenze e l'affermazione dell'architettura razionale in Italia," in *La stazione e la città*, Gangemi, Rome 1990, pp. 93–98).
Public opinion—and the city's press—were so hostile to Mazzoni's ideas that the political authorities were obliged to call a public competition for designs on August 20, 1932. The committee that would judge the entries was chaired by Cesare Oddone and included Cesare Bazzani, Armando Brasini, Marcello Piacentini, Romano Romanelli and Tommaso Martinetti, with the Italian Ministry of Communications reserving the final say to itself. The material supplied to applicants in the competition included the ground plan drawn up by Mazzoni, which gave a precise description of the exact area of the site, and the specifications required architects to design "a building solely for the housing of passenger services," laying down that "the project must be compatible with the work that is already underway. The buildings for postal services on Via Alemanni will be modified to make them in keeping with the winning design" (Belluzzi, Conforti 1986, p. 96). The actual cantilever roofs to be raised over the individual platforms were, however, to be built according to the designs proposed by Mazzoni.
Sixteen designs were selected for final consideration, and that submitted by the Gruppo Toscano was then declared the winner; however, the jury's decision was again criticized by local associations: the Reale Accademia delle Arti e del Disegno, the Sindacato Fascista Ingegneri and

The station gives onto a sloping trapezoidal piazza. A "cascade" of glass runs down the *pietra forte* façade to then continue over the covered area of the driveway.

the Associazione Leonardo da Vinci all made official complaints about the running of the competition to the Ministry of Communications and to the head of Government. The Engineers Union criticized the winning design on various grounds: technical considerations of the construction itself; its environmental impact; the distribution of traffic flow and services it envisaged. Such criticisms were though judged unfounded by the authoritative engineers Nervi and Fiori, with the competition and its result ultimately being declared valid by the Fascist minister Galeazzo Ciano in summer 1933.
Founded on the occasion of the Third Italian Exhibition of Rationalist Architecture (MIAR), held in Florence in 1932, the Gruppo Toscano brought together a number of very young architects—Nello Baroni, Pier Niccolò Berardi, Italo Gamberini and Leonardo Lusanna—who (with the exception of the latter) had all studied under the head of the group, Giovanni Michelucci, at the Florentine Scuola Superiore di Architettura. The project they subsequently presented for the Santa Maria Novella competition was inspired largely by the graduation designs drawn up by Lusanna and Gamberini; the latter had actually graduated in 1932 with a project for a passenger-terminal building for the station of Santa Maria Novella, which dealt not only with the actual design of the building but contained a technical and functional study of such a facility. The fundamental importance of Gamberini's role has been emphasized by Koening, who identifies the "cascade" of glass in the façade, the low cantilever roof, the use of horizontal bands of *pietra forte* and the layout of the terminal concourse as all being features of the young architect's graduation project. In the final designs, his work underwent only such insignificant variations as "the elimination of the windows in the façade and the suppression of a section at the front of the building to contain the structure within the site limits set by the competition specifications" (Koening 1968).
In the presentation of their project, the Gruppo Toscano wrote that "no architectural problem is perhaps so difficult of solution as the reorganization of the layout of the Florence station" (*Eclettica* 1933, p. 38), because the designers had to meet the conflicting needs of city planning and railway services. One of the first issues to be tackled was the alignment of the new building in relation to the tracks themselves. At the same time, the ground plan drawn up was heavily influenced by the need for work to be carried out in two stages so as not to totally interrupt the normal working of the station; the competition specifications had explicitly required that the two phases be distinctly marked, respecting a division already indicated on the plan that gave the precise perimeter to be respected by the new building. The group decided to "locate on one side of this separating line the departures atrium and the ticket office, which were conceived of as a wide space 'laid out with the greatest clarity' so that travelers would be able to get their bearings as easily as possible" (*Eclettica* 1933, p. 41).
The general layout used in Florence recalls that of nineteenth-century terminal stations, with the transversal concourse between passenger reception building and platforms envisaged as a sort of covered street with shops and facilities. As in nineteenth-century stations, this terminal concourse was open at either end so that passengers could gain direct access to it without having to pass through the reception building. This latter structure was a volume aligned lengthwise, with an ample atrium-ticket office (33 × 28 meters) around which were laid out other station facilities: on the Via Valfonda side there were most of those for arriving passengers, on the Via Alemanni side, those for departing passengers. The former, therefore, had the baggage deposit, the restaurant, the buffet and tourist information areas—as well as the first- and second-class waiting rooms. "Behind these rooms, in the section of the building looking onto the forecourt, were a restaurant dining room, a small private dining room and the offices of the Wagon-Lits Company. On the departures side of the station, there were the rooms housing telephone services, a buffet and the third-class waiting room" (Belluzzi, Conforti 1986, p. 97).
The front of the station gave onto a sloping trapezoidal area, with a "cascade" of glass falling down the façade and then projecting forward over the outer wall of the covered section of the driveway, where cars could drop off or pick up passengers. Alberto Baratelli sees the use of *pietra forte* as inspired by the desire to establish some sort of dialogue between the new station and the nearby apse of the church of Santa Maria Novella, one imposing mass of such stone, interrupted solely by a large window of light-reflecting glass. Seen from the piazza before it, the station embodies "a typical Florentine use of solid walls, reminding one of the material presence of the stone in the apse of the church" (Baratelli 2003, p. 18).
The compact mass of the building is cleanly emphasized by the cantilever roof. Interrupted solely from the projecting central block, this roof runs the entire length of the façade over the windows of the restaurant and the other entrances to the station. The solid wall forming the upper

part of the face is interrupted solely by seven vertical bands of Termolux glass which, as has already been mentioned, then extend forward over the projecting volume which "covers part of the driveway" (Belluzzi, Conforti 1986, p. 98). Held in place by vertical iron girders and supports, this double wall of glass runs across the entire width of the large departures hall.

Placed off-center within the façade, the "cascade" that flows over the concourse and the atrium-ticket office sets up a vertical contrast with the horizontal bands of stone. The actual form and location of the covered car entrance were largely determined by "considerations of urban planning": to prevent traffic congestion, the architects decided to create in front of the atrium of the departures hall a covered glass gallery, open at either end, through which "there would be one-way traffic flow running parallel to the layout of the building" (*Eclettica* 1933, p. 43). Incoming cars would drive in directly from Via Valfonda and exit into Via Panini, leading in the direction of the city center.

For "environmental" reasons, the Gruppo Toscano decided that the new station building should be in keeping with the "markedly horizontal character" of most of the buildings around the piazza, which was "dominated by the harmonious upward thrust of the apse and bell tower of Santa Maria Novella"; by marking off the far side of the piazza with another horizontal structure, the station would allow the full "monumentality" of the church apse to emerge. (*Eclettica* 1933, p. 44). The new station, conclude the architects, harmonizes with its surroundings not only because of its elevation, but also because of the materials used (the same *pietra forte* as that of the church apse).

But within that homogeneous and simple exterior is an interior of rich and varied marble, glass and metal. The atrium-ticket office (departures hall) is divided into three aisles: two side aisles of ten meters in height, and a central aisle of twelve. These are entirely faced with different kinds of marble: the walls in yellow Siena; the floors and pilasters in green Alpine serpentine. The ceilings of the side aisles are in white Carrara held in place by metal T-brackets painted white, while the door and window frames are also outlined in white marble; Claudia Conforti speaks here of "an unreal white light flooding down from the ceiling of glass, which is held in place by black frame structures in copper-finished iron"(Belluzzi, Conforti 1986, p. 98). The gigantic marble portals then lead through onto the platform-head concourse, the roofing of which is in part also of glass. One end of the reticular roofing rests on the reception building, while the girders are dog-legged at the other end, due to the difference in height between the platform cantilever roofs and the covering of the concourse.

This transitional space of the concourse makes skillful use of facing materials. The iron girders of the roofing are finished with patinated laminate sheeting—"fitted into the wall at one end, these beams gradually taper towards the other end" (Belluzzi, Conforti 1986, p. 98), so that their appearance actually "contradicts" the reality of the weight-bearing structure—while the inside ceiling of the concourses is made up of translucent glass panels. The floor comprises lengthwise alternate strips of Calacatta and Amiata red marble. The end wall, which is 106 meters long and 7 high, "is laid out like a sort of large departures board in its own right, with a series of portals each surmounted by inscriptions in patinated copper" (Belluzzi, Conforti 1986, p. 98).

At the end of the building housing the offices, on Via Valfonda, is the Royal Pavilion, intended to provide hospitality for the king and his entourage. Given its very special function, this is an independent entity with respect to the rest of the station. It was already included in the competition project, but then the designs for it were reworked in 1934 by Michelucci and other members of the group; as the group's representatives, Italo Gamberini and Niccolò Berardi chaired the two committees which had to assess proposals for the "painted decoration" of the ceremonial reception room and the "group sculpture" for the large outside water basin. Two sides of the pavilion are faced in white Carrara marble with a stylized sequence of pilaster strips, and the drive approach to the building is delimited a semicircular space, at the centre of which stands the water basin of light blue tesserae with Griselli's allegorical figures of *The River Arno and its Valley*.

The pavilion itself is approximately 28 meters square, with the central reception hall extending the full height of the building (10 meters) and being enclosed on two sides by vestibules: one opens onto the giant portico of the entrance, the other gives access directly onto the platforms; the entrance portico itself is linked to the platforms by a gallery that gives onto the arrivals area on the Via Valfonda side of the station.

Inside, the decor makes ample use of precious marbles and wood paneling. The two vestibules have floors in Levantine red marble and walls in Roman stuccowork and walnut; the gallery and the portico have walls in peach-flower Carnic marble and floors in green Alpine serpentine. However, the most careful combination of colors and materials comes in the ceremonial reception hall: the walls here are in slabs of red marble and the floor, as in the neighboring rooms, is in parquet of different woods (walnut, oak and olive), with the fillets laid out in various geometrical designs (a detailed description of the materials can be found in Belluzzi, Conforti 1986, pp. 95–101).

Equal care to detail can be seen in the fittings that the architects designed for all the various areas of the station building and in the various "emblematic" features that are part of any station; see, for example, the clocks, the signposting, the continuous bands of framed photographic enlargements and even the original system of seats-suitcase stands that are fixed to the pillars of the cantilever roofs by means of copper bands. Even here the design respects the principles of balance, linearity and gravitas that had inspired the entire project. "The general appearance of the construction," wrote the Gruppo Toscano, "is, as befits a generation that aims to give vigorous expression to its own age, resolutely modern... However, it is also in keeping with that clear, calm, sharp sense of mass that is a feature of Florentine architecture in general. That architectural spirit will be clear to anyone who knows how to look at Palazzo Pitti, Palazzo Strozzi, Palazzo Riccardi or the greatest churches in the city and see how their mass and volume is built up through the majestic composition of horizontal components. The harmony and beauty of each of these works arises not from frivolous delight in charming decorative details but from their gravitas—that is, their massive clarity and directness" (*Eclettica* 1933, p. 45).

Bibliography

"La stazione di Firenze. Progetto del Gruppo Toscano vincitore del concorso," *Eclettica*, March 1933, reprint 1988.

G.K. Koening, *Architettura in Toscana. Il concorso per la stazione di Firenze*, ERI Edizioni Rai, Turin 1968.

V. Savi, *De Autore*, Edifir, Florence 1985.

A. Belluzzi, C. Conforti, *Giovanni Michelucci. Catalogo delle opere*, Electa, Milan 1986.

F. Bandini (ed.), *La Stazione di Santa Maria Novella 1935–1985, Italo Gamberini e il Gruppo Toscano*, Alinea, Florence 1987.

M. Dezzi Bardeschi, *Giovanni Michelucci. Il progetto continuo*, Alinea, Florence 1992.

A. Baratelli, *Giovanni Michelucci. La stazione di Firenze*, Alinea, Florence 2003.

The solid stone exterior is broken by the seven vertical strips of Termolux glass, which then continue over the covered section of the driveway.
At the end of the office buildings, on Via Valfonda, stands the Royal Pavilion, intended to provide hospitality for the king and his entourage. Given its very special function, this is an independent entity with respect to the rest of the station. Two sides of the pavilion are faced with Carrara marble—in stark contrast with the *pietra forte* of the station proper—and adorned with stylized pilaster strips.

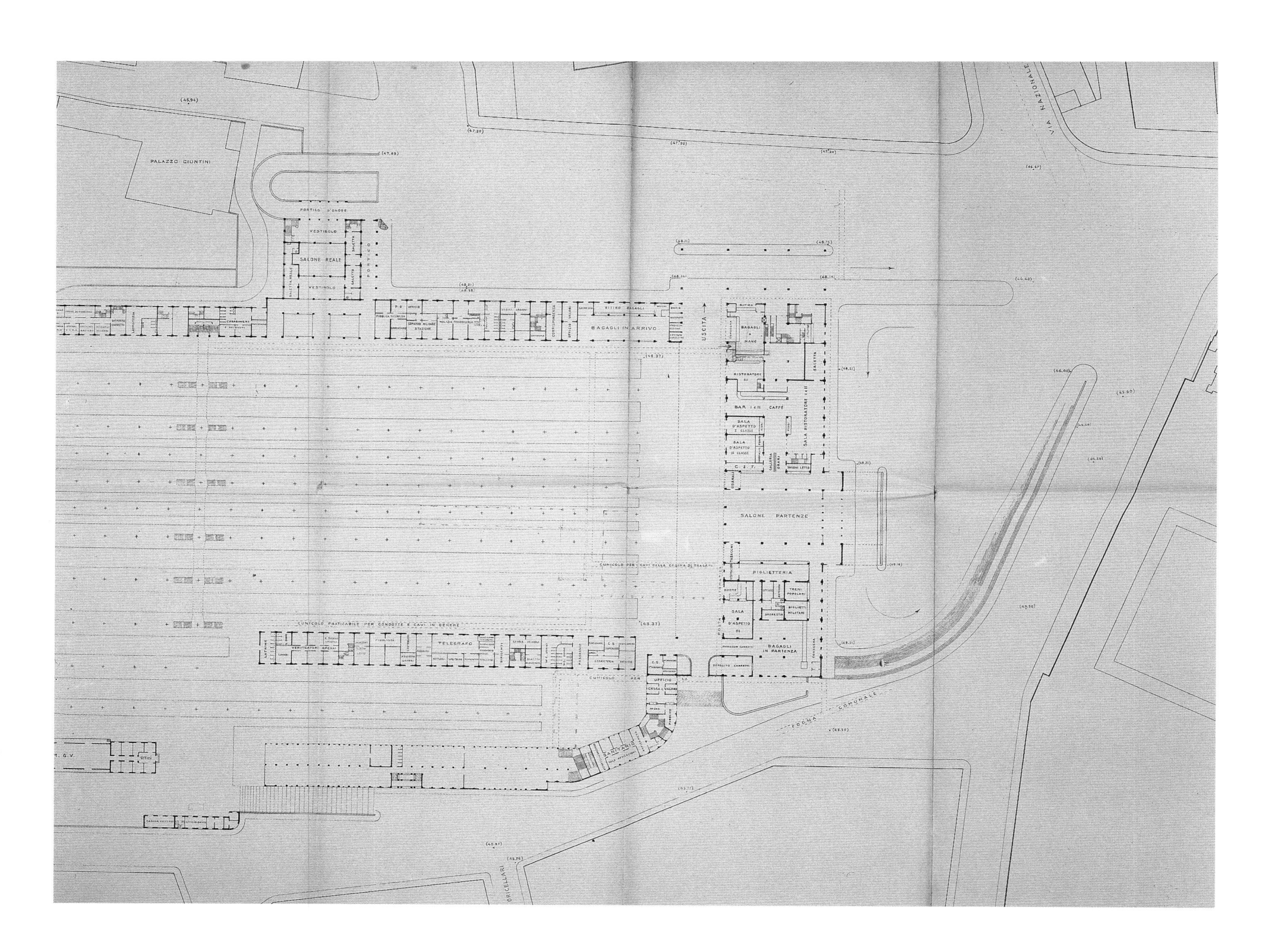

PALAZZO GIUNTINI
VIA NAZIONALE
PORTICO D'ONORE
VESTIBOLO
SALONE REALE
SALETTA
PORTICO
BAGAGLI IN ARRIVO
USCITA
BAGAGLI A MANO
RISTORATORE III
SALETTA
BAR I e II CAFFÈ
SALA D'ASPETTO I CLASSE
SALA D'ASPETTO II CLASSE
SALA RISTORATORE I e II
SALONE PARTENZE
BIGLIETTERIA
SALA D'ASPETTO III
BAGAGLI IN PARTENZA
TRENI POPOLARI
BIGLIETTI MILITARI
TELEGRAFO
CUNICOLO PRATICABILE PER CONDOTTE E CAVI IN GENERE
UFFICIO CASSA E VALORI
SANITARIO
FOGNA COMUNALE
ORICELLARI

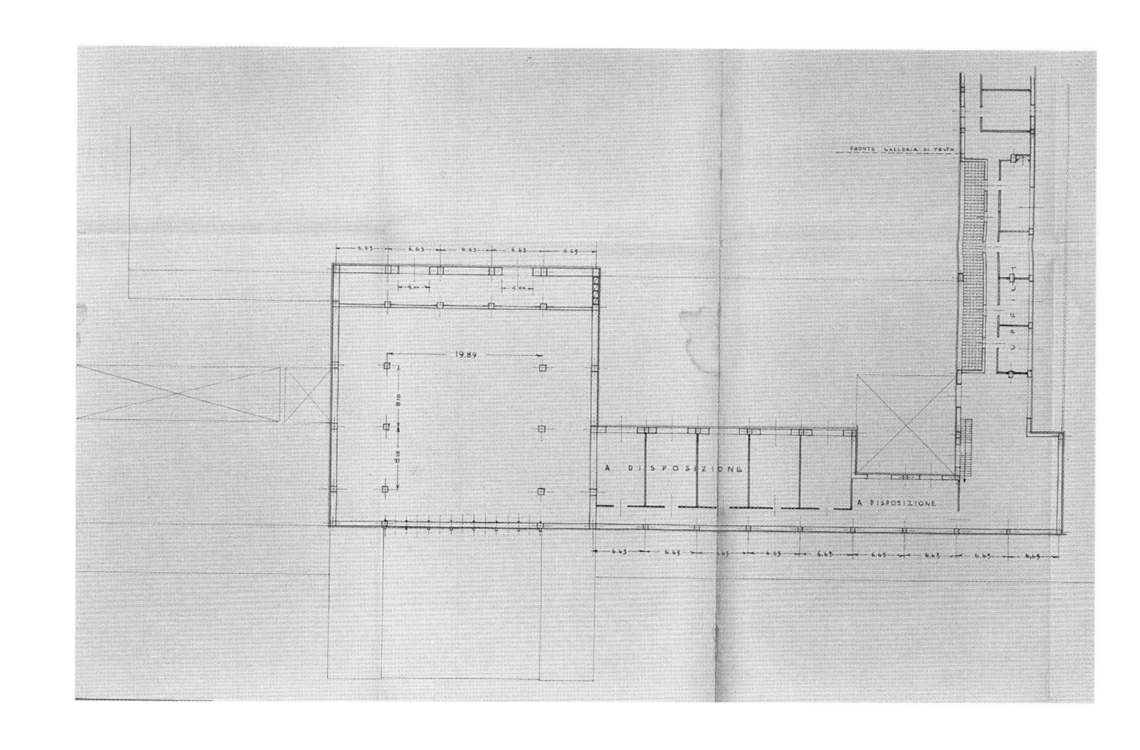

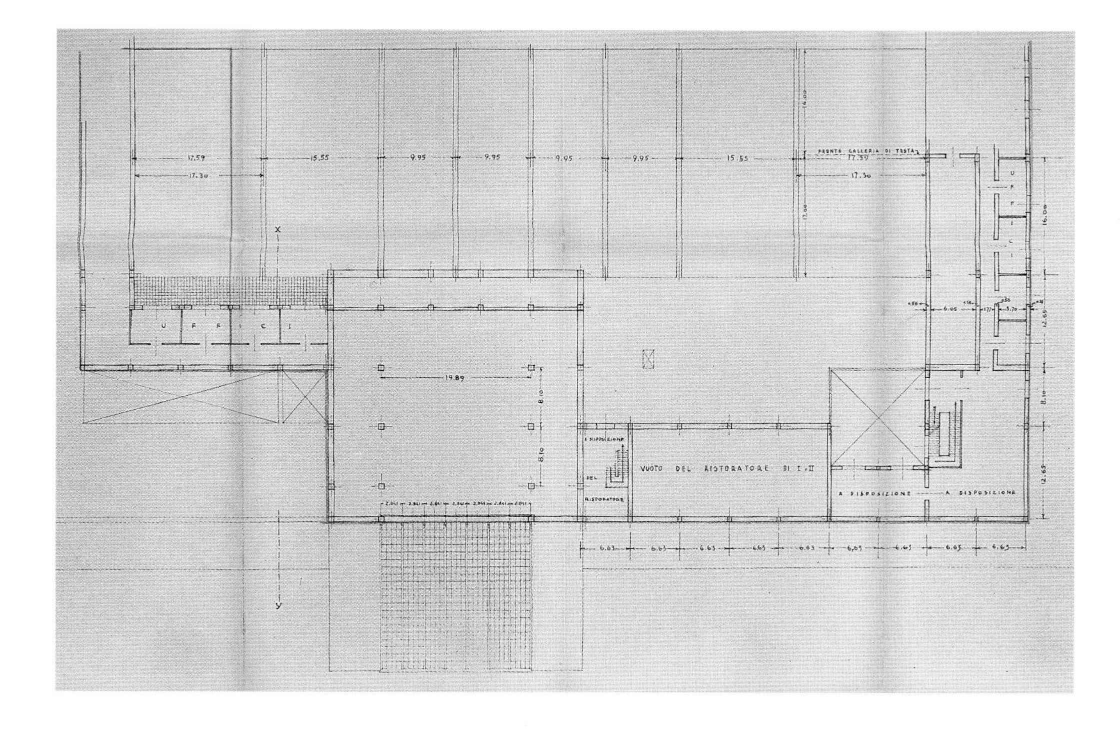

General plan, with the layout of the ground floor.

Plans of the third and first floors of the passenger building.

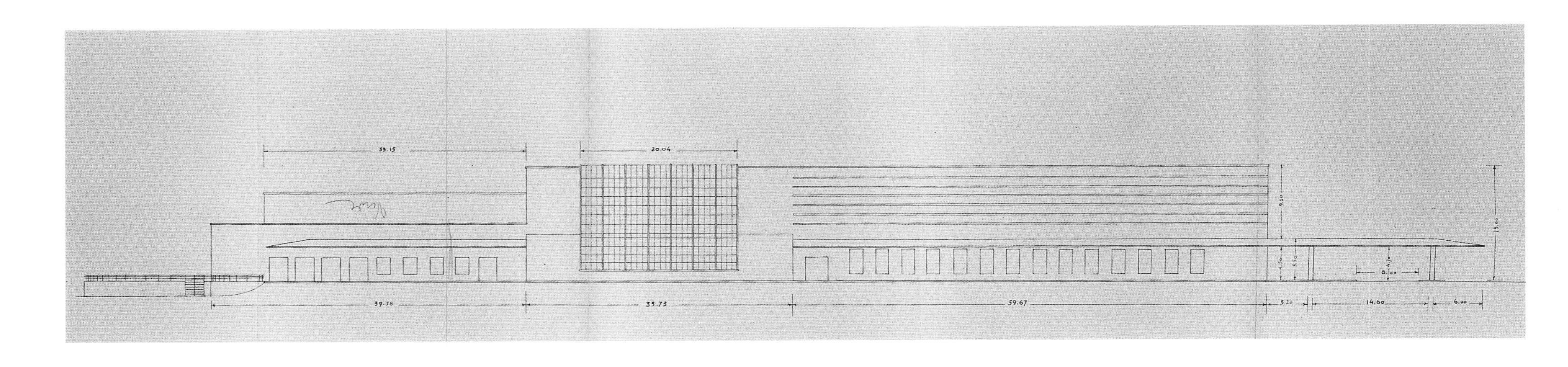

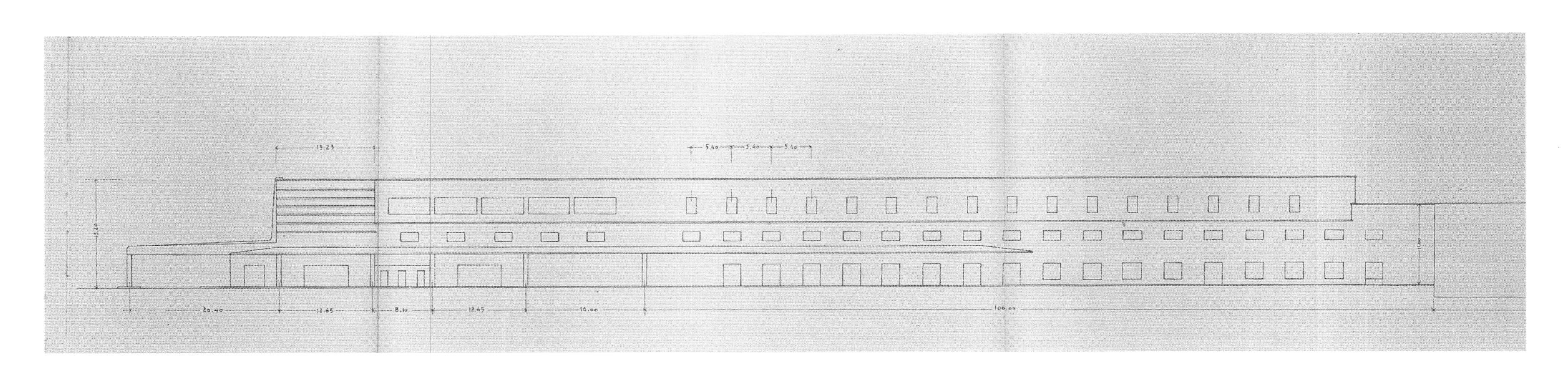

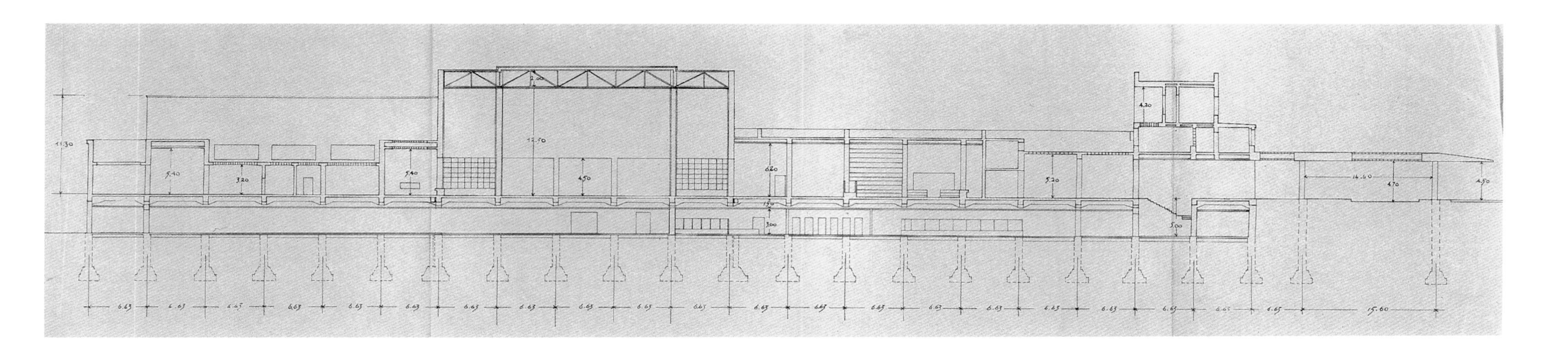

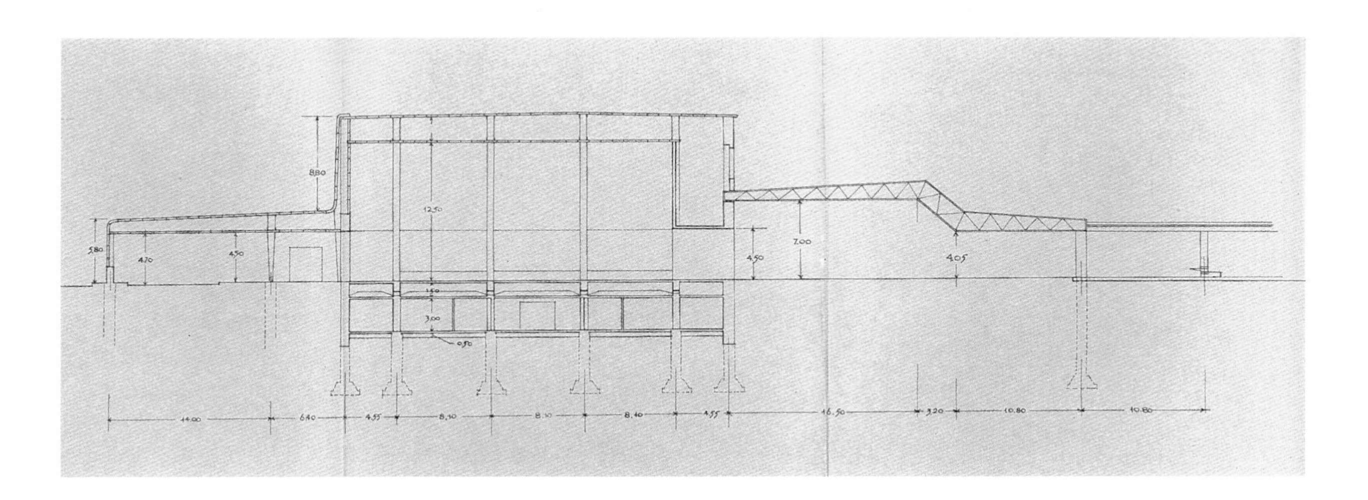

Main elevation giving onto Piazza Santa Maria Novella.
Side elevation giving onto Via Valfonda.

Longitudinal and cross sections.

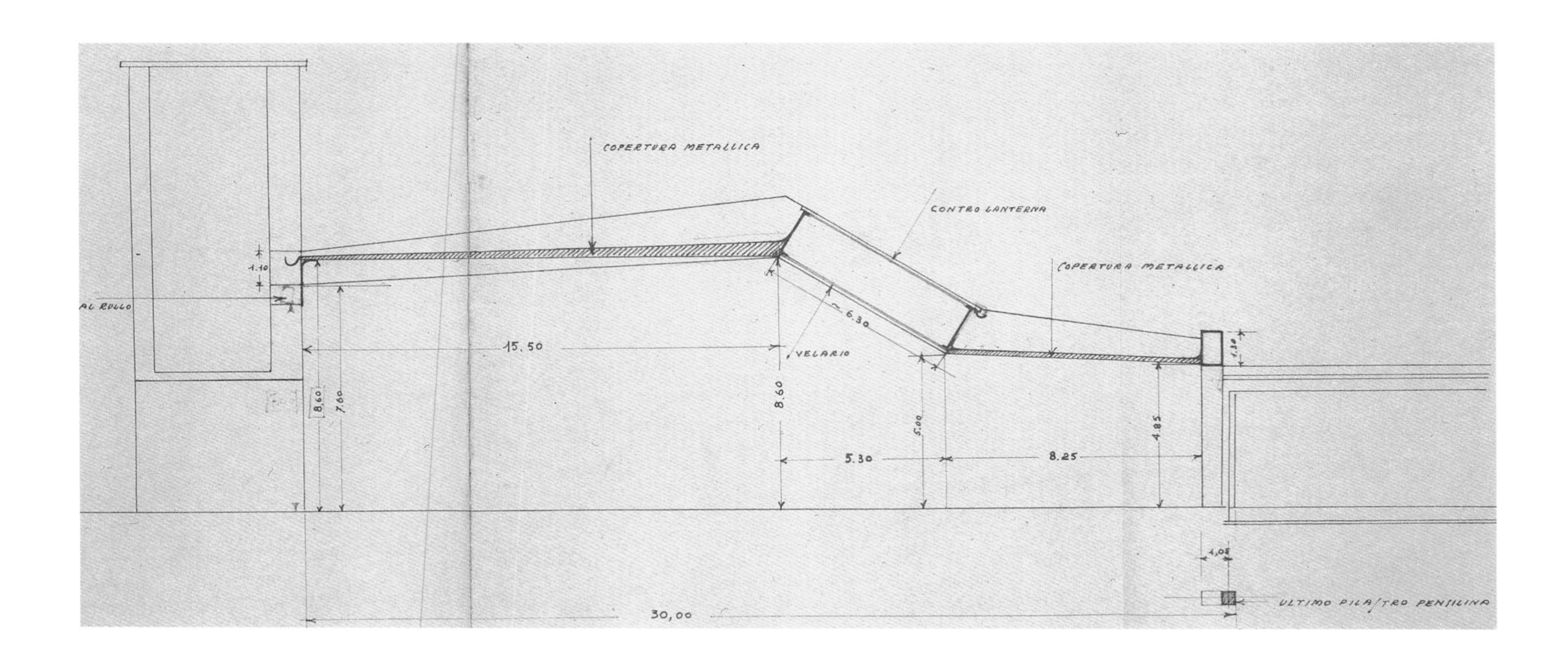
COPERTURA METALLICA
CONTRO LANTERNA
COPERTURA METALLICA
AL RULLO
1.10
15.50
6.30
VELARIO
8.60
7.60
8.60
5.00
4.85
1.30
5.30
8.25
1,05
ULTIMO PILASTRO PENSILINA
30,00

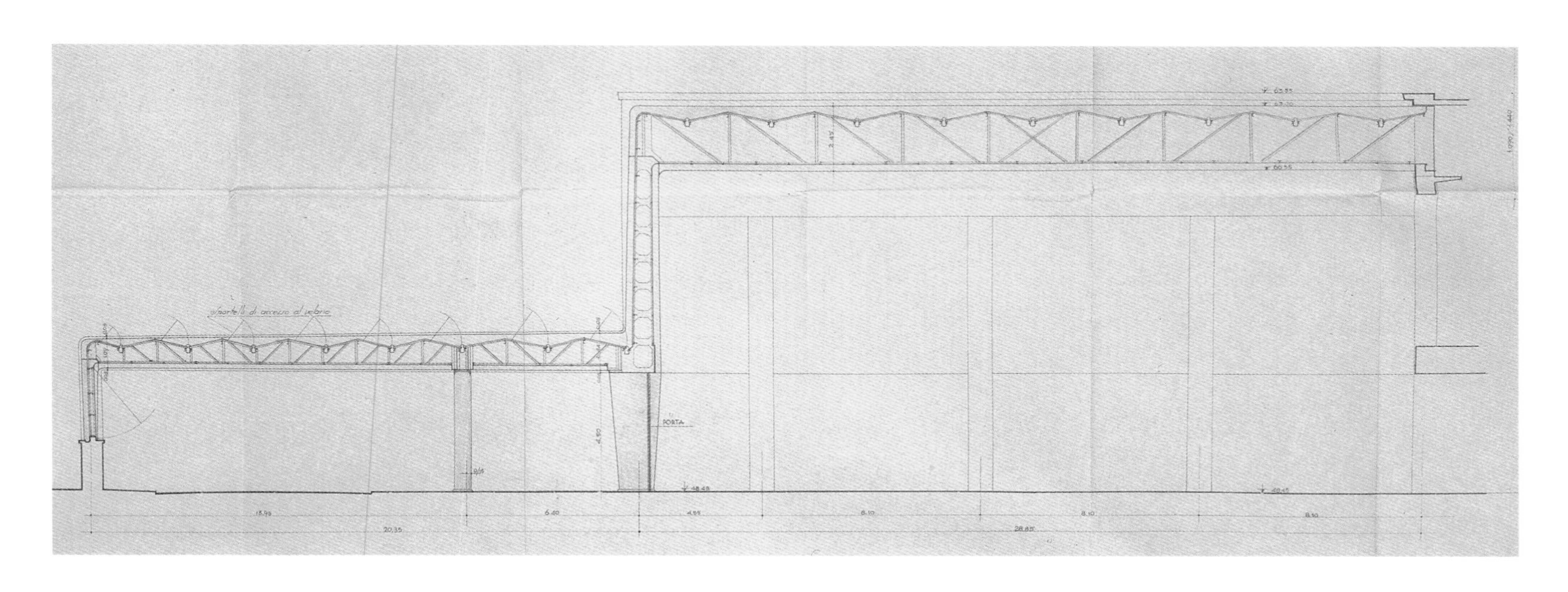
PORTA

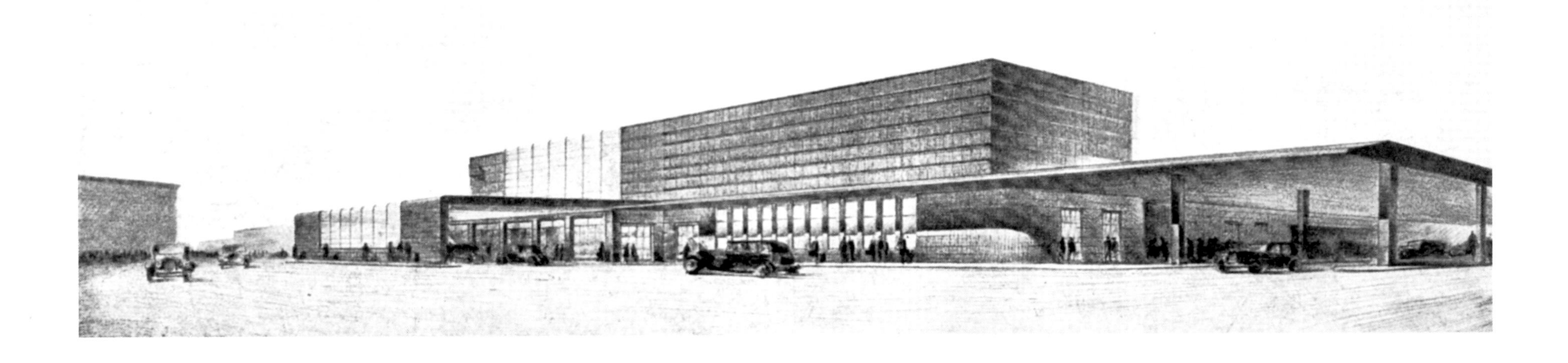

Diagram showing the metal roofing of the main concourse and smaller concourse linking the platforms; longitudinal section of the glass roofing.

Views of the passenger building.

The "cascade" in Termolux glass runs across the top of the covered section of the driveway and up over the main atrium; placed off-center in the façade, it marks a strong vertical contrast with the horizontal bands of *pietra forte*.

The "cascade" of glass seen from inside the atrium/ticket office. Divided into three aisles—one of 12 meters in width between two of 10 meters—the atrium is entirely faced in different types of marble.
The glass section of the roof of the main concourse is made up of reticular girders, dog-legged at one end due to the difference in height between the cantilever roofing of the platforms and the concourse itself.

4 santiago calatrava

bahnhof stadelhofen

zurich, switzerland 1983–90

project
Santiago Calatrava
with
Arnold Amsler (redevelopment of existing building), Werner Rüeger (layout of park areas)
client
Swiss Federal Railways, Bern
location
Stadelhofen Square, Zurich, Switzerland
chronology
1983: open competition for designs
1983-86: project
1986-90: construction

The extension work on the Stadelhofen railway station was part of an overall plan drawn up by the Swiss Federal Railways to redevelop and exploit the potential of a number of stations in medium-large cities (Basle, Bern, Lucerne) and the various transit stations of the Zurich urban rail network. The redeveloped buildings were to serve as new poles of activity within the city, housing a number of commercial and service-industry facilities. A common feature of all the schemes was the decision to focus on underground levels for the location of shopping facilities; without in any way disturbing the character of the old city center, these levels thus became true shopping malls, with "limited intervention at ground level being necessary to resolve the problems caused by underused or badly exploited nodes of pedestrian and other traffic" (Saggio 1994, p. 102). The building for this extension, designed by Santiago Calatrava, became an important model for such projects.
Given the sloping terrain of the site, the architect decided to organize the functions on different layers, with both materials and structures becoming lighter as one moved upwards. From the light beams in the upper sections to the powerful arches of the underground sections, the different construction techniques adopted offer a visual demonstration of the play of forces within the structure and of the different locations of the various functions it houses. The need to create a third rail track also meant that part of the hillside had to be excavated for the train tunnel to be widened; and as "embankments" for this excavated area, Calatrava designed a series of walls against which he raised the various new additions that artificially "redraw" the slope of the hillside: the raised garden; the footpath/belvedere; the third track that runs into the tunnel; the inclined pilasters and the bridges spanning the tracks.
With his background in both architecture and engineering, Calatrava always combines a practical and conceptual approach to any project; as Mirko Zardini comments, "natural forms" and the possibilities provided by engineering science are inexhaustible sources of inspiration for his designs, "with the abstract calculations of the engineer taking on formal significance, and architect's exploration of form revealing itself once again to have a structural *raison d'être*" (Zardini 1991).
This double background is the real strong-point in Calatrava's approach to architecture; his designs combine both natural forms and complicated engineering structures in works that are characterized by technical mastery and originality of language. In the Stadelhofen station, for example, the structural components function as works of sculpture, around which the various parts of the project are articulated. It is no accident that it was the work on this train station which first established Calatrava's international reputation.
Used by regional and metropolitan rail traffic, the Stadelhofen railway station stands in the center of Zurich, between Stadelhofenplatz and the Hohenpromenade hill (formerly one of the bastions of the city's defenses). The project for the extension envisaged the conservation and redevelopment of the small, old two-floor station building, the increase in the number of tracks and platforms and the creation of shopping facilities. The design group also included Arnold Amsler, who worked on the redevelopment of the existing station building, and Werner Rüeger, who designed the layout of the green areas;

Santiago Calatrava himself was responsible for the new rail infrastructures and the road and pedestrian links between the two sides of the station.
To meet the first requirement in the specifications of the design competition—the provision of a third rail track—the architect proposed a compromise between the two equally feasible suggestions of an underground tunnel (more complex in execution but less disruptive in the existing urban fabric) and open-air tracks (much easier and quicker to build). Respecting the slope of the terrain, he opted for a open-air platform, that would run into a tunnel created by partially excavating the hillside and then "re-creating" its slope in man-made structures. At the level of the tracks themselves, the existing containment wall was replaced using box girders in reinforced concrete with a curved inner surface; these would be supported by a wall strengthened with struts in the back and a system of inclined, tapering three-point pilasters along the front. This entire structure runs for 270 meters in a curve of a 400-meter radius, following the line of the tracks. Transparent roofing in a dynamic-looking frame of filiform steel covers the first platform. Above the box girder (at a height of 7.8 meters) runs a covered walkway under a metal structure, "a sort of transparent green vault" which facilitates the assimilation of the new infrastructures within the existing urban landscape, establishing a link with the nineteenth-century park area behind the station. Along this "balcony," at five-meter intervals, are steel spider braces that serve as supports for both the handrail and the open pergola arching above. Here, Calatrava has designed a three-hinged arch that gives a visual rhythm to the whole and serves to create a hybrid space that is neither open nor enclosed; its outline is defined by "curved metal components which project undulant geometrical forms down onto the ground and inclined surfaces" (Saggio 1994, p. 104). From this raised walkway, passengers can reach the platforms by stairs, elevators or the footbridges that span the tracks. A bridge for road traffic, identified by its more robust "pier," follows the incline of the hill further down from the station, while the first footbridge (the Olgasteg) rests on a triangular structure and a second (the Falkensteg) develops as a sort of curved projection in reinforced concrete from a very "sculptural" base that extends beyond the station towards Stadelhofenplatz. All three bridges appear to rest lightly on the hillside at one end and rise from visually-striking bases on the city side of the station. At the highest level above the station (12 meters) there is a garden that serves to link the new structure with the fortifications at the top of the hill which dominate the city.
To fully exploit the commercial potential of the site, the client suggested linking together all the various pedestrian underpasses to form an ample underground shopping mall. Reminiscent of the ribcage of some enormous animal, this underground space is in reinforced concrete (required so that it could support the weight of the slabs bearing the first two sets of tracks). The concrete supports were cast on site using single-block molds, which were gradually shifted forward and adapted to the incline of the tunnel. At each entrance, where there were no such supports, the structure is held by covered tie-rods. Although one single surface, the concrete seems to be made up of two separate components that meet in the center; the advantage of this design is that the vibrations in the upper slab, due to the passage of trains, are absorbed and not transmitted to the rest of the structure. The shops occupy the spaces between the vertical supports, which are 8 meters apart; side openings between the supports also let natural light into the gallery and reinforce the visual rhythm of the composition. The supports for the hinged leafsprings that make up the structure become deeper towards the end of the underground level, where—aligned along the same axis as the existing station building—they provide support for the curved girders of the shafts which house stairs, elevators, escalators and the rotating doors that serve to close the station during the night.
The Stadelhofen project is of great interest not only as a scheme of urban planning but also because it moved towards the definition of a new model of station. Calatrava "reconstructs" part of a hillside without engaging in formalistic excess or disturbing the rich variety of the existing urban fabric. The idea of juxtaposing a series of autonomous structural components (the glass-covered platform which stands independent of the station building; the shopping mall created within the underpasses; the walkways raised over the platforms) makes the whole more like a project of urban planning than the design of a single infrastructure. As required by the specifications, the underpass that links the station building to the central platform was widened to make it into a shopping mall, thus becoming an area that brings together commuter and rail traffic, shopping and free-time activities. And both this underground mall and the raised pergola walkway link the station with the roads, city squares and shopping facilities of the surrounding neighborhood. Bridges and entrances to underground areas become defining features of this whole network of raised and sunken walkways; the varied designs and construction techniques used in each makes them important points of reference for those using the station.
Stadelhofen is, in effect, a series of different interconnected places serving different functions, each of which makes a contribution to the quality of the urban area in which the station is located. As already mentioned, it is no coincidence that it was this project which played a decisive role in establishing Calatrava's international reputation. True, he had designed a number of important buildings before 1983; but it was here that he first fully demonstrated his extraordinary ability not only to combine architectural and structural design but also to give a new interpretation of the very concept of urban space. And in doing this, Calatrava managed to transform the stereotype of the train station. The form and functions of the features he designed here can be seen as a celebration of the railways; yet the architect takes the characteristic features of such architecture and "reinvents" them, providing an original and innovative new model for the stations of the Swiss railway network. As Antonio Saggio puts it, at Stadelhofen "the transformation of a rail junction into a fully-equipped channel for pedestrian-rail traffic brings together achievements in architectural design with innovative ideas regarding urban layout and the distribution of facilities. Quite apart from the explicit intentions of the designer, the project marked a distinct evolution in a certain type of architecture and set a standard for new designs of transit rail stations" (Saggio 1994, p. 107).

Bibliography

M. Zardini, "The Stadelhofen Station in Zurich by Santiago Calatrava. From Designing Railways to Designing the City," *Lotus*, 69, 1991, pp. 6–29.
Santiago Calatrava. Bahnhof Stadelhofen, Zürich, Wasmuth, Tübingen-Berlin 1993.
A. Saggio, "Zurigo, Lucerna, Lione. Tre progetti di Santiago Calatrava," *ArQ 13*, monographic issue, *La stazione ferroviaria. Verso un nuovo modello d'uso*, December 1994, pp. 102–07.
Stazione ferroviaria Stadelhofen, in S. Polano, *Santiago Calatrava. Opera completa*, Electa, Milan 1998, pp. 44–55.
L. Molinari, *Santiago Calatrava*, Skira, Milan 2000.

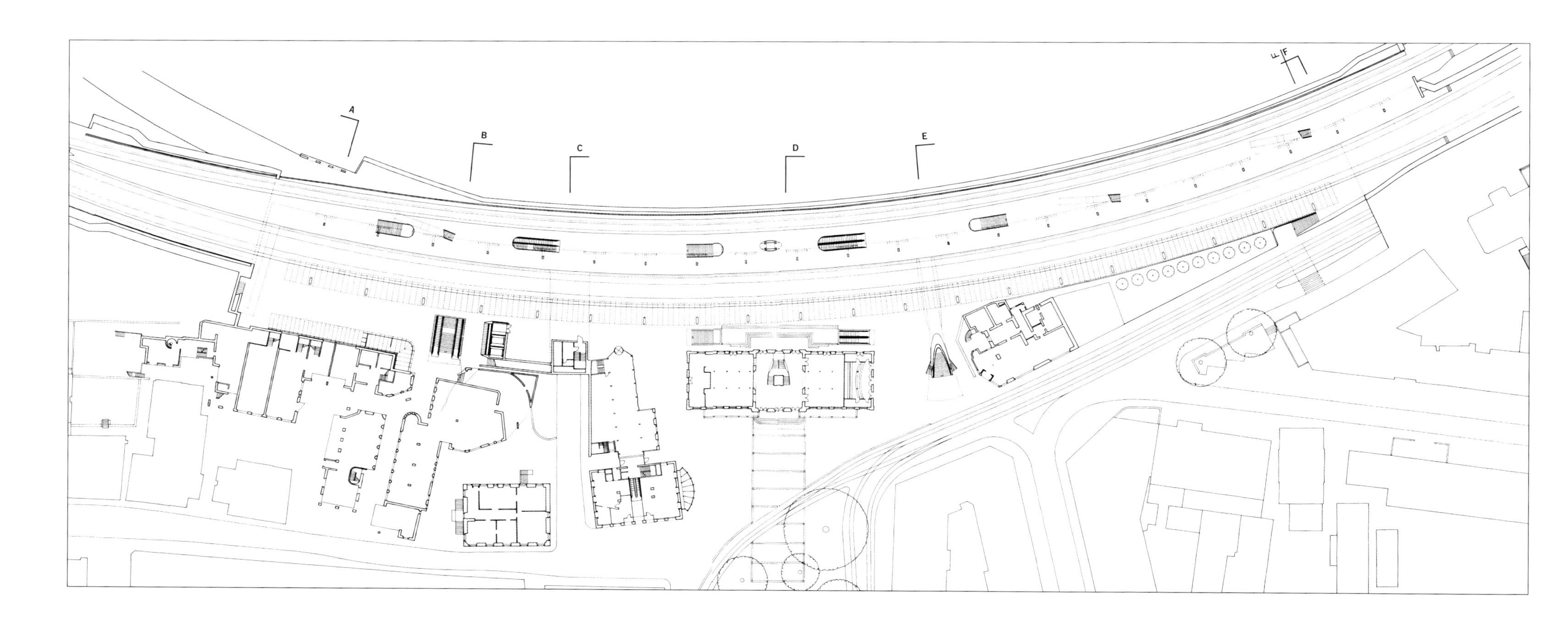
A
B
C
D
E
F

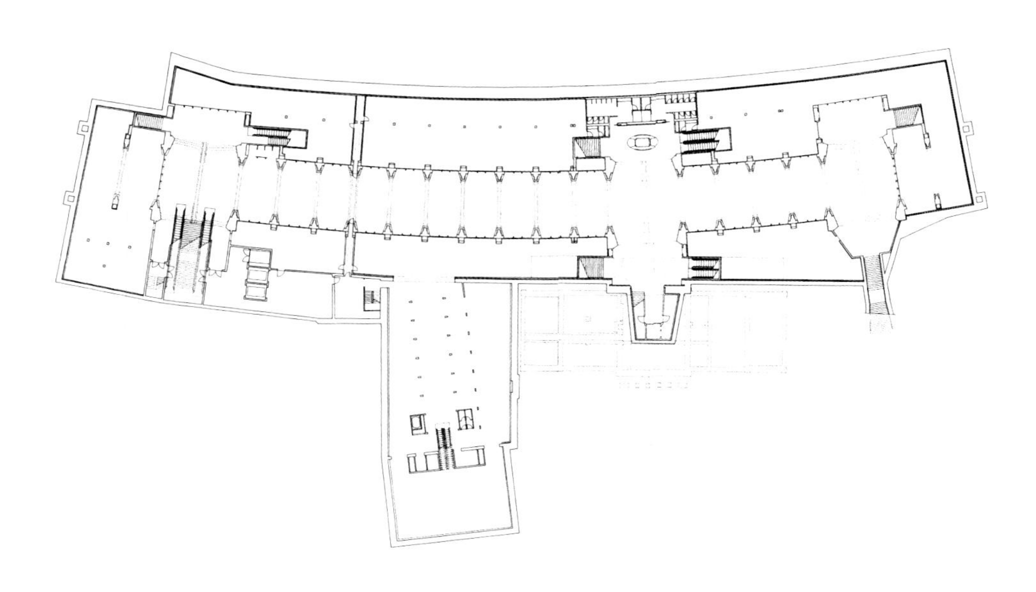

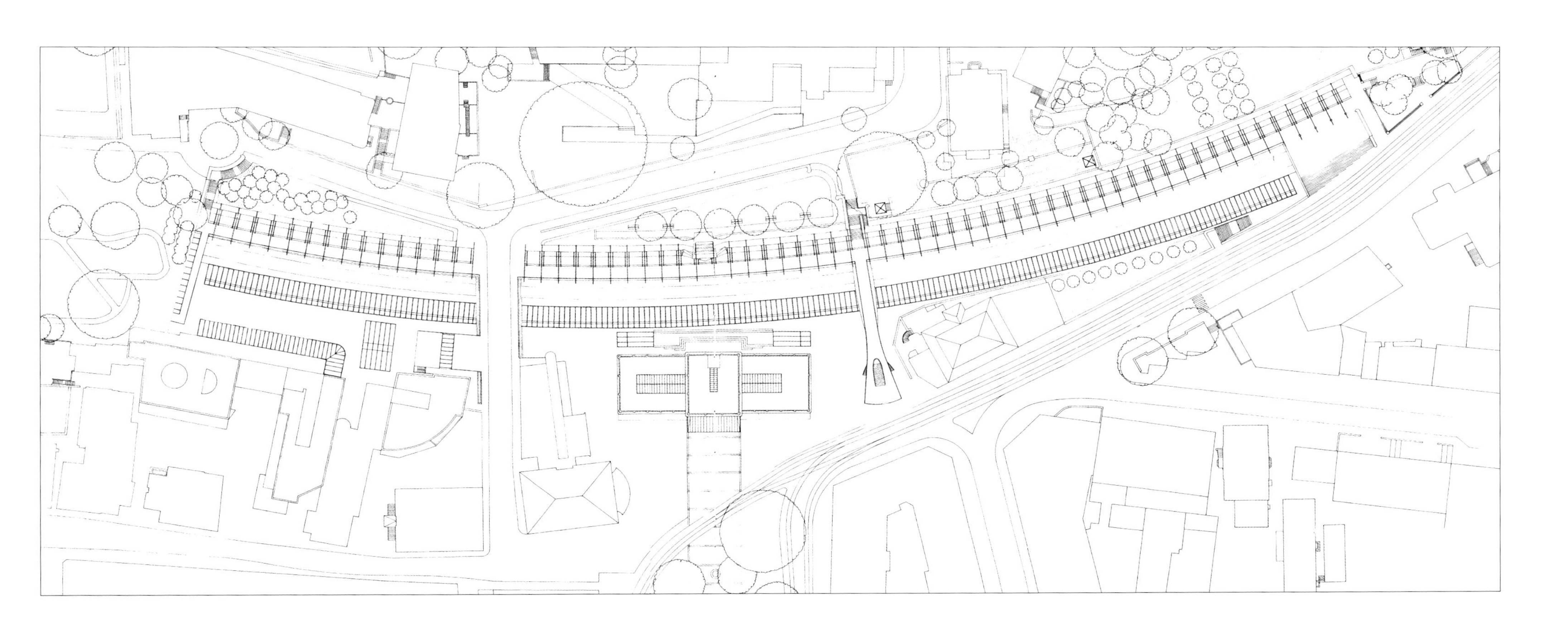

Plan of the ground floor and underground gallery.

Plan of the raised walkway.

Previous page
The juxtaposition of volumes compensates for the difference in level between the hillside and the existing station.

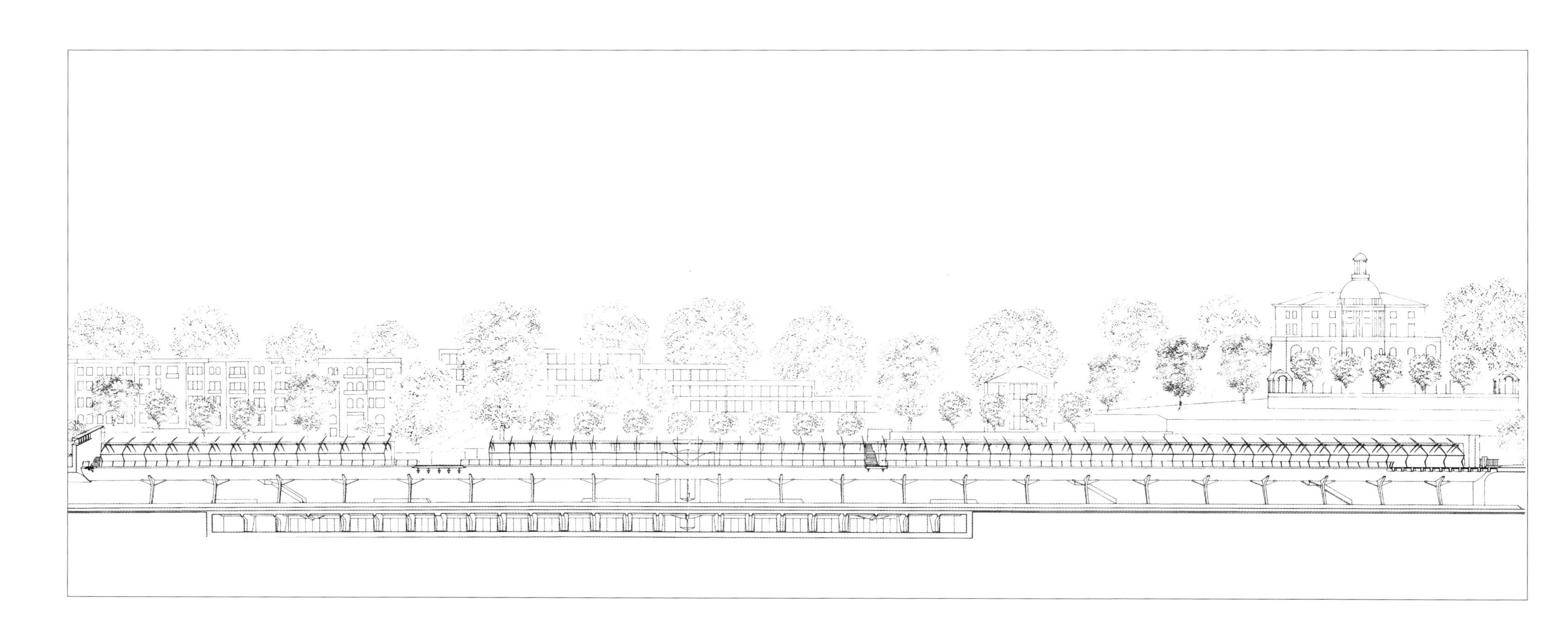

Longitudinal elevation/section.

Cross sections.

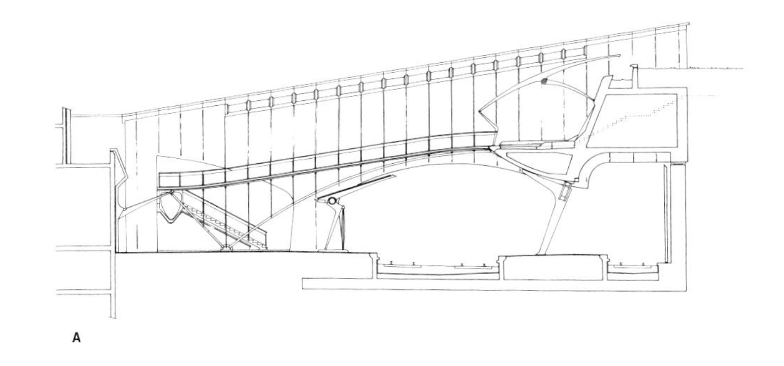
A

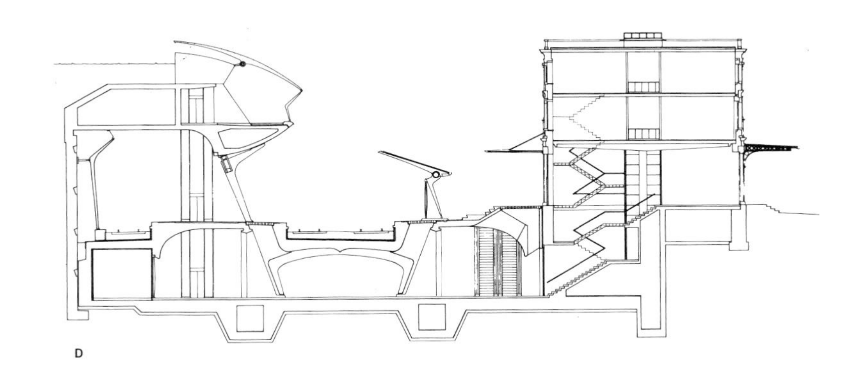
D

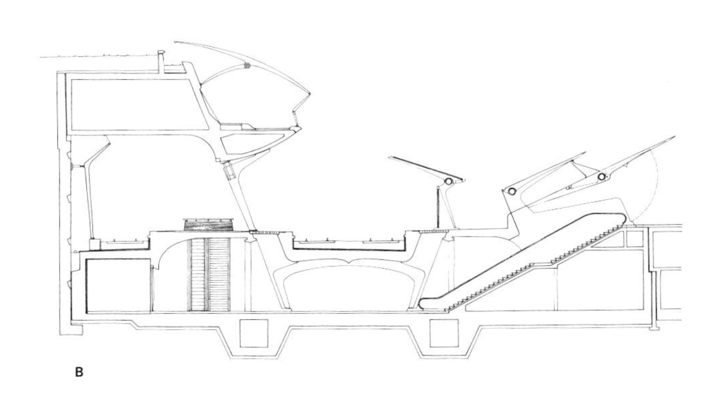
B

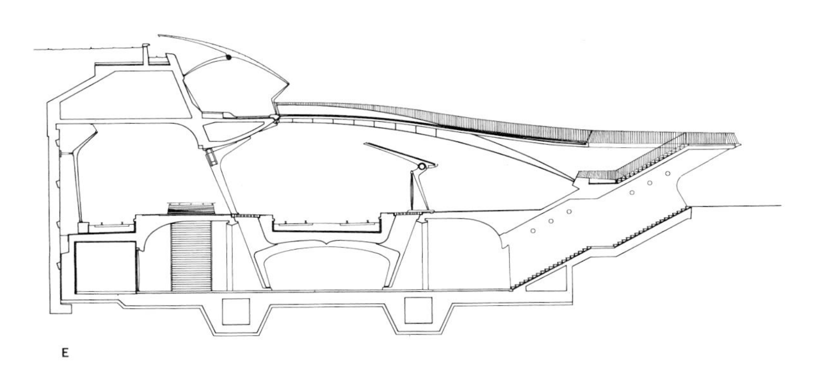
E

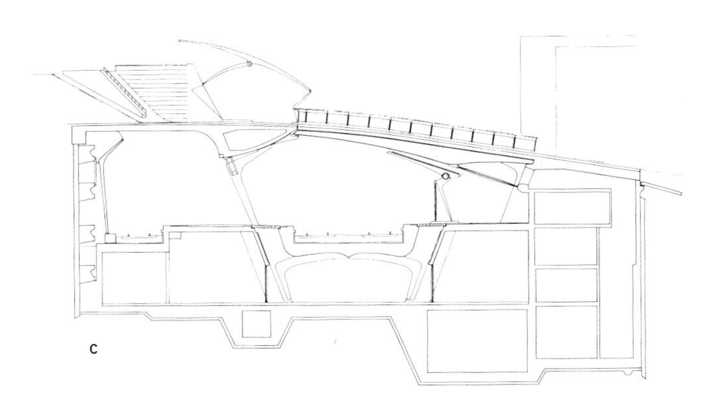
C

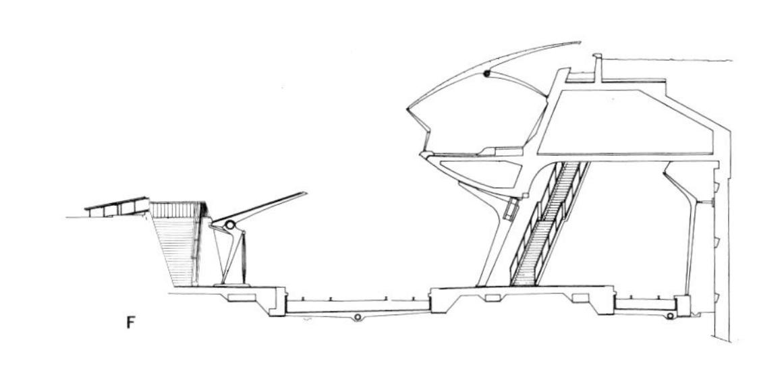
F

Two views of the raised walkway that "re-creates" the hillside.

The first platform is protected by transparent roofing supported by a dynamic filiform structure in steel.

Sektor
C
Gleis
2
11.44
S7
Winterthur
1
B
1
KIOSK
B
2
2
11.45
S7
SEKTOR B
Meilen Stäfa

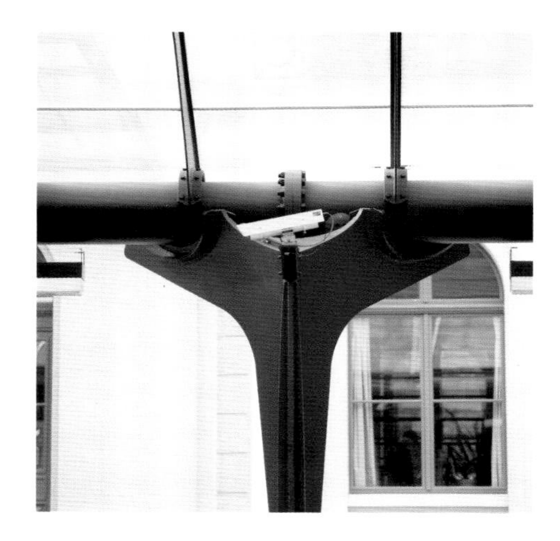

One end of the bridges rests lightly on the hillside, the other—on the city side of the station—arises from bases that have a powerful visual impact.
At five-meter intervals along the "walkway" are steel braces that serve as supports for both the handrail and the open pergola arching above.
Detail of the roofing structure over the platforms.

Entrance to the train tunnel.

Gleis
1
Sektor
C
3
Überschreiten der Gleise verboten
Défense de traverser les voies
Vietato traversare i binari
Do not cross the railway lines

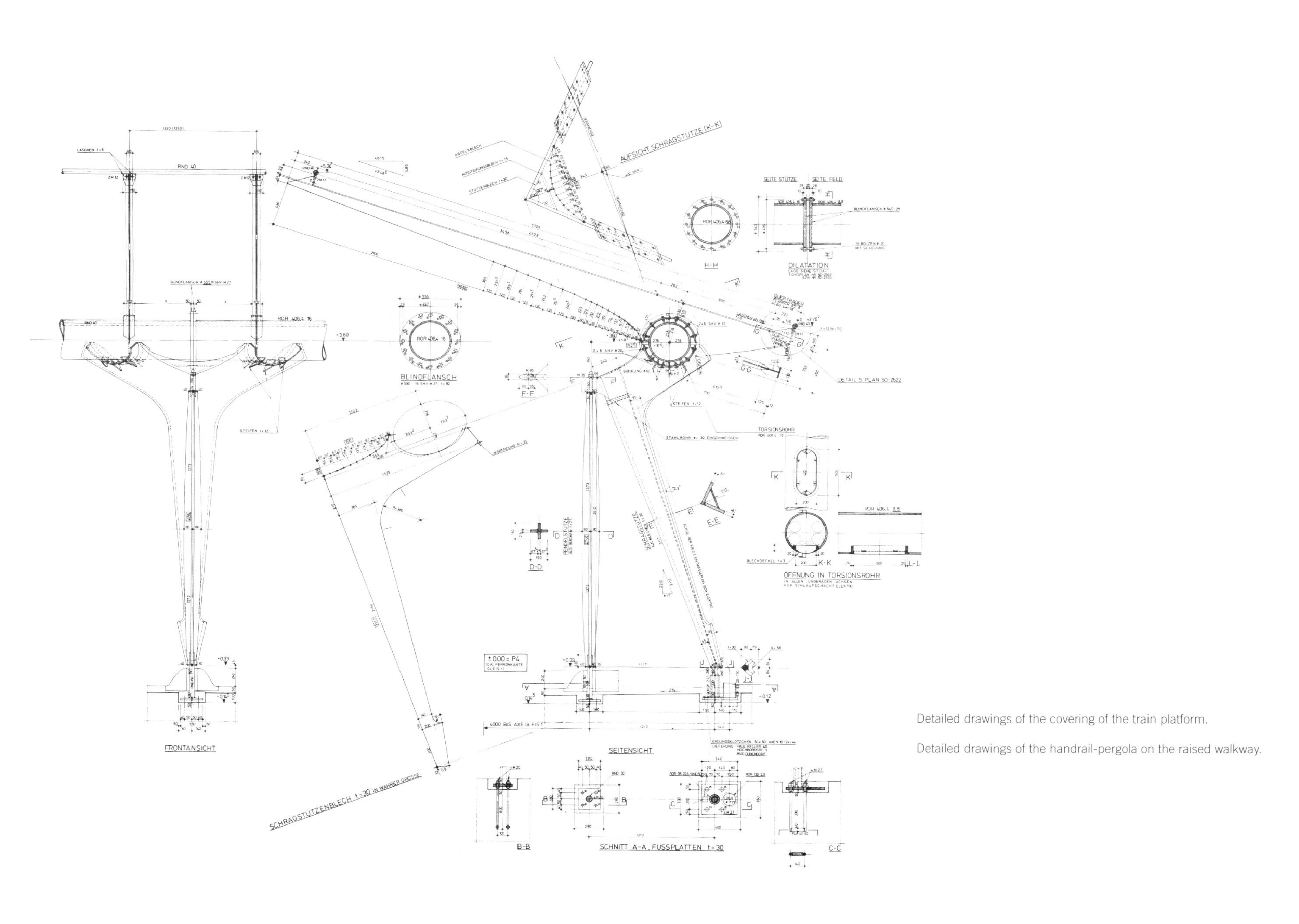

Detailed drawings of the covering of the train platform.

Detailed drawings of the handrail-pergola on the raised walkway.

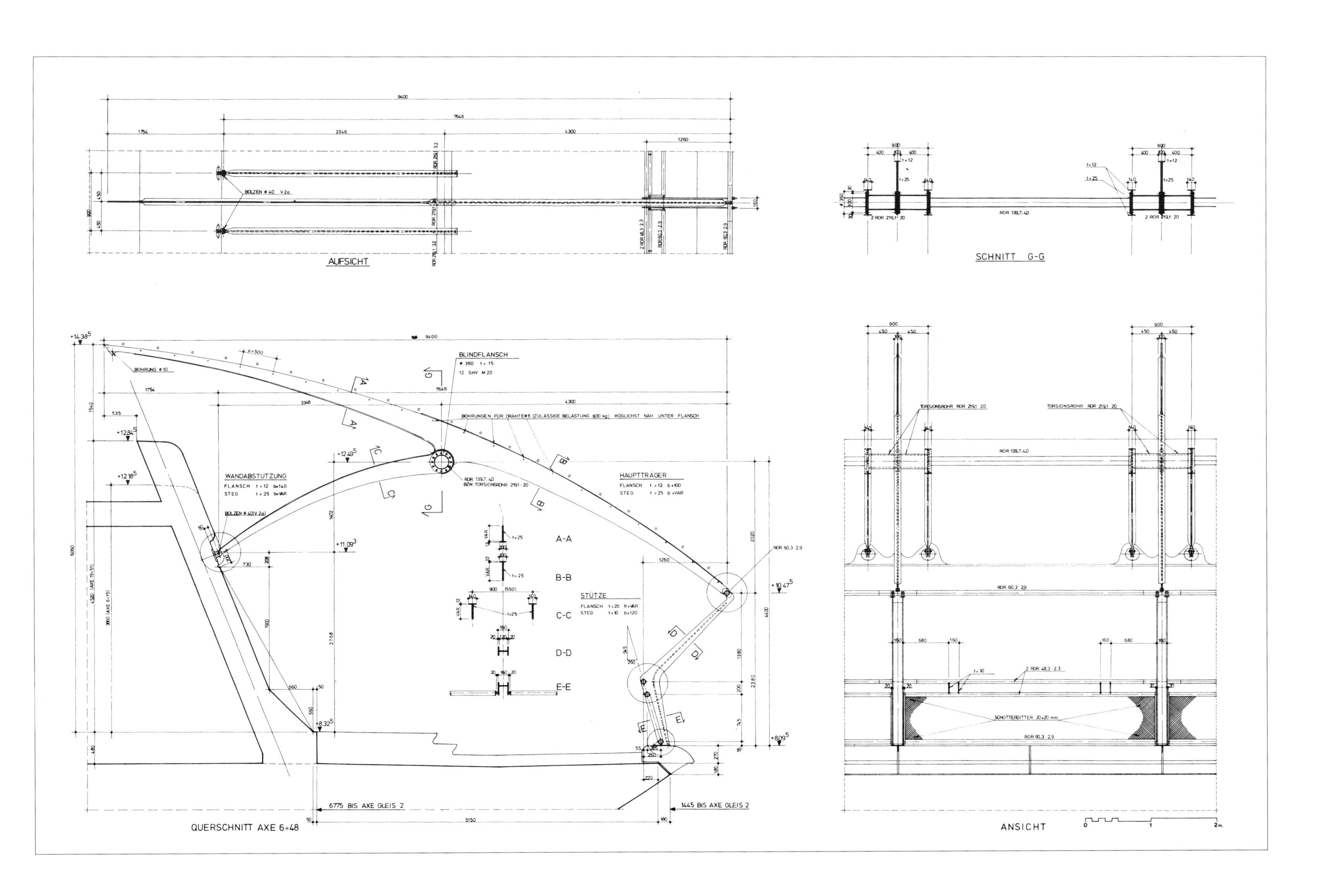

AUFSICHT
BOLZEN ø 40 V 2a
SCHNITT G-G
ROR 139,7. 4,0
2 ROR 219,1 · 20
BLINDFLANSCH
ø 360 t = 15
12 SHV M 20
BOHRUNG ø 10
BOHRUNGEN FÜR DRAHTE ø 6 (ZULÄSSIGE BELASTUNG 800 kg) MÖGLICHST NAH UNTER FLANSCH
WANDABSTUTZUNG
FLANSCH t = 12 b = 140
STEG t = 25 b = VAR
BOLZEN ø 40 (V 2a)
ROR 139,7 · 4,0
BZW. TORSIONSROHR 219,1 · 20
HAUPTTRÄGER
FLANSCH t = 12 b = 100
STEG t = 25 b = VAR
A-A
B-B
C-C
D-D
E-E
STÜTZE
FLANSCH t = 20 b = VAR
STEG t = 10 b = 120
ROR 60,3 · 2,9
6775 BIS AXE GLEIS 2
1445 BIS AXE GLEIS 2
QUERSCHNITT AXE 6÷48
TORSIONSROHR ROR 219,1 · 20
ROR 60,3 · 2,9
2 ROR 48,3 · 2,3
SCHOTTERGITTER 20 × 20 mm
ANSICHT

Reminiscent of the ribcage of some enormous animal, the underground shopping mall is in reinforced concrete so that it can support the weight of the slabs bearing the first two sets of train tracks. Side openings between the vertical supports let natural light into the gallery, thus reinforcing the rhythm of the composition.
At each entrance, where there are no concrete supports, the structure is held by covered tie-rods.

The shops occupy the space between the vertical supports, which are 8 meters apart.

View of the raised walkway, with its distinctive metal pergola. Like some sort of "transparent green vault," this covering facilitates the assimilation of the new infrastructures within the existing urban landscape, establishing a link with the nineteenth-century park area behind the station.

5 antonio cruz and antonio ortiz

estación de santa justa

seville, spain 1987–91

project
Antonio Cruz and Antonio Ortiz
collaborators
B. Sánchez, J.R. Galadí, M.A. Maese,
C. Castro, M. Velasco, J.C. Mulero, L. Gutiérrez
site direction
Jefatura de Construcción de Transportes
Terrestres (Rafael Morrá)
building contractor
Fomeno y Construcciones, S.A.
signposting, fittings and shop design
Addison España
client
Direccìon General de Infraestructura,
Ministerio de Transportes
location
Seville, Spain
dimensions
12,000 sq.m: built-up area
chronology
1987: project
1988-91: construction

Occupying the vast site of a demolished goods yard, the Santa Justa station was built for the 1992 Seville Expo and stands in an area that is relatively close to the city center yet of low urban development; the new station itself was intended to be the catalyst for the growth of the zone. The architects took the redevelopment of the site as an opportunity to create a "station neighborhood" that would link together the city areas on either side of it; this goal was in part possible because a number of the roads that had long marked a rupture in the urban fabric here were now redirected underground.
The project defines a large enclosed area that houses parking lots and service facilities, with the station as one single free-standing block within it. To obviate the possibility of the tracks creating a break within the area, these were lowered, with part of them being entirely underground; the trains running south from the station pass through an underground tunnel, which leaves the surface area entirely free. However, in appearance Santa Justa strikes one as a terminal rather than a through station, with the tracks aligned behind a large façade with projecting roof, beyond which lies a vast forecourt. This choice of design means that, in terms of clarity, the layout is comparable to best such terminal stations in Europe. In effect, this large-scale project not only marked a turning point in the development of the architects Cruz and Ortiz but also provided an important opportunity for reflection upon railway architecture as such. In the words of Rafael Moneo, the Santa Justa station "reveals the architects' sensibility and sensitivity in identifying the strategy that should be adopted when tackling an architectural project whose very scale necessarily implies a powerful impact upon the city as a whole" (Moneo 1996, p. 13).
Continuity within the whole design relies on the "concatenation" of elements within it. Santa Justa could, in fact, be broken down into a series of components associated with various aspects of rail travel: the platforms, the escalators, the *tapis roulants*, the waiting rooms, the ticket office and the arrivals/departure hall. The unity of the whole is in part guaranteed by a clear identification of function, in part by the design of the roofing; the variations in this latter reflect the changes encountered as one moves uninterruptedly from one area of the station to the other. To quote Moneo once again: "What is new about this design is its use of 'conjunctions.' The single components are autonomous in form and function and yet skillfully linked together by the flow of roofing, which gives Santa Justa a 'unique aura.'"
The system adopted is very clearly illustrated when one looks at a side elevation of the building, which underlines how the different volumes/functions fit into each other. Above the roofing of the entrance space arises the volume of the main atrium; above that, arises a higher volume, whose sloping roof runs down to the level of the covering over the platforms. Tracing a sort of ideal curve, which runs from the entrance cantilever to rise and then fall to the level of the platform roofing, this design emphasizes the markedly horizontal layout of the building, giving tangible expression to the idea of fluid movement through it.
Cruz and Ortiz have themselves said that their design aims to be an architectural metaphor of movement. According to Juan-José Lahuerta, one gets the first reference

to this metaphor in the main façade of the station, where the curve of the cantilever roof and the roofing of the entrance form two great arcs which, if protracted, would seem to meet the ground at the same point, as if they were invisibly anchored there. The result is a fusiform horizontal figure cut through by two parallel planes that curve outwards as they project from the façade. The form seems to be one that is contained within itself, like something "that rises and folds back along the curve of its own outline, thus offering minimum resistance to the motive force within it."

In the interior, it is the various modulations of natural light which further develop this metaphor of movement, differentiating between the various spaces of the station. Cruz and Ortiz described their intention here as "to design a building that does not look imposing from the outside, but reveals all its grandeur on the inside, through the very division of its spaces" (Ortiz 1994, p. 76).

For functional reasons—the trains arriving from the north are at 8.40 meters above ground but must then proceed south by passing under the building—the atrium was constructed 14.65 meters above road level. From the outside, one passes up to the main entrance hall (marked externally by the large curved cantilever roof). Two wide galleries—lined with bars and shops and overlooked by administration offices—lead to the atrium were there are ticket offices, information desks, waiting areas and various kiosks (newsagent's, tobacconist's, foreign currency exchange).

The rectangular form of this atrium would seem to contradict the notion of movement and flow that is the entire basis of the project, thus becoming—in the works of Cruz and Ortiz—one of the "surprising" features of the building. From the outside, in fact, the atrium emerges as a rectangular block bound between the entrance and the roof which slopes down to the train platforms. On the inside, a high wall of glass, interrupted at regular intervals by the square brick-built shafts housing the elevators, separates the atrium from the area of the platforms. The natural light which filters through the openings in the external brick walls floods the entire space. Having moved beyond this massive wall of glass and brick, one reaches the transverse concourse; a contemporary reading of this key feature of nineteenth-century stations, this not only links the two sides of the building (with an ample portico at either end) but also houses the escalators that lead down to the train platforms. Corridors, bound by brick walls with massive square openings, run from either end of that concourse along the sides of the station to a walkway (again linked to the platforms by means of escalators) which runs the entire width of the station (east-west) and provides an interesting observation platform for the whole of the space. These four "linking" features—the transversal concourse, the walkway and the two side corridors—all mark the boundaries of an open rectangular-shaped well occupied by the escalators; this is covered above by a sloping roof supported by a series of reinforced concrete plates aligned with the the elevator shafts.

Here the cross section of the building becomes particularly important. Having passed through the atrium and reached the zone for embarking passengers, one is in an area where the roofing is designed in such a way that natural light provides atmospheric illumination for each of the individual spaces. Lit directly from above, the walkway running east-west seems here to float unsuspended. The angle of the natural light from the roofing is determined by a series of horizontal cement slats, while the side walls in brick are illuminated by the daylight that enters indirectly, after having first passed through the outlying areas of the station.

Elegant coverings of modest span provide shelter for the railway platforms, extending for quite some distance. These form six aisles with elongated arch barrel vaults—one for every double set of tracks; the metal arches rest on girders of reinforced concrete, themselves on elliptical pilasters in the same material which are faced with metal paneling. The fall of the light into the space is designed to enhance the impression that the aisles are independent of each other. The diagonal light, which filters in through metal blinds placed along the lower part of the arched roofing means that each individual aisle is sharply lit, but the area when one joins the other is left in a sort of penumbra.

To the sides of the tracks—at the heights of 8.4 and 11.50 meters—are the various facilities reserved solely for rail company staff. There are also secondary entrances, involving the use of staircases and ramps to the sides of the building (for example, the latter might provide access for vehicles to be loaded onto trains). External galleries also double circulation within the building and provide direct access to certain specific areas. All around there is a shopping area, which though easily accessible is sharply distinguished from the spaces used by passengers; the distinctive character of a railway station is thus maintained and the structure can in no way be confused with a shopping mall. It is also envisaged that the two upper levels of the outer block of the building will house further shopping and service facilities, in keeping with the now prevalent idea of using stations for urban facilities that can serve passengers and non-passengers alike.

As for the materials used, brick—a durable material of low-cost maintenance—is the one which establishes the overall unity of the entire complex. Most of the surfaces in the travelers' part of the building are faced with this material. However, the pilasters of the entrance portico, the plates supporting the concourse, the walkway and the sloping roof, the pillars for the arched roofing over the tracks, and various details on the façade (for example, the long cantilever roof) are all in reinforced concrete.

As Javier Cenicacelaya claims, "in Santa Justa one does not see an exhibition of designed components ... but rather the containment of the different elements of construction within the various surfaces. The overall effect depends upon the simplicity of materials and on the play of light."

The limited number of constructive components used in this composition reveals this project to be not a demonstration of conspicuous design but of what can be achieved through very careful attention to every minor facet of a building. As an example of this close attention to detail one might cite the perfect harmony between the metal components and the overall structure of the building.

Bibliography

P.A. Croset, "Nuova stazione a Siviglia di Cruz e Ortiz," *Casabella*, 556, April 1989, pp. 40–41.

"Estación de Santa Justa. Antonio Cruz y Antonio Ortiz," *El Croquis*, 48, 1991.

J.-J. Lahuerta, "The New Station of Seville: An Underground Movement," *Lotus*, 70, 1991, pp. 6–22.

J. Cenicacelaya, "Cruz & Ortiz. Stazione di Santa Justa, Siviglia," *Domus*, 736, June 1992.

A. Ortiz, "La stazione di Santa Justa a Siviglia," *ArQ 13*, monographic issue *La stazione ferroviaria. Verso un nuovo modello d'uso*, December 1994.

"Santa Justa. Seville, Spain," M. Binney, *The Architecture of Rail*, Academy Editions, London 1995.

R. Moneo, "Tra il gesto e la norma," *Cruz/Ortiz*, Logos-Tanais, Madrid-Modena 1996.

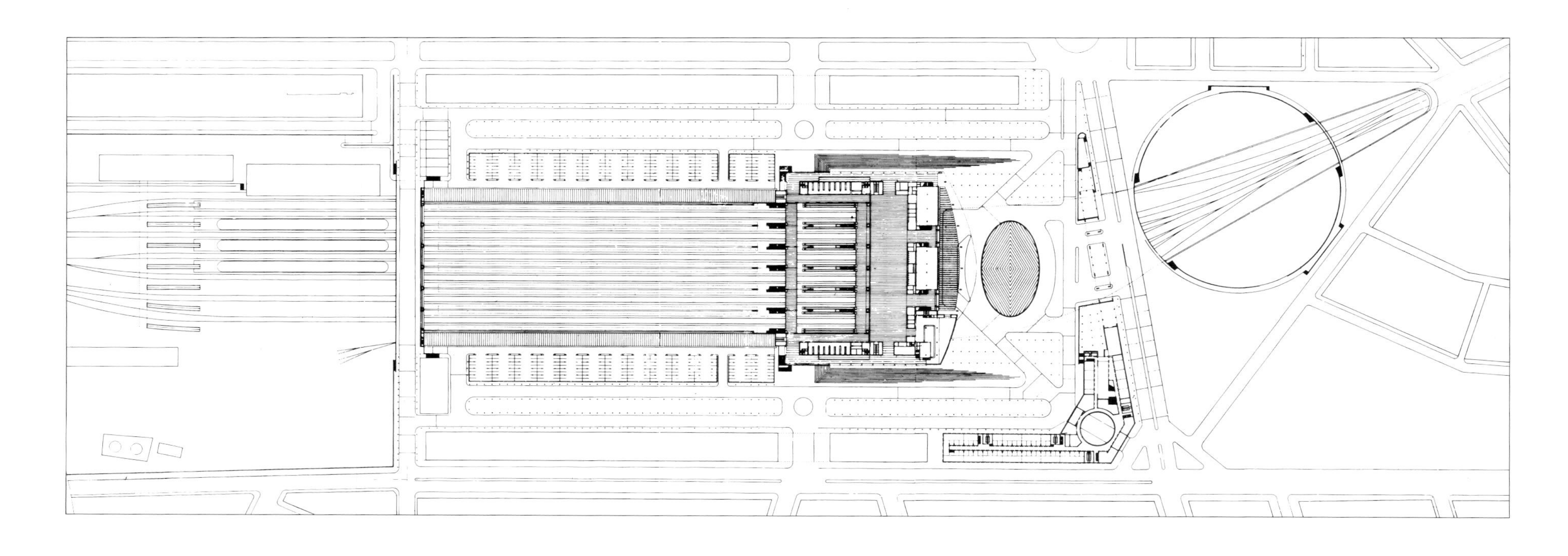

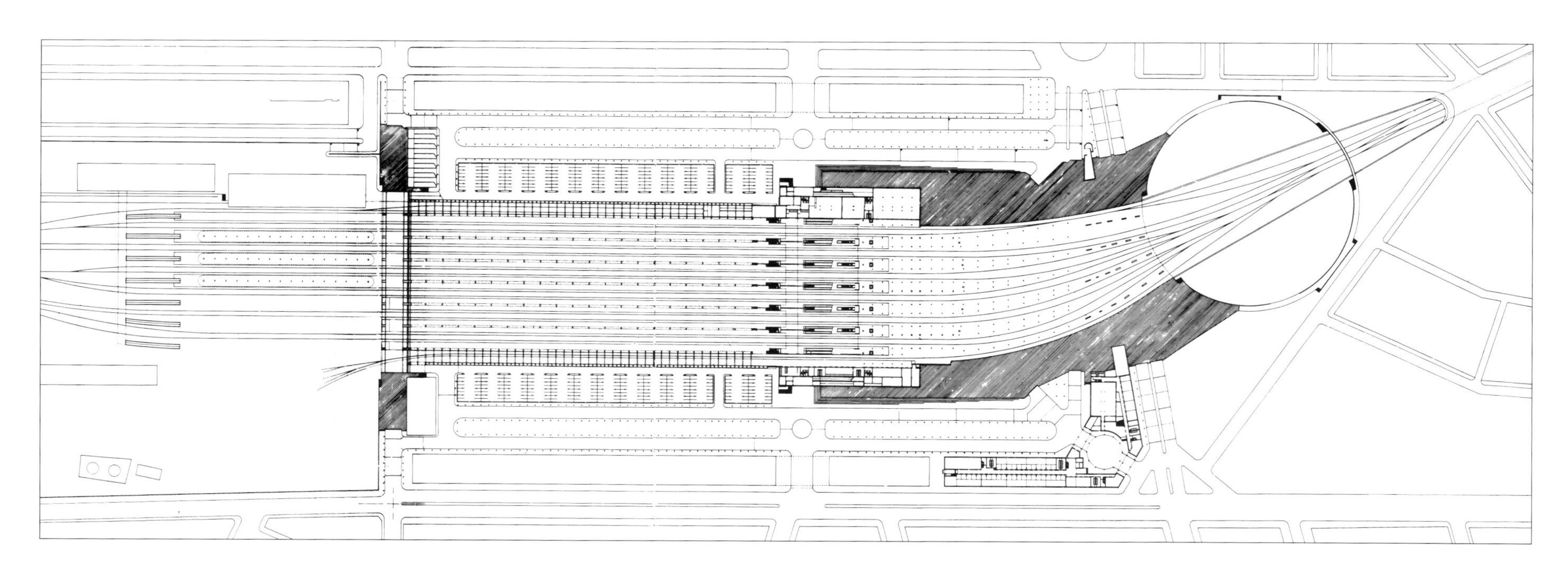

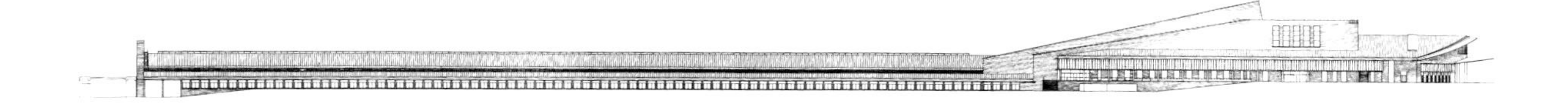

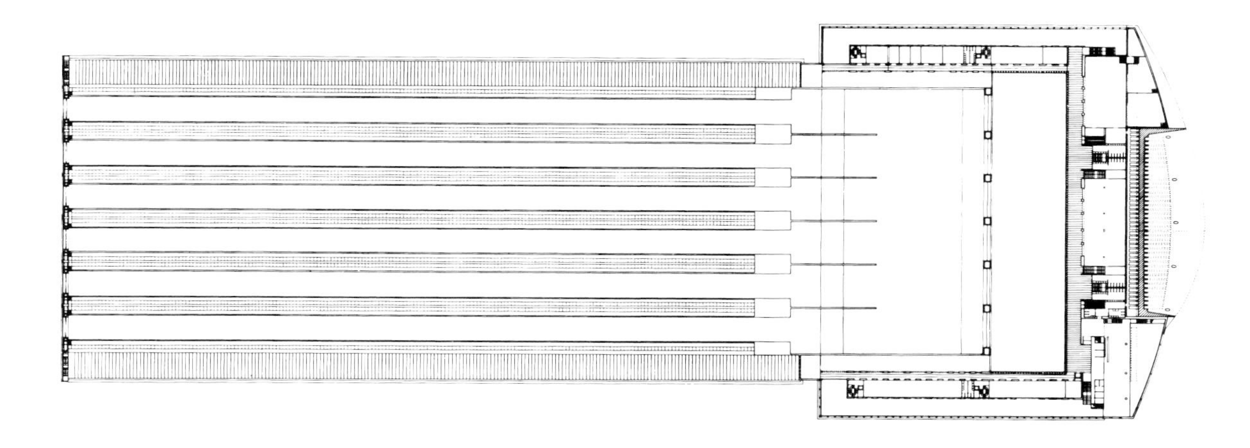

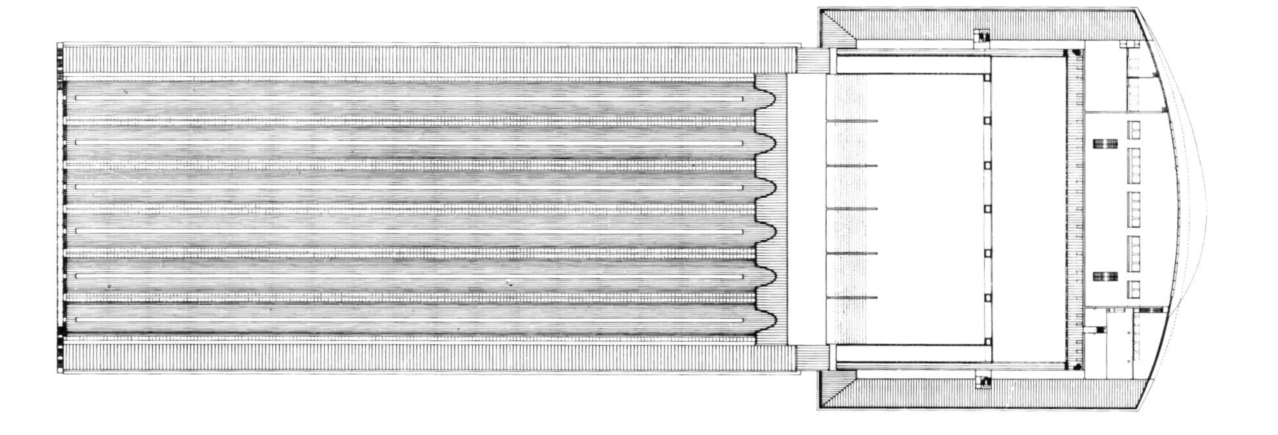

Plans of the floors at 14.65 meters and 11.5 meters above ground level; the former is the actual entrance level.

Side elevation at 19.15 and 23.65 meters above ground level.

Previous page:
Situated in an area of low urban development, the Santa Justa station is a catalyst for extensive expansion in the future.

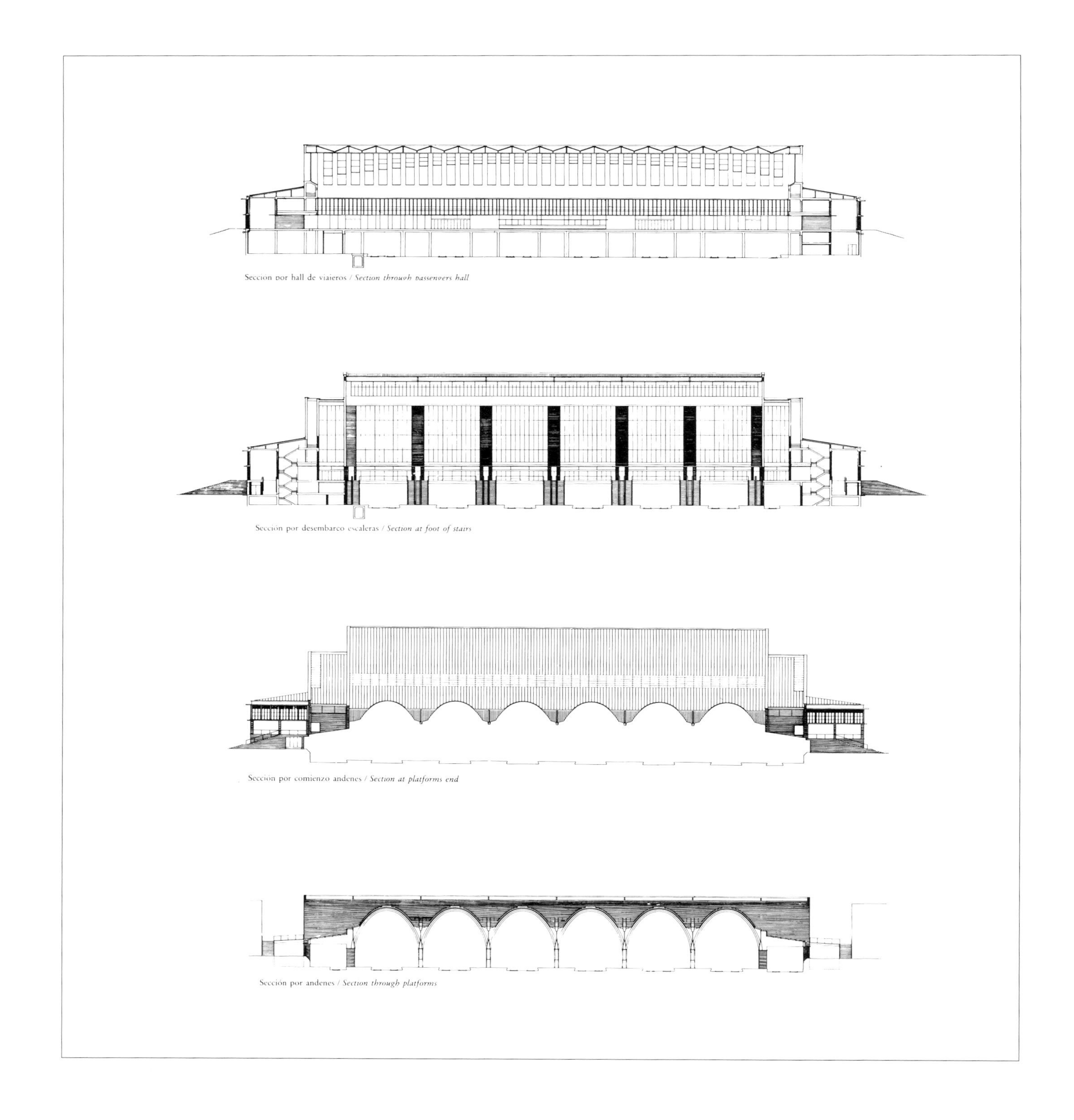

Sección por hall de viajeros / *Section through passengers hall*

Sección por desembarco escaleras / *Section at foot of stairs*

Sección por comienzo andenes / *Section at platforms end*

Sección por andenes / *Section through platforms*

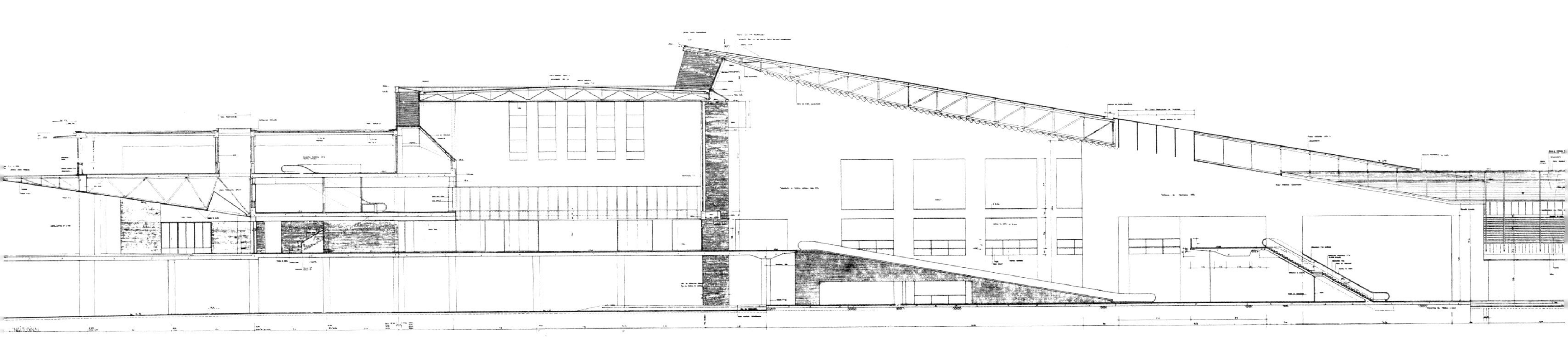

Cross sections. Top to bottom: the passenger hall; the top of the stairs; the end of the platforms; the platforms.

Longitudinal section.

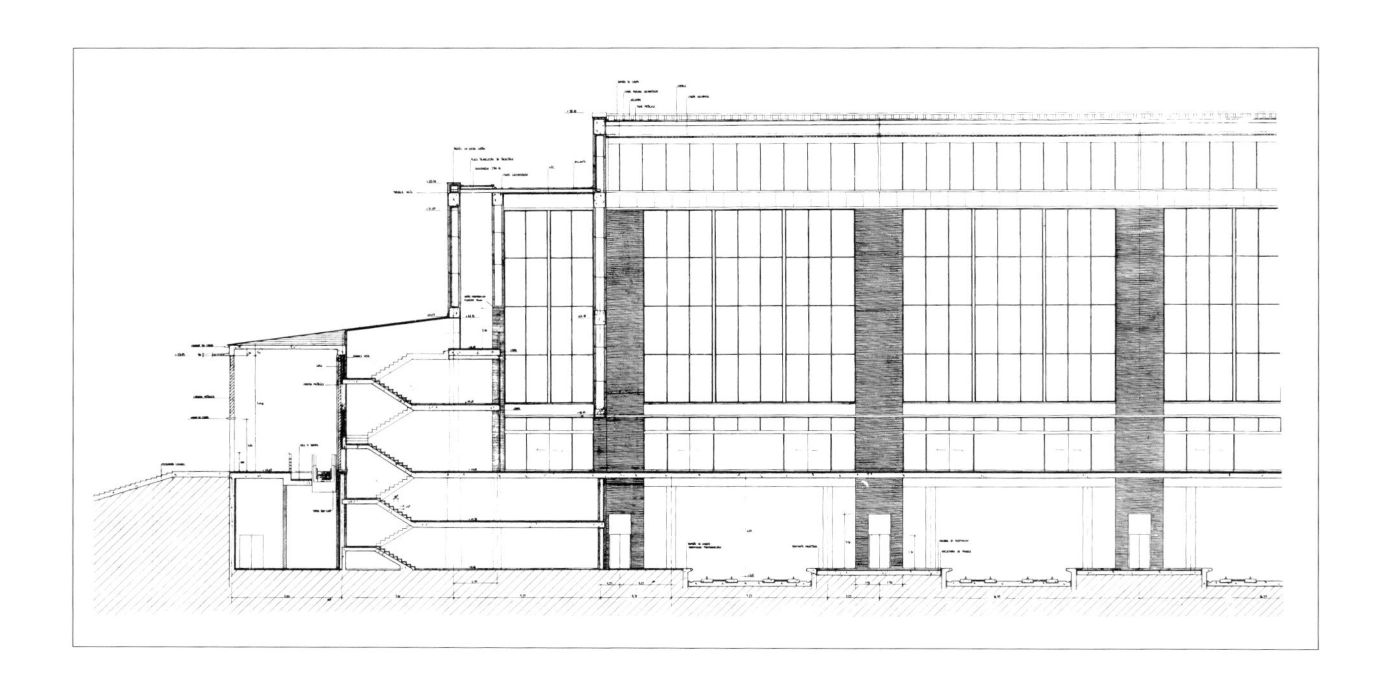

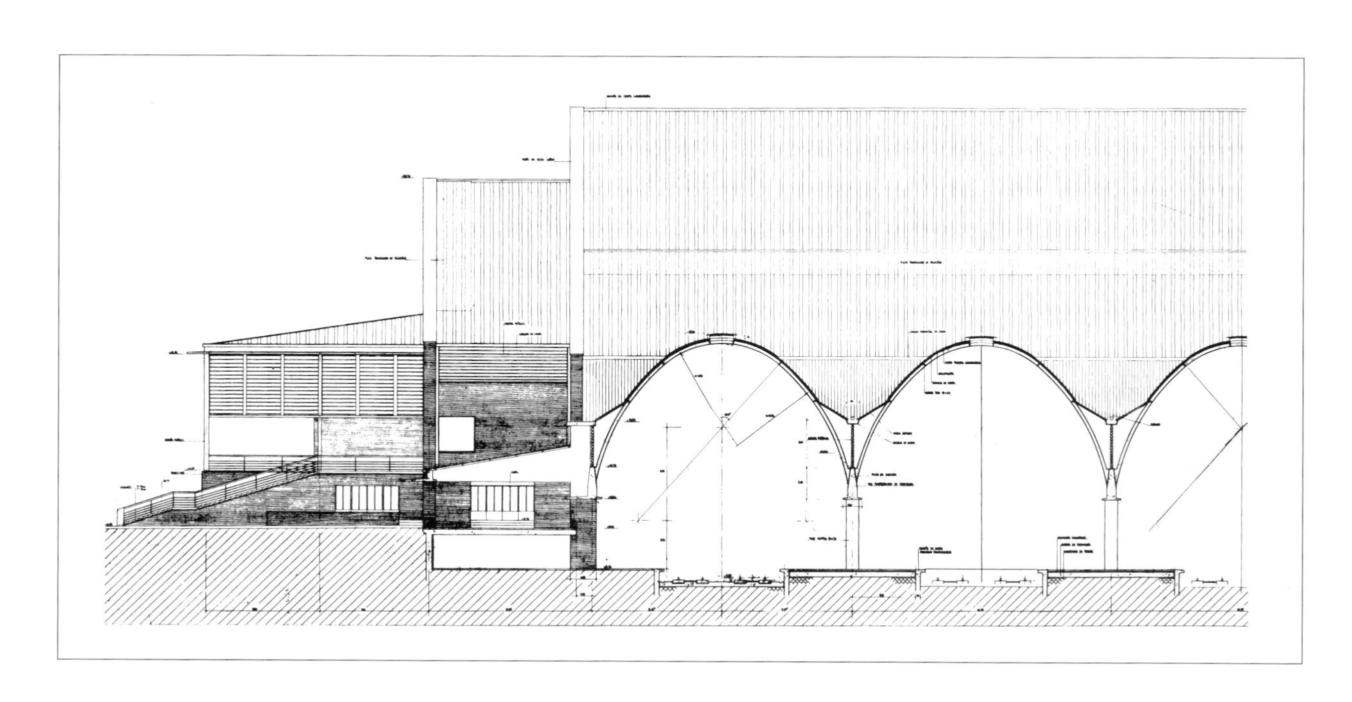

Detailed sections of the passenger hall and the platform roofing.

The long façade seen from the forecourt, with the cantilever roof over the main entrance.
A side view reveals how the different volumes fit into each other.

Overall view of the atrium.

One of the side corridors, with the distinctive square openings
in the brick walls.
A glass wall, divided by brick-built elevator shafts, separates the atrium
from the escalators leading down to the platforms.

The raised walkway which runs east-west across the building commands an interesting view of the interior.

View of the tracks and platforms.

Of modest span, the graceful vaults over the platforms and train tracks extend for some distance.

6 santiago calatrava

gare tgv de lyon-satolas

lyons, france 1989–94

project
Santiago Calatrava
with
Agence des Gares SNCF
collaborators
L. Burr, A. Burret, D. Long, S. Mémet
contractors
reinforced concrete: Entreprise Industrielle / GFC / Maïa Saunier
metal structures: CFEM
clients
Région Rhône-Alpes
SNCF Lyon
Conseil général du Rhône
Chambre de Commerce et de l'Industrie de Lyons
dimensions
5,830 sq.m: total covered area
location
Lyons, France
chronology
1989: open competition for designs
1989-92: project
1992-93: construction

In middle of the nineteenth century railway stations and lines changed the form of cities, particularly of their central areas; in the early 1980s, renewed interest in this form of transport meant that train stations—those serving commuter, intercity and airport lines—once more became the hub of areas of urban development. This was the context in which Santiago Calatrava designed his station for the Saint-Exupéry airport at Satolas near Lyons. An architect and engineer who was a recognized—and much appreciated—"expert" in the field of railway architecture, Calatrava proposed a form of great visual and urban impact, which would have a decisive effect upon the redevelopment of the area within which it stood. Located on the high-speed line from Marseilles to Paris, this station set previously unimaginable standards that subvert the cliché of the "amorphous suburbs."
In 1989, as part of a general program intended to stimulate trade by providing modernized transport services, the Regional Government of the Rhône-Alpes and the Lyons Chamber of Commerce and Industry (CCIL) called an open competition for the design of a station serving the new rail link between the city and its airport, located in the Satolas district. The specifications laid down that the building should be an efficient junction for traveling passengers as well as "the gateway to the region," a structure of powerful visual and symbolic impact. The station was, in fact, to serve not only as an interface between the airport and the railway but also as a major stop on the TGV line running eastwards over the Alps; hence it was to be a major traffic junction on a European scale. Satolas, in effect, answers to two groups of priorities: the functional requirements of any train station, and the more specific requirements of a space that mediates between the airport and the urban area around it. It is this concentration here of railway, airport and local transport which makes the station into a "particularly efficient" system (Jodidio 1998, p. 18).
The various parts of the stations are characterized by those anthropomorphic forms that have become such a hallmark of Calatrava's architecture. In the initial sketches one can see how the final form of the building was inspired by images of the human eye and by that sculptural form which the architect refers to as "the bird": the main elevation of the station recalls the image of a bird about to rise in flight, the side elevation seems a stylized geometrical rendition of the eye enclosed beneath its eyelid and brow. Calatrava himself has commented: "The eye is the true instrument of the architect, and this idea has historical roots that go back to the culture of the Babylonians" (Jodidio 1998, p. 22). But while anthropomorphic metaphors, plant structures and anatomical forms provide the inspiration for the project, that which makes it "live" are the elaborate calculations of the statics of the structure, the design of the balancing polygonal forms which made it possible for the original vision to become a reality.
The Lyons station is made up of two main parts: a passenger building, which contains the atrium for arrivals and departures, and the vault over the platforms which incorporates the gallery used by passengers. 120 meters long, 100 wide and 40 high, the passenger terminal rises above a central steel core. The large atrium then runs into the center of the vault over the tracks and platforms, dividing it into two symmetrical wings. Triangular in form, the atrium directs passengers from the main entrance towards the service facilities area, the airport check-in desks

and the long gallery over the tracks. Aligned with the airport building—to which it is linked by a raised channel for passenger flow—the central hall has a walls of glass and a curved roof that rises eastwards; beneath this there is a multi-level concourse with various services and facilities: ticket offices, shops, restaurants and bars, temporary exhibition space, access to the airport, station-master offices, airport police station and the designated areas of the SNCF and the CCIL. The wedge shape of the ground plan is then developed further by the roofing, which opens up into two widely spread wings that recall the alpine nature of so much of the Rhône-Alpes region. This roofing is composed of four steel arches which converge in a curved and tapering spine. The two inner arches, which support the central spine, spring from an architrave aligned transversally to the elevator shafts; the two outer arches extend from two tapering spurs in reinforced concrete, placed to the far eastern side of the building. A single V-shaped abutment in reinforced concrete supports the arches to the west. The vertical surfaces between the concrete arches of the hall and the two external steel spans of the atrium roofing are enclosed by glass panels that stabilize the structure. The arches to the two sides of the central atrium are also the points of access to the platforms.
The six sets of railtracks that run under the building occupy a covered structure that extends for some 500 meters. As in the Zurich Stadelhofen station, Calatrava creates a system of concatenated forms which offer an ideal image of the function of this space. Throughout its length, the structure that bears the railtracks is in fact two-tier: the lower level—some 8 meters below ground level—houses the six sets of tracks; the central ones, for high-speed trains, are enclosed within a separate concrete tunnel. Intersecting diagonal arches of reinforced concrete extend over all the tracks, forming a lamellar covering some 53 meters wide. All of the structures in reinforced concrete, including the niches for the lighting, were created on site, using the "slipform" technique which makes it possible to produce fluid, continuous forms of almost perfect finish. On the extrados of the tunnel over the high-speed lines runs a raised walkway connected to the platforms by stairs, escalators, elevators and bridges in reinforced concrete.
The main materials used are reinforced concrete (about 10,000 cubic meters), steel (1,300 tons) and glass (the walls of the hall and the 160 panels in the covering of the platforms). The general use of slabs of granite (40 × 80 centimeters) for the paving and floors adds to the homogeneity of the entire structure, while the use of local white sand in the mix of the concrete tends to give this latter the appearance of a natural material.
The various spaces of the finished building seem to be comprised of unfolding anthropomorphic forms; for example, a series of metal posts above the two hollow arches in reinforced concrete, which themselves echo the form of the lower vault over the train tunnel, provide a sort of lateral framework rising alongside the central aisle of the hall to a height of more than 30 meters. The roofing of that central atrium, which opens out in a triangular form, is made up of a reticular structure of W-shaped components supported by two split steel arches that reproduce the stylized image of an enormous bird spreading its wings; a structure in reinforced concrete supports the covering over the platforms and passenger gallery, while the characteristic feature of the central train tunnel and side walls consists in the inverted V components on whose tip arise the concave piers for the lower vaulting with its lozenge motif.
Each of Calatrava's station designs reveals a very refined technical approach to the problems posed; for example, there is an original and surprising reinterpretation of the tunnel as the locus of train movement here. Perfect examples of how the architect uses sculptural structural frameworks and daring individual components, Stadelhofen and Satolas both show Calatrava rejuvenating the idea of the railway station as such—a building whose architecture is once again identified with a structural skeleton.
Triangular in form, the concourse directs passengers from the main entrance towards the service facilities area, the airport check-in desks and the long gallery over the racks.

Bibliography

M. Bédarida, "On the Wings of the TGV," *Lotus*, 86, 1985, pp. 32–49.
W. Blaser (ed.), *Santiago Calatrava: Ingenieur-Architektur Engineering Architecture*, Birkhäuser, Basel-Boston-Berlin 1989.
L. Gazzaniga, "Stazione per il TGV Lyon-Satolas," *Domus*, 763, September 1994, pp. 38–47.
A. Saggio, "Zurigo, Lucerna, Lione. Tre progetti di Santiago Calatrava," *ArQ 13*, monographic issue, *La stazione ferroviaria. Verso un nuovo modello d'uso*, December 1994, pp. 102–07.
P. Jodidio, *Santiago Calatrava*, Taschen, Cologne 1998.
"Stazione Tgv Rhône-Alpes," S. Polano, *Santiago Calatrava. Opera completa*, Electa, Milan 1998, pp. 154–63.
L. Molinari, *Santiago Calatrava*, Skira, Milan 2000.

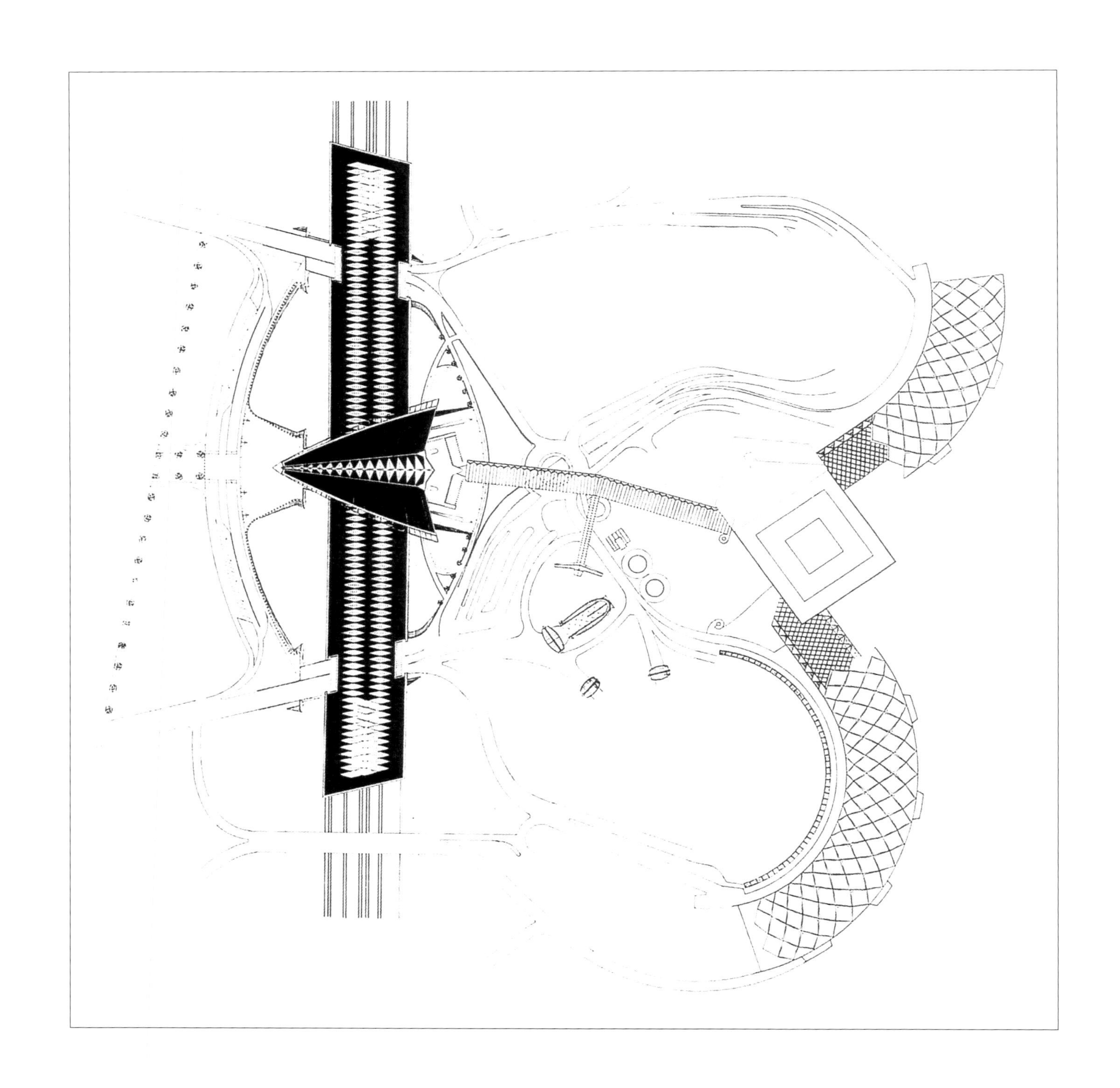

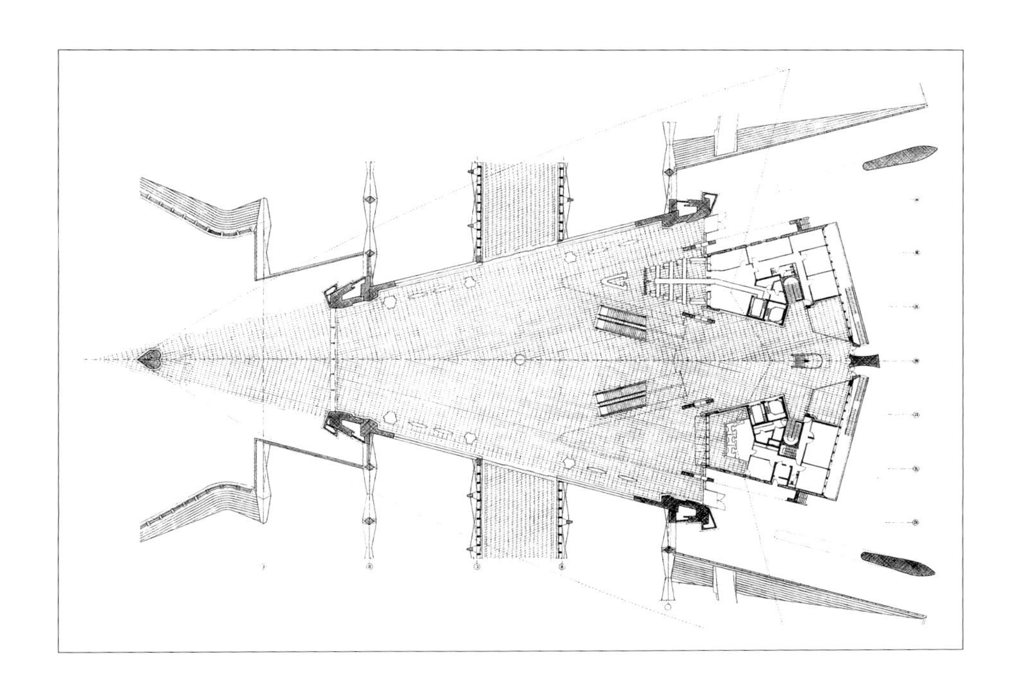

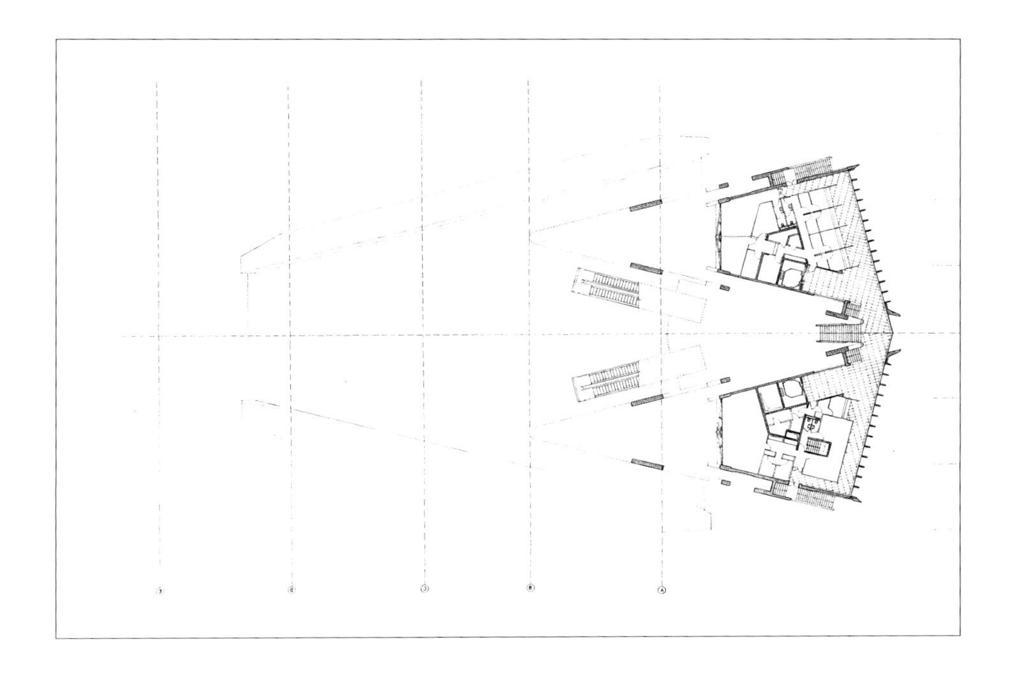

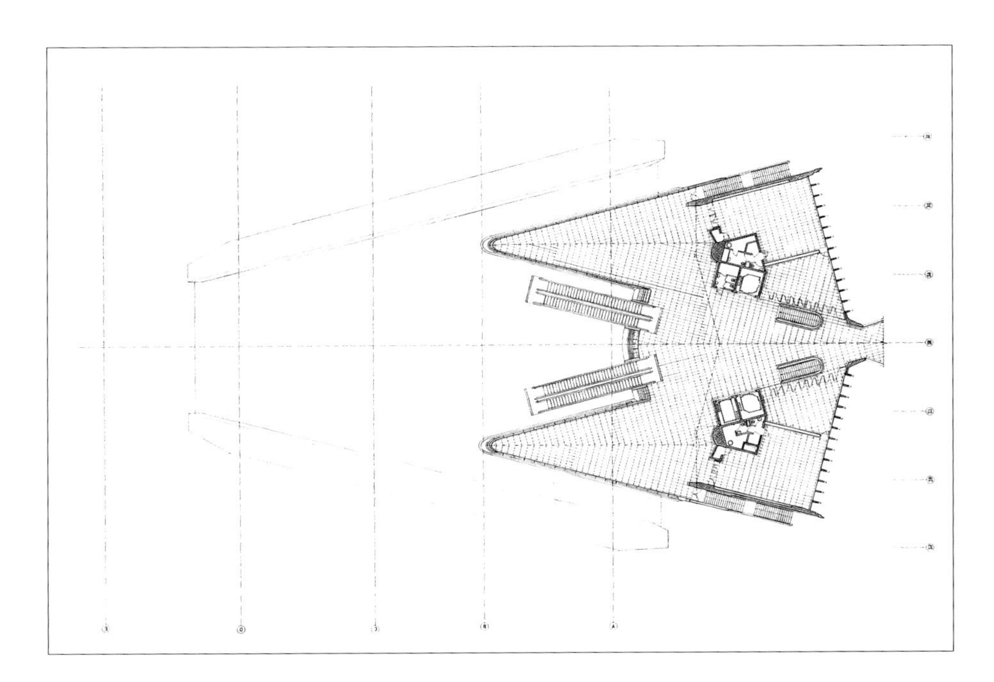

General ground plan.

Plan of the second and first ground levels.

Previous page
The main elevation recalls the sight of a bird spreading its wings in flight.

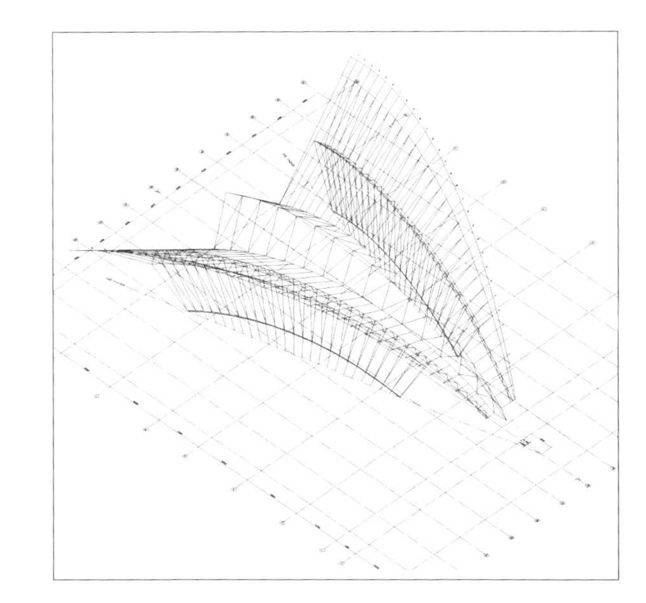

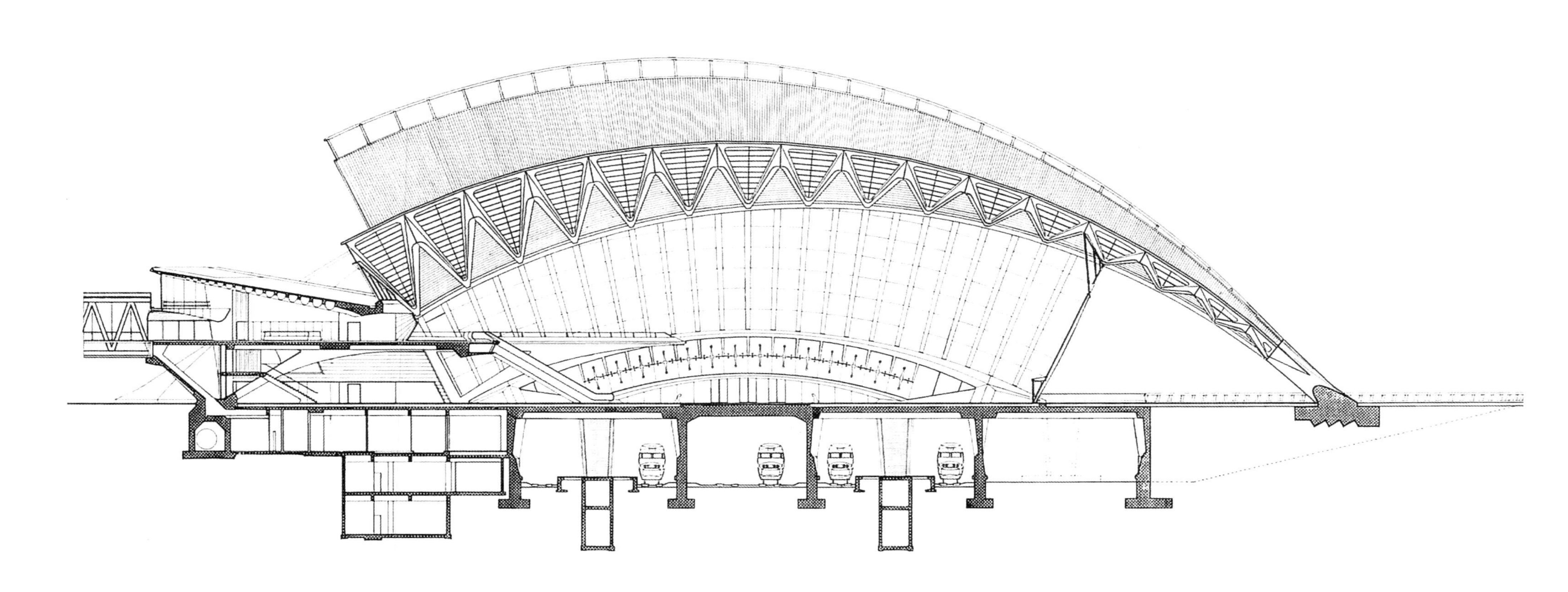

94

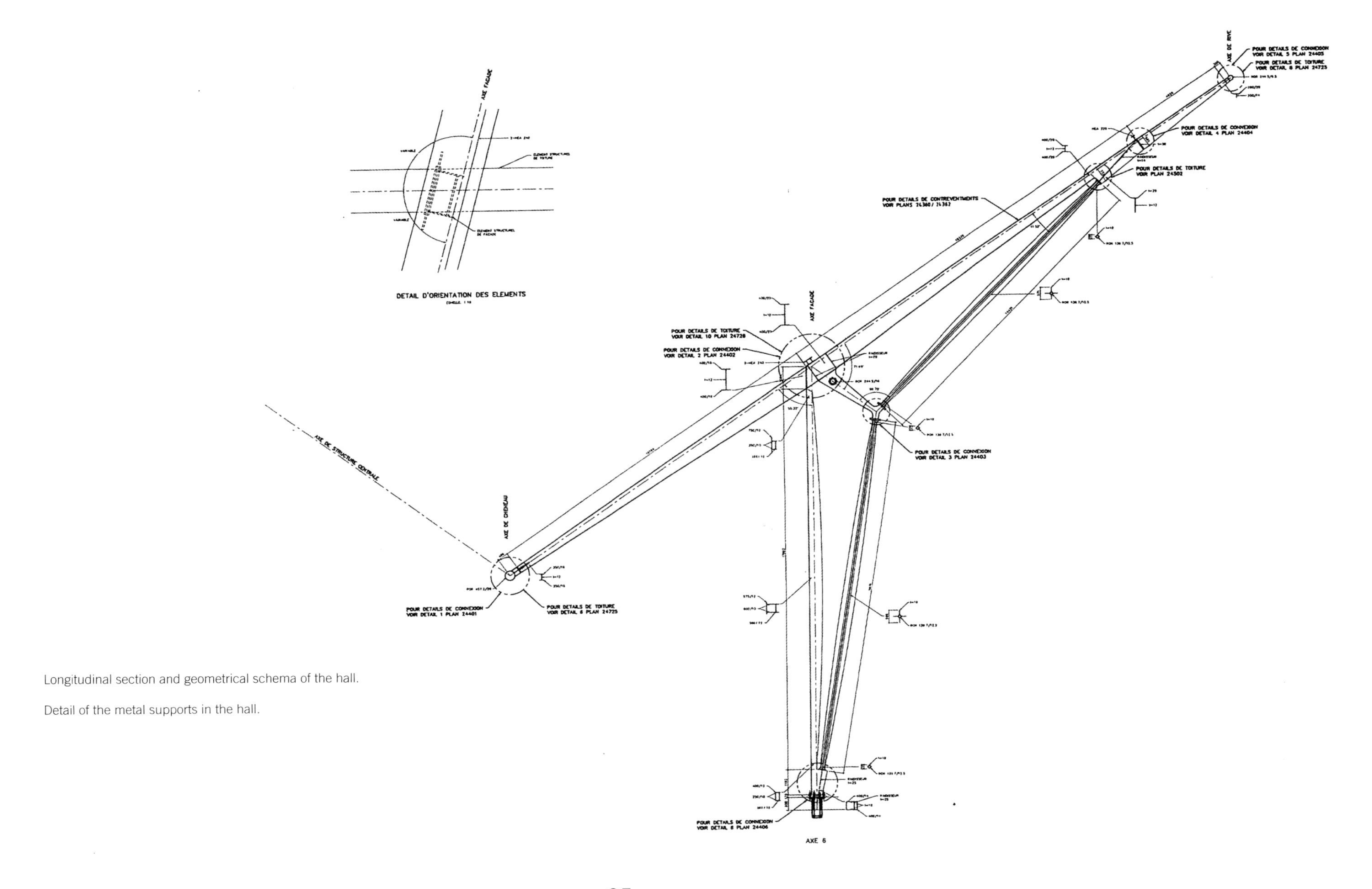

Longitudinal section and geometrical schema of the hall.

Detail of the metal supports in the hall.

A raised channel links the central body of the station to the airport.

Details of the reinforced concrete base for the large metal arches.

RHONE
Trains au Départ

The roofing is composed of four steel arches which converge in a curved and tapering spine.

Triangular in form, the concourse directs passengers from the main entrance towards the service facilities area, the airport check-in desks and the long gallery over the tracks.

Aligned over the tracks, the concourse looks like a large stylized eye from the outside. The rail tunnel is a two-tier structure; the central tracks, for the high-speed trains, are enclosed in their own concrete-built tunnel.

Intersecting diagonal arches of reinforced concrete extend over all the tracks, forming a lamellar covering some 53 meters wide.

The openwork structure of the train tunnel reveals the complex network of weight-bearing components.

A system of escalators links the parking lot and the large concourse with the platforms below.
The side walls of the train tunnel are composed of inverted V-shaped components.

7 hiroshi hara

kyoto station building

kyoto, japan 1991–97

project
Hiroshi Hara
with
Atelier 5
structures
Kimura Structural Engineers
acoustics
Tachibana Lab, Institute of Industrial
Science University of Tokyo
plant installations
Inuzuka Engineering Consultants,
Akeno Mechanical and Electrical Installation
Engineering Co. Ltd.
contractors
JV of Obayashi, Tekken, Daitetsu Kogyo,
Fluor Daniel Japan, Khosei
client
Kyoto Station Building Development Co. Ltd.,
West Japan Railway Company
dimensions
38,076 sq.m: area of site
32,351 sq.m: area of building
237,689 sq.m: total floor area
at different levels
64.3 m: maximum height
location
Kyoto, Japan
chronology
1991: open competition for designs
1991–94: project
1993–97: construction

Opened in 1997, the new Kyoto railway station is a multi-level structure that houses different functions organized in conjunction with each other. Defined as a "monster-city," Kyoto is a metropolis of 26.5 million inhabitants in a Far East which is internationally recognized as being the new frontier in urban development. However, in the presentation of his project, the architect Hiroshi Hara—together with the Atelier 5 studio, the winner of the competition for designs for the new station —observes how the city has still maintained the grid layout of the original Kyoto, founded some 1,200 years ago; in effect, temples, gardens and historic homes still survive not only within the reticular layout of the city center but also in the outlying suburban areas. Thus Kyoto is a place of dual character: a city that has maintained the most sizable traces of medieval Japanese culture, and a modern international metropolis which attracts visitors and tourists from all over the world. Hiroshi Hara, therefore, sees the city not simply as a container of disparate components, each with its own autonomy and identity, but rather as a phenomenon of continuous development and transformation. It is this idea which inspired his notion of a station that would reflect the "aesthetic spirit" of its context, without however in any way "deliberately" trying to establish a historic continuum with the existing urban fabric of the city. On the other hand, as the architect himself observes, a clear effort was made to "place" the new building within the history of railway-station design at the same time as "identifying" it as an unmistakable work of contemporary architecture.
Occupying an east-west rectangular site of around four hectares in area (longest side: c. 450 meters), the station is located between the districts at the foot of the hills and the new zone of shopping and technological facilities. From the point of view of city-planning, the project and the concomitant redevelopment of the surrounding area are intended to redraw the limits between these different zones and improve links between the northern and southern sections of the city. The design envisaged the construction of one large building which would house various facilities: railway station, hotel, shopping mall, conference center, museum and multistory parking lot. Seen from the temples and gardens of the hills beyond, the structure is a gigantic yet compact form that is aligned with the train tracks themselves.
The complex as envisaged by Hiroshi Hara and Atelier 5 was one in which those using the various facilities would constantly be aware of the presence of the station, even if that facility itself only accounts for just over ten percent of the total surface area within the building. To this end, the architects designed a structure that extends lengthways, with the interior gradually stepped downwards in the center; the different facilities are organized on the various levels which outline this internal V, the base point of which is occupied by the railway station atrium. Hara describes the whole layout as the creation of a "geographical concourse." Opening upwards to the glass roofing of the building, this multi-level internal piazza is designed to be the complement to the external piazza in front of the station building. At street level, a series of doorways—leading to the bus and taxi ranks—bring one through into the arrivals and departures atrium, around which are laid out the various facilities for travelers. From this space, one may proceed to

the platforms, to the subway trains or to the large shopping mall overlooking the atrium from the terraces to either side (these are reached by a large central staircase or by long side escalators). To the western end of the building, beyond the shopping mall, is the multi-story parking lot, while to the east the upper floors are occupied by a large hotel. The aligned blocks containing the bedrooms and the long communication corridors define the outside appearance of the building, with the central opening at the end of the steel and glass gallery being occupied by a terrace. The public walkways and interiors are characterized by weight-bearing columns that provide a leitmotif and framework for the project.
Resting on the long sides of the building, the glass roofing was inspired by that of the historic train sheds of nineteenth-century stations, and was designed to create a covered piazza that allowed some sort of permeability between the interior and exterior of the building. The space under that roofing is designed by the architect as a "semiotic field": it houses the reference points for orientation (signposting, the circuits for passage through the building, etc.) and the areas reserved for leisure activities. Thus, 15 meters above ground level, there is an artificial "ground floor" which is designed for the various mechanical systems of vertical, horizontal and inclined links between the different parts of the structure; this is what the architect defines as the "matrix" of the entire project, the fulcrum of the polyfunctional structure. In effect, the central concourse is conceived of as a sort of covered piazza that serves as a hub in the system of circuits and spaces that extend throughout the building. Along its walls are illuminated advertising hoardings with reproductions of the works of such famous artists as Roy Lichtenstein, Robert Longo, Kokyo Hatanaka, Thomas Shannon and Joseph Kosuth.
Monumental in scale, the building takes its place in the urban fabric as an actual chunk of the city itself; its various internal spaces are easily identifiable, celebrating the railway station as a part of the city at the same time as they perform the different functions of an urban area. Overall, the composition is identified by a series of what the architects call "attractors": the illuminated towers, the vents for the air-conditioning, the cantilever roofs, the vertical links between the floors.
The outside surfaces are uniform and make large use of reflecting materials such as glass. The vast façade in the latter material reflects the sky and surrounding air, so that one's perception of the solid structure varies according to weather conditions. Alongside the north side of the façade, covering the lobby of the hotel conference hall, the reticular girders form irregularly arranged triangular components, thus creating a "sky collage" whose different facets reflect the sky in different directions. In the forecourt in front of the station building the cascade of polygonal glass surfaces forms a series of shifting mirrors that reflect the surrounding area; at the same time, a central opening cut in the façade is aligned with Karasuma Dori Street, establishing a visual link between the Muromachi Square within the building and the city beyond.
All the latest generation of such buildings in Japan have taken this Kyoto project as a model, incorporating railway services within a complex of leisure facilities which are placed in direct relation to the city itself. As in all the new rail station infrastructures created in the country, here too it is the shopping and leisure functions which predominate.

Bibliography

Y. Futagawa, "Intervista a Hiroshi Hara," *GA Document*, 47, p. 20.
H. Hara, "Kyoto Station Building," *GA Document*, 52, August 1997, pp. 76–107.
N. Pollock, "Kyoto Station makes a major impact," *Architectural Records*, July 1998, p. 31.
The New Kyoto Station - 1997, Sheri Blake, Kyoto 1997.

JR
デパート

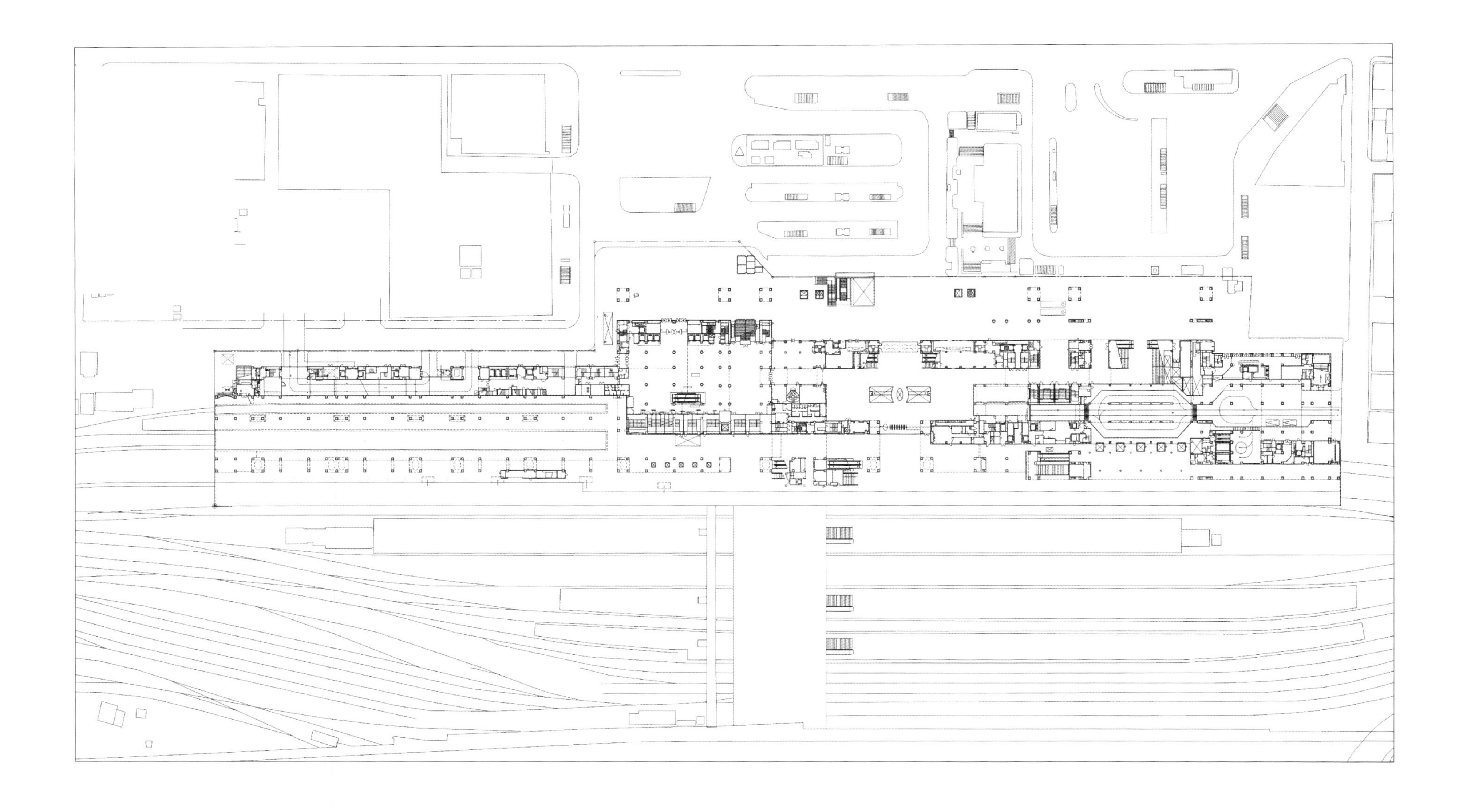

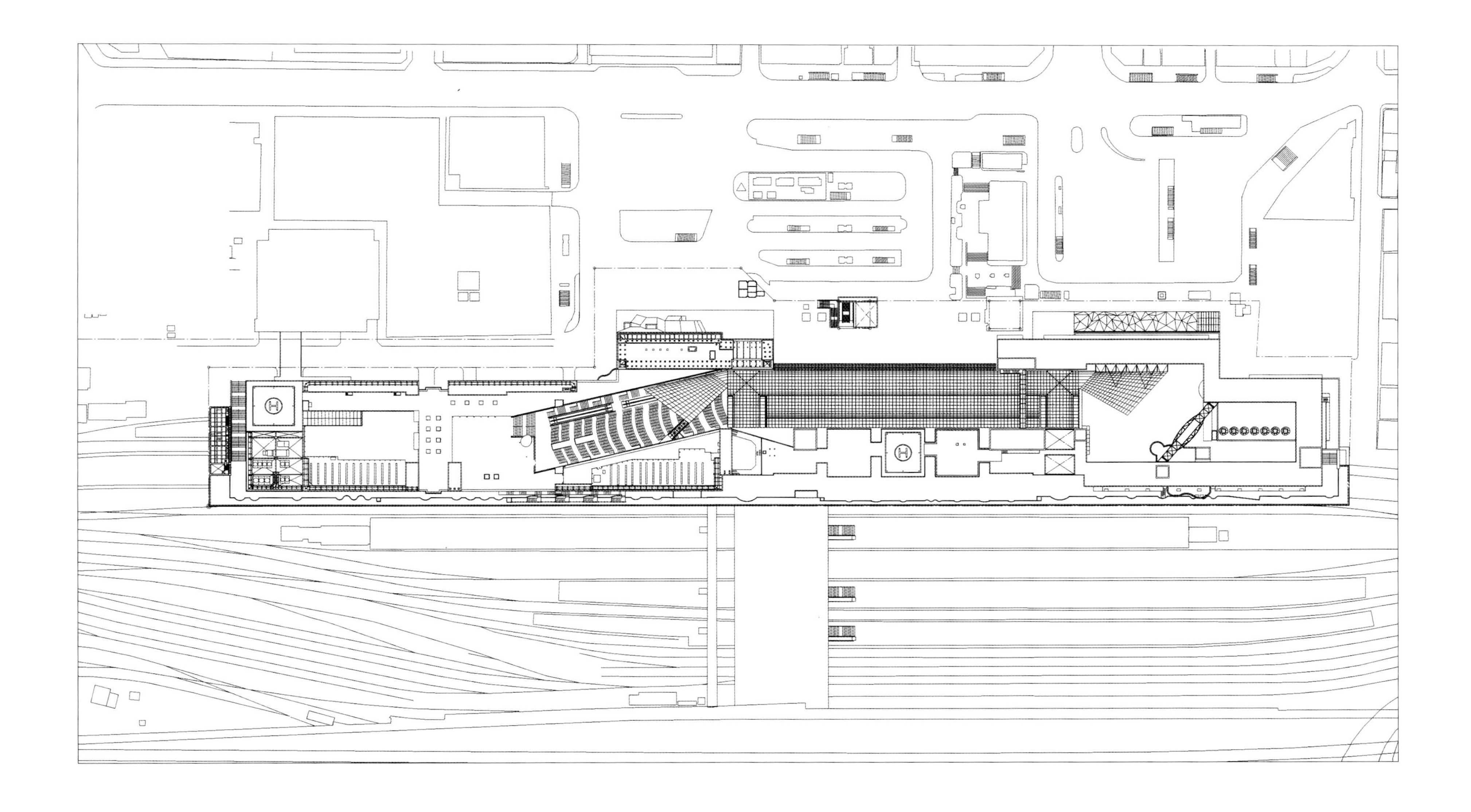

General plan of the ground floor.

General plan of the roofing.

Previous page
The north façade of the building seen in sunlight from Karasuma Square.
The predominance of glass makes the façade one vast reflecting surface.

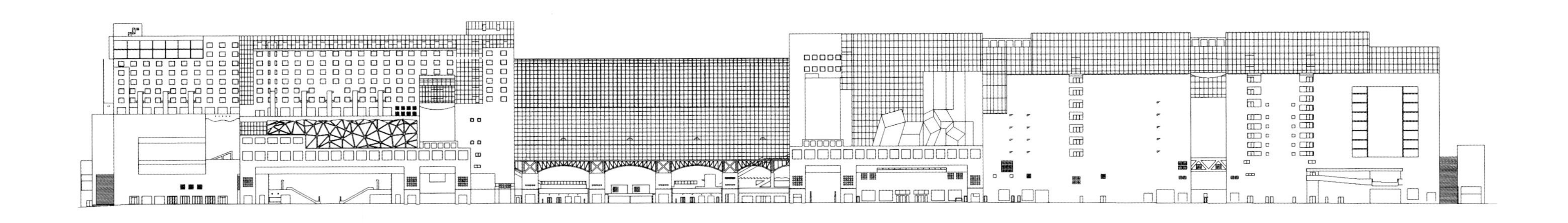

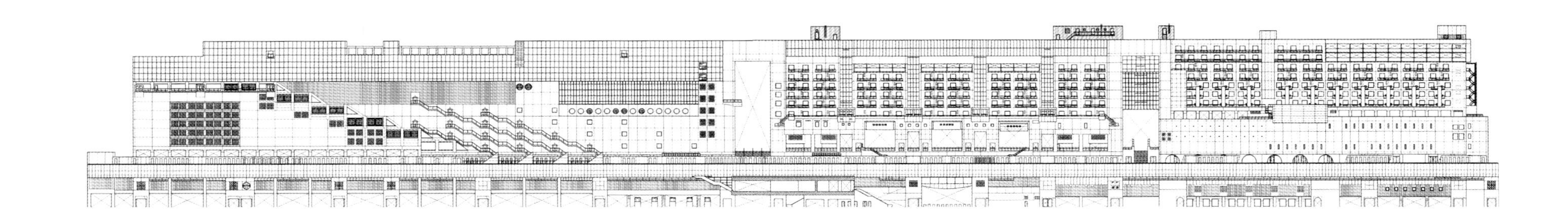

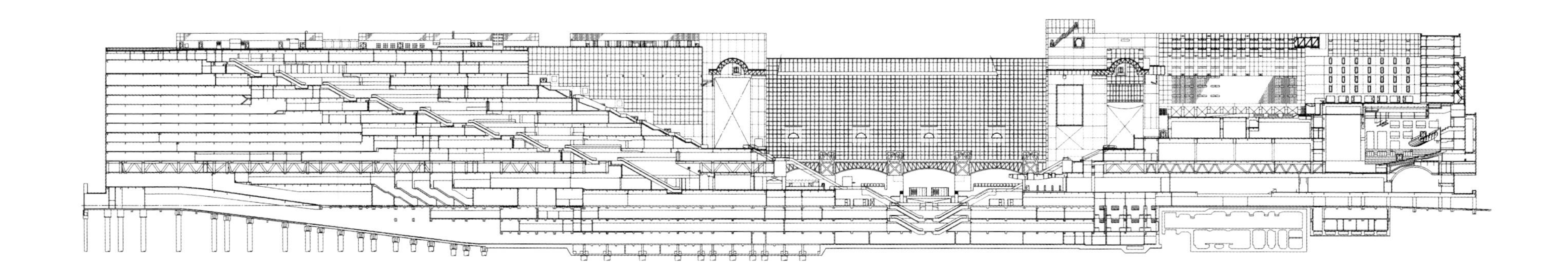

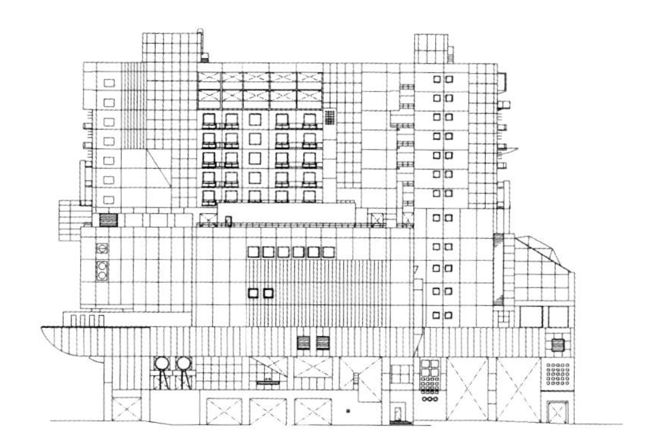

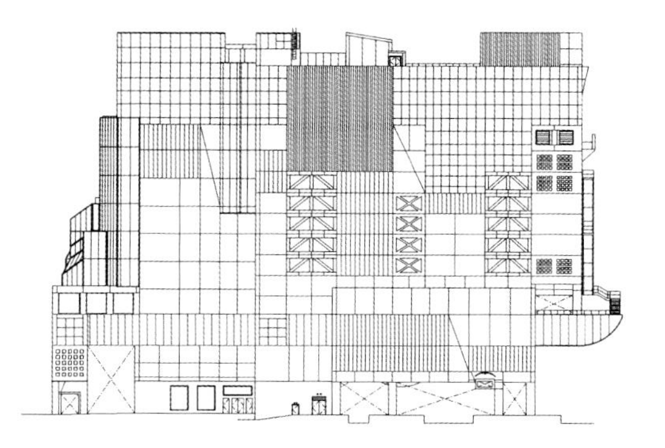

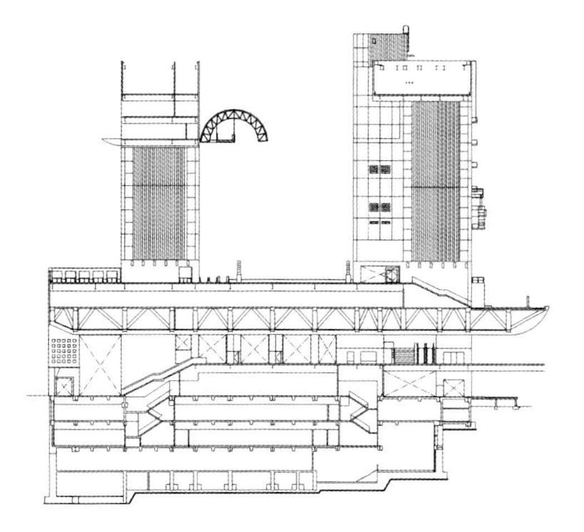

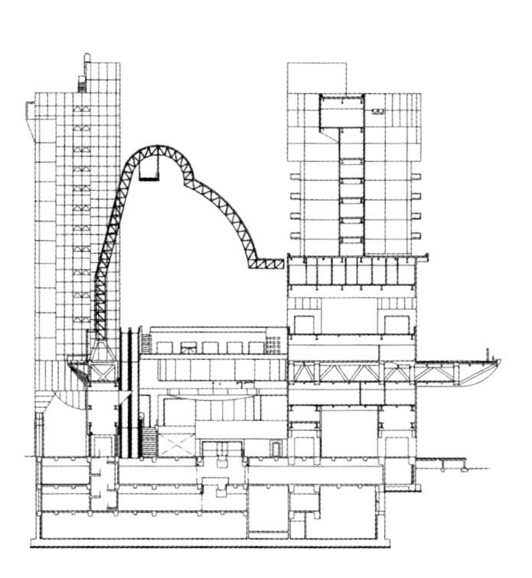

North and south elevations and longitudinal section.

East and west elevations and cross sections.

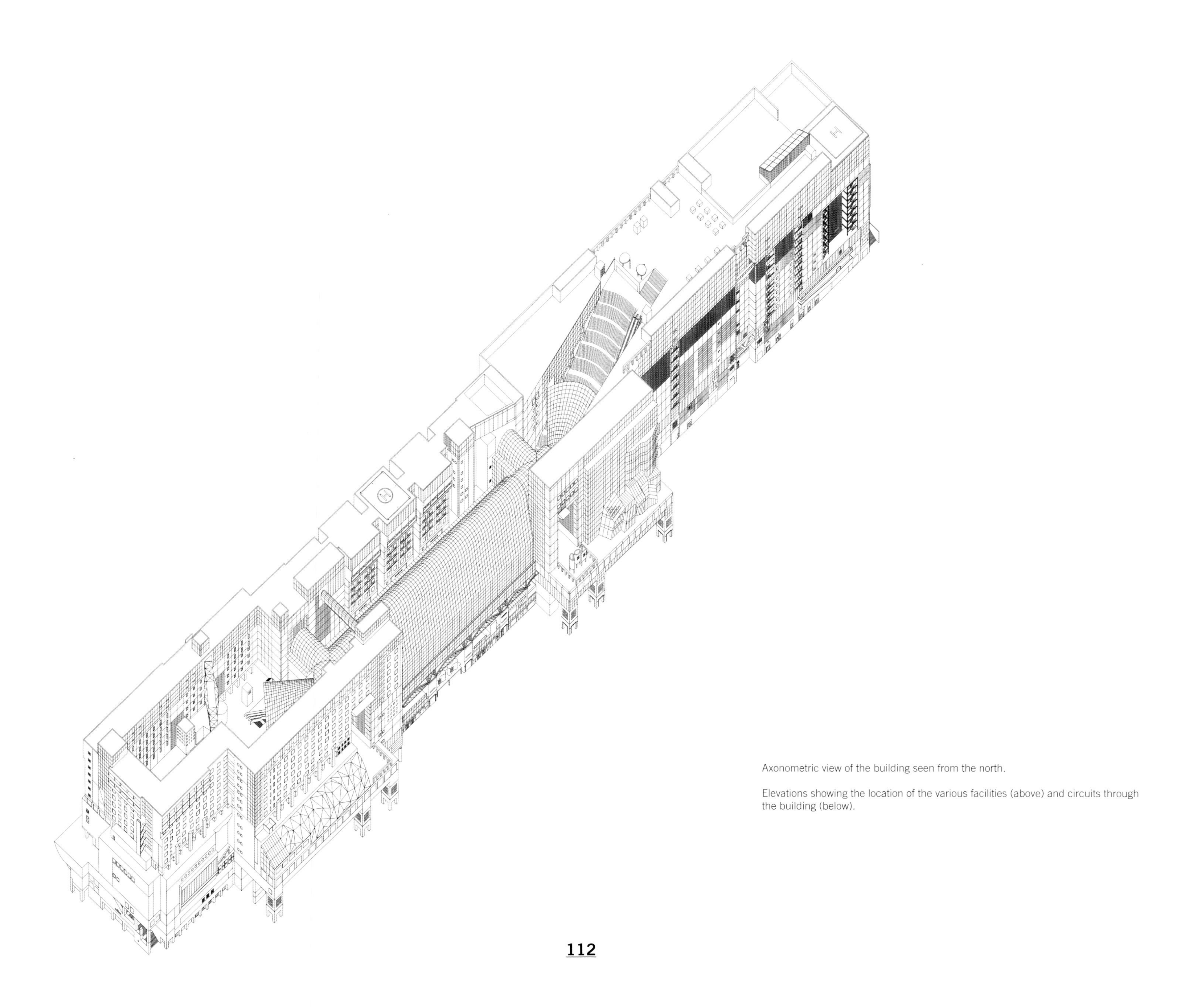

Axonometric view of the building seen from the north.

Elevations showing the location of the various facilities (above) and circuits through the building (below).

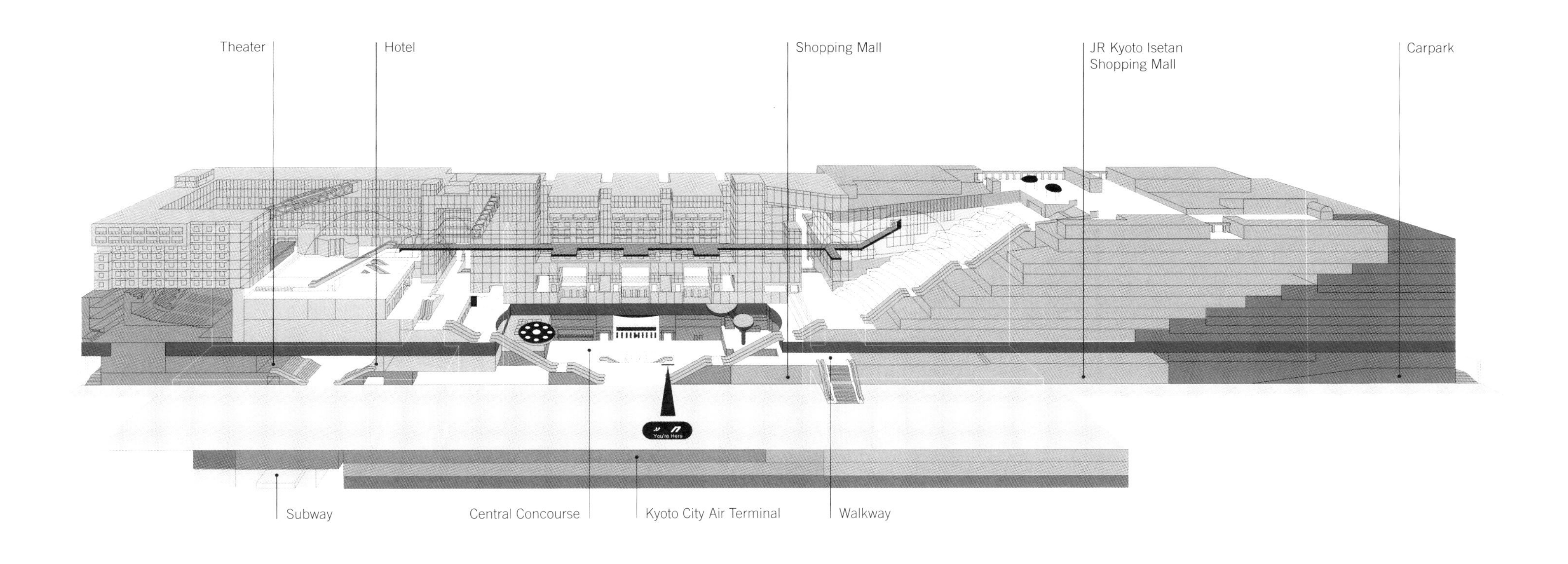

Theater
Hotel
Shopping Mall
JR Kyoto Isetan Shopping Mall
Carpark
Subway
Central Concourse
Kyoto City Air Terminal
Walkway

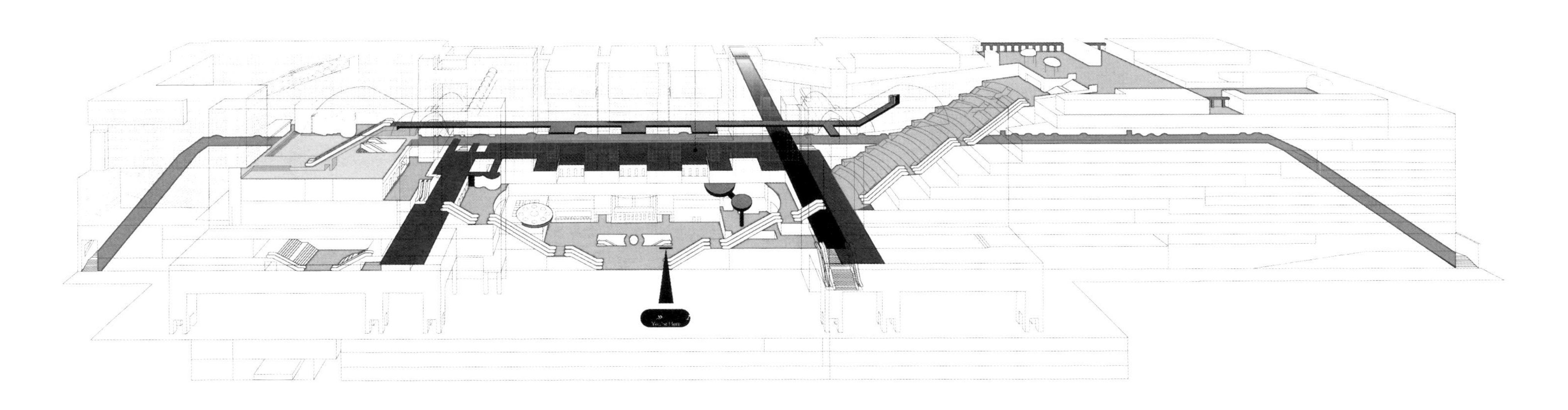

View of the north façade and the glass roofing of the geographical concourse seen from above.

View of the train tracks. The area occupied by the station accounts for only a small part of the entire project. The Karasuma Central Railway links the train platforms with the central concourse.

View of the south façade showing the west wing destined to house a shopping mall.

Entrance to the JR Kyoto Isetan Shopping Mall seen from the walkway; the nine levels of the mall are linked by escalators.
The central concourse forms a sort of valley; below the yellow disk is the hotel tearoom.

Looking west across the central concourse. The Muramachi Square escalators lead up to the hanging garden. The stairs are organized on an axis inclined 136 degrees south.

8 wilkinson eyre architects

stratford regional station

stratford, london, united kingdom 1994–99

project
Wilkinson Eyre Architects
architects
M. Barron, D. Bettison, S. Critchlow,
J. Edwards, J. Eyre, S. McGill, C. Poulton,
R. Troup, O. Tyler, C. Wilkinson
structures and plant installations
Hyder Consulting Limited
civil engineers
Ove Arup & Partners
contractor
Kvaerner Trollope & Colls
metal structures
Tubeworkers
clients
London Underground Limited
Jubilee Line Extension Project
Stratford Development Partnership Ltd
London Borough of Newham
dimensions
3500 sq.m: covered area
14 m: maximum height
location
Stratford, London, United Kingdom
chronology
1994–99: project
1996–99: construction

In the early 1990s, at the same time as the redevelopment of the docklands, work began on the Jubilee Line Extension (JLE), which was intended not only as an addition to the city's subway system but also as a boost to urban development in the East London. The JLE was to run from Green Park, in the very center of the West End, to Stratford, located in the heart of East London.

Following his work as head of the architectural project for the new Hong Kong subway, Roland Paletti was appointed as Architect-in-Chief for the JLE project, and it is to him that one owes the decision to commission each of the eleven stations on the new stretch of line from different British architectural studios, with the result that this challenging technical undertaking ultimately produced an important compilation of contemporary British architecture. Various of those who Paletti chose—for example, Wilkinson Eyre Architects, Alsop and Störmer or Ian Ritchie—were at the time just establishing their reputation, and for each of them this commission turned out to be a very important "test" of their abilities. The end-results are brilliant demonstrations of design, with each station becoming a sort of "reflection" upon the very art and practice of architecture. In effect, the JLE provides the plot structure for a number of different "stories," the final one being the Stratford Station for which Wilkinson Eyres Architects won the commission in 1994.

Founded by Chris Wilkinson in 1983, the studio of Wilkinson Eyre Architects now enjoys a solid national and international reputation thanks to a number of important projects. Its first major commission was for the Stratford Market train depot on the Jubilee Line, and this was followed by various schemes of great interest—for example, the South Quay Footbridge in the Docklands area and the Floral Street Bridge, which links the new block of the Royal Ballet School with the Royal Opera House in Covent Garden (in 2003, this latter bridge won not only the British Construction Industry Award for design and execution, but also the Aluminium Imagination Award for the innovative use of aluminum). The most recent projects undertaken by the studio give even sharper expression to its aim of producing "spare" functional structures in which architectural form becomes the clear expression of structural core, in which questions of statics (for example, concerning the frame and roof) are the dominant theme in the story the building has to tell. The Stratford Station is a perfect example of the studio's attempts to combine this originality in structure with designs that are environmentally "sustainable."

The new building replaces the old underground station and serves as an important terminal for the JLE. Defined by the architectural critic Ian Nairn as "the true heart of the East End" (Powell 2000, p. 152), Stratford has, in spite of the scarce development in the area over the last thirty years, managed to maintain a vital local identity. The railway here is an important presence: cutting across the urban territory, it would seem to separate Stratford from the rest of East London—an impression made all the stronger by the multiple tracks serving the local goods yard. The first rail line here—the Eastern Counties Railway, subsequently renamed the Great Eastern Railway—was built in 1840, following the construction in the zone of various factories for the manufacture

of locomotives. Gradually that line was joined by other rail and subway lines, creating a complex network of train tracks that cut across Stratford both east-west and north-south; even before the arrival of the JLE, the area covered by the project saw the intersection of the North London Line, which runs approximately north-south, the Central Line of the subway system, which runs east-west, and a surface line of the national rail grid running parallel to the Central Line. After the Jubilee extension, which was to run alongside the tracks of the North London Line as far as Stratford, the situation in the area would be even more complicated.
The project hinged on two main issues: the first was predominantly a question of urban planning, concerning the site of the station and the key role it played in the surrounding urban fabric; the second was more strictly a question of architectural design and structure, regarding the problems posed by the differences in level between the tracks of the mainline railway, the North London Line and the new Jubilee extension, and—above all—the need to prevent the North London Line from sharply dividing the concourse of the new station into two distinct zones (that train line runs right through the internal space enclosed by the metal and glass shell of the station).
To the west and east of the North London Line, the architects created two different concourses that are linked by a raised mezzanine which can be reached by stairs, escalators and elevators (the latter enclosed in glass shafts). This mezzanine backs onto a Victorian railway embankment and rests on a block foundation in cement. Two pedestrian underpasses connect the two concourses with the Central Line subway. One of these (now serving the east concourse) already existed, the other was built as part of the project; to avoid interruptions in rail traffic during building work, it was constructed by using hydraulic hammers to drive prefabricated box sections into the embankment.
The side elevation of the building is a quarter ellipse, which opens south towards the Jubilee Line Extension. The curving surface is anchored to the outside edge of the concrete floor of the mezzanine and then extends over the wide glass façade; the structure itself is formed of curved box girders in steel that taper towards the upper end. At the entrance side of the building these are hinged with the tapering pilasters that rise up the inclined façade; horizontal tubular components and diagonal tie-bars link the end of these sloping pilasters, forming one reticular framework along the length of the glass wall. This entire structure rests on four massive pillars which are placed in such a way that they do not interfere with the surface or underground rail lines and are designed to meet the very high standards required by railways regulations: they must be capable of resisting structural damage to the façade and the impact which might result from an accident on the train line which runs through the station.
The two layers of the roofing are separated by a cavity; this design was adopted to provide a natural ventilation system and temperature regulator for the enclosed space beneath. When the outer layer is heated by the sun, the spaces between the ribs serve as natural draft ducts drawing cooler air from underground and outside into the upper part of the structure, thus reducing the temperature. This system, whose efficiency is in direct proportion to the heat of the sun, also works to expel smoke from the building should there be a fire.
The predominance of glass and the "extravagant" form of its roofing make the Stratford Regional Station a building whose powerful visual impact is ideally suited to its role as a hub for the urban redevelopment of the surrounding area. In the words of K. Powell, the entire building becomes a "shining jewel" when seen at dusk. In fact, the lighting both within and around the structure has been carefully designed to create this atmospheric effect: wide strips of lighting on the service walkway that runs along the lower framework of the Vierendeel truss cast light up onto the roofing, while other fixtures facing downwards throw light onto the interior.

Bibliography

K. Powell, *The Jubilee Line Extension*, Laurence King, London 2000, pp. 152–56.
B. O'Looney, "Jubilee Line Extension," *Frame*, 4, vol. 2, 2000, p. 64.
K. Powell, *New Architecture in London*, Merrel, London 2001.

STRATFORD STATION
DLR
Stratford

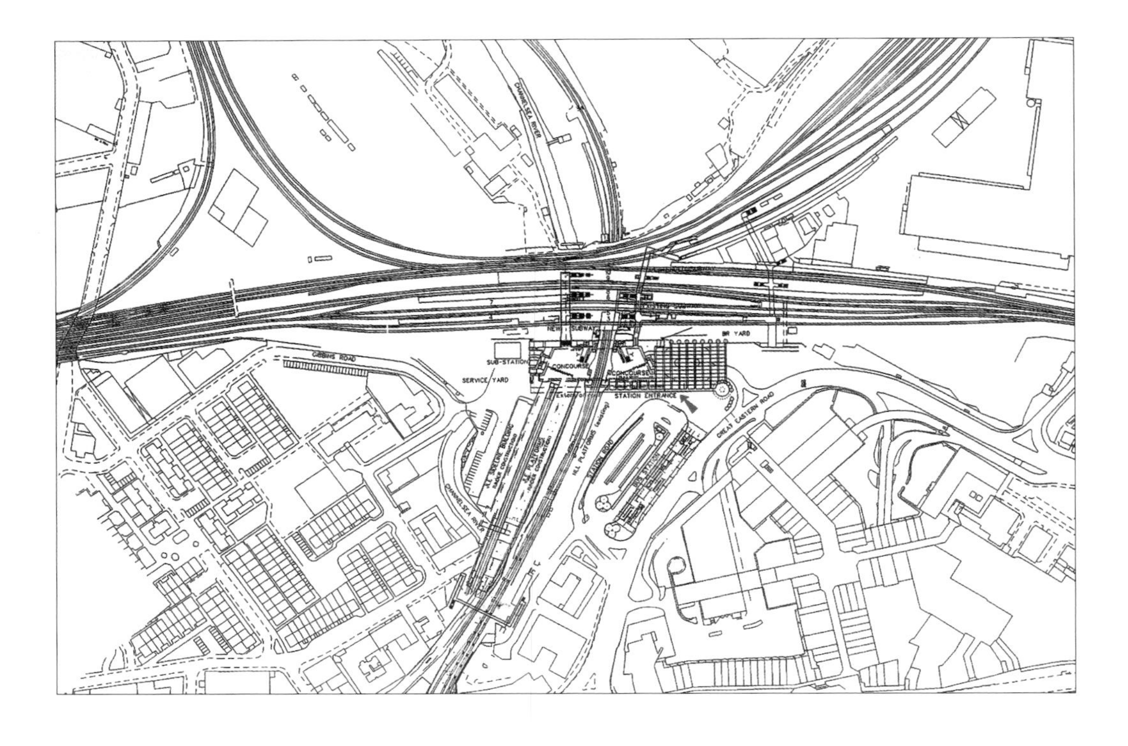

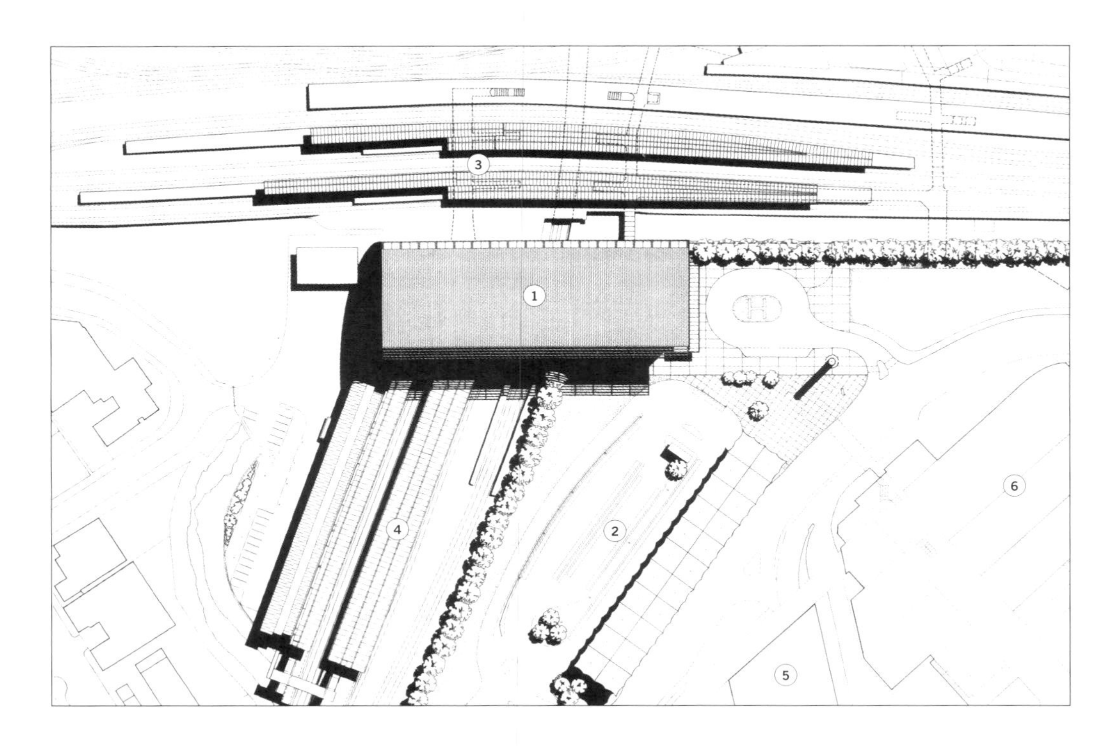

General layout and volumetric plan of the site.
Key: **1** station **2** bus station **3** central line and British Rail platforms **4** Jubilee Line Extension platforms **5** parking lot **6** town center.

Diagram of the functioning of the roof to ventilate the station and control daylight heating; north-east elevation and cross section.

Previous page:
The glass façade uses the most advanced technology for maximum transparency and luminosity.

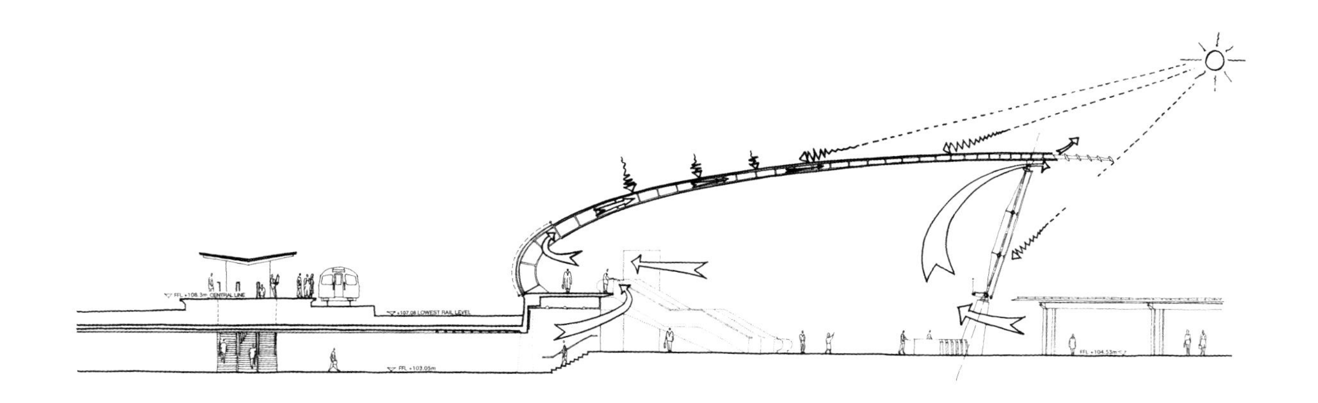
FFL +108.3m CENTRAL LINE
+107.08 LOWEST RAIL LEVEL
FFL +103.05m
FFL +104.53m

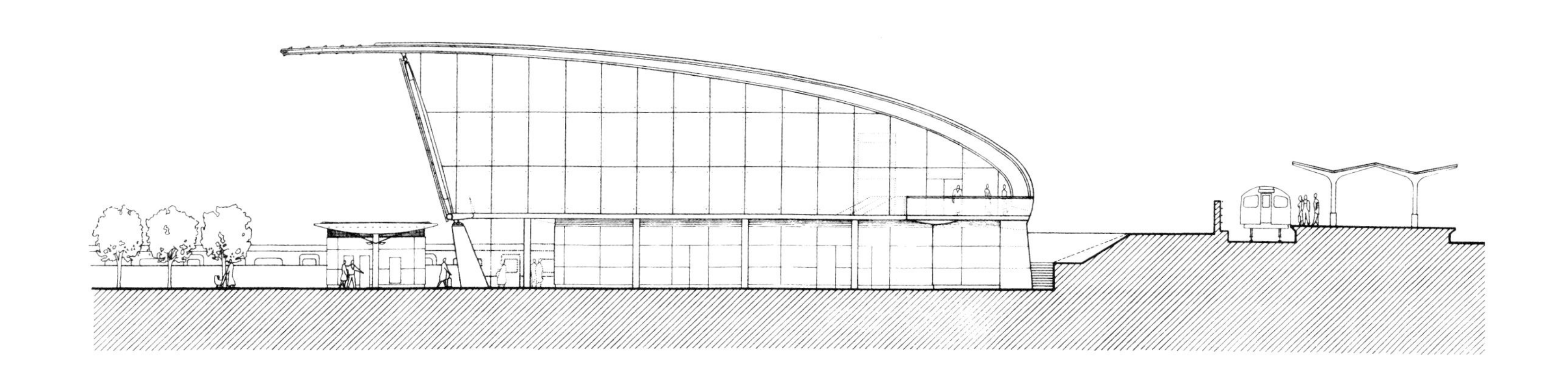

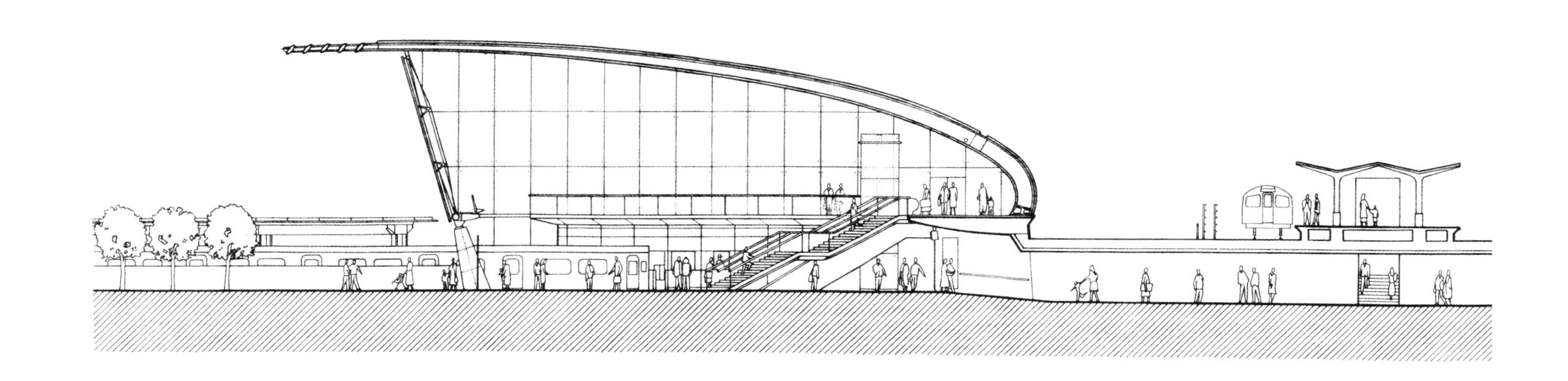

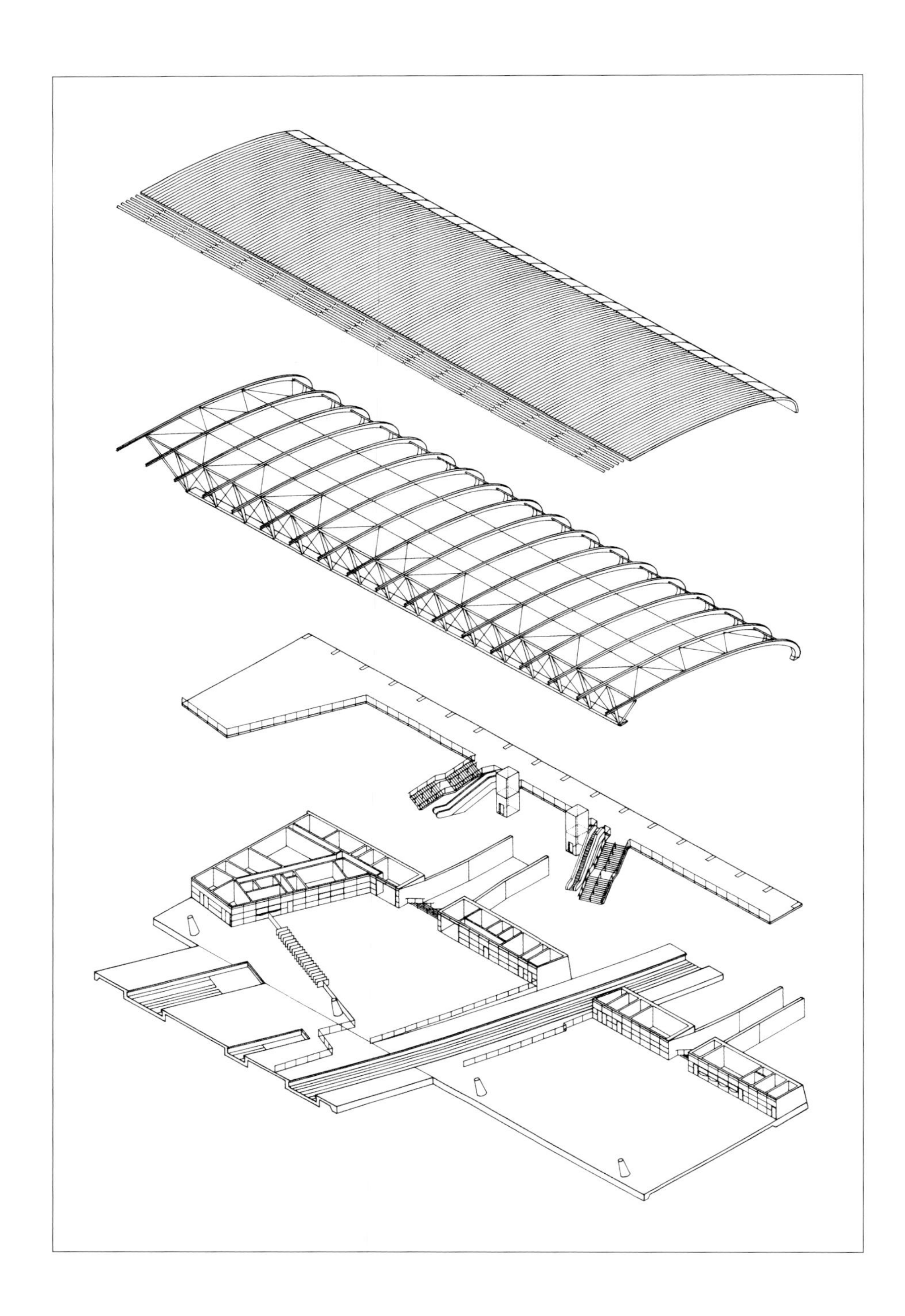

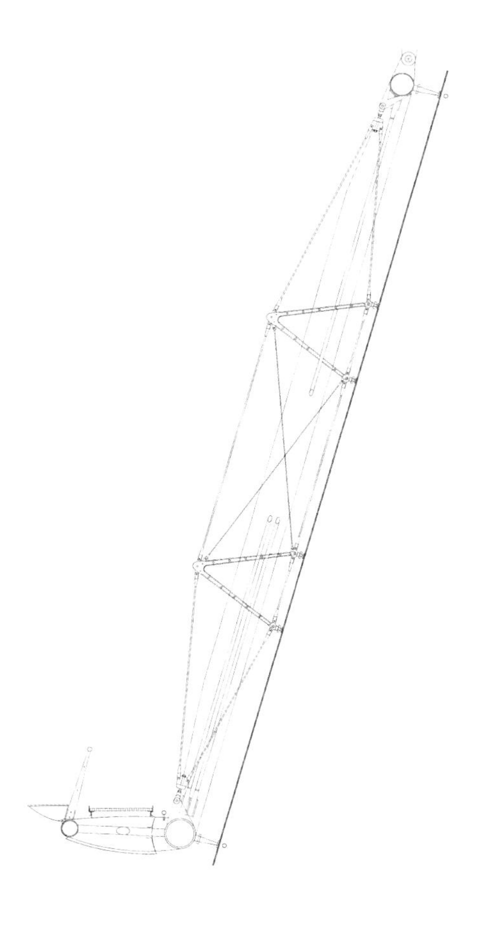

Exploded axonometric diagram of (from bottom): the platforms and concourses, the raised mezzanine running the length of the station, the roof structure and covering.
Detail of the glass façade.

Under its covering of glass and metal, the internal space of the station is cut by the twin tracks of the North London Line, to the sides of which are the two concourses.

The west concourse is linked to the atrium by a mezzanine reached by stairs and elevators.

Backing onto a Victorian railway embankment, the mezzanine rests on a concrete foundation block. The curved roofing/wall is anchored to the outside edge of the raised level, forming a visual link between the station and the rail lines behind.

9 brt architekten

flughafen fernbahnhof

frankfurt-am-main, germany 1996–99

project
BRT Architekten (Bothe, Richter, Teherani)
design team
B. Staber (architect-in-chief), C. Feck, L. Gnosa, F. Görge, M. Horn, W. Labsch-Boga, K. Pahl, A. Pakrooh, M. Pfretzschner, C. Springmeier, P. Weiß, C. Wilford, A. Woelke
client
Deutsche Bahn AG
dimensions
4,755 sq.m: atrium level
7,500 sq.m: lounge level
22,500 sq.m: platform level
3,400 sq.m: service facilities level
38,155 sq.m: total area
location
Frankfurt-am-Main, Germany
chronology
1996–99: construction

Built by the Hamburg architectural studio BRT Architekten, the high-speed rail station at the airport of Frankfurt-am-Main (1996–99) offers an original and innovative interpretation of the concept of a railway station. The markedly horizontal character of the entire station is broken solely by the large elliptical cupola of steel and glass which arises in the middle of the vast slab of concrete extending some 700 meters over the tracks and platforms. All in all, the structure has an aura of the indefinite and incomplete, which seems deliberately intended to negate its function.

The station is one component of an urban planning scheme that involves the entire surrounding area. Starting from an analysis of the density of urban development within the zone and the precise functions that were to be located within the building, the specifications provided by the clients for the project called for a building that would provide a flexible structure that can be extended in the future (almost as if the site were totally free of previous development). Hence, the station is designed to be the "foundation structure" for future extension; in fact, the present covering over the tracks can become the base for a multi-story structure above.

Handling forty million passengers a year, the Frankfurt airport is one of the largest in the world and one of the most important hubs in Europe. Since 1972 it has been served by a local train line to the city, and is now the first airport in Germany to have a high-speed train link. The entire project is the fruit of an agreement between the German Federal Railway, the Deutsche Bahn and the Frankfurt Airport Authority, which envisages the construction of a large facility in various stages. The winner of the open competition for designs was the BRT (Bothe, Richter and Teherani) studio in Hamburg. Founded in 1991, the studio has worked on various station projects which are, in the words of Dirk Meyhöfer, distinguished by their futuristic—not to say "preposterous"—appearance. In the 1997 project for the Dortmund station, for example, the three architects created a cylindrical volume of 240 meters in diameter and 60 meters in height, providing some 40,000 square meters of floorspace that would house cinemas and shopping malls above ground, with the rotating platform deck of the station below. The same extravagance and delight in gigantic conceptions can be found in the work on the extension of the Stuttgart Station and the redevelopment of that in Hanover (for this latter, the architects proposed a giant glass roof over the tracks and platforms). The Frankfurt design and all of the above-mentioned schemes have a certain approach in common: as Hadi Teherani puts it, they are airports for trains. Reevocations of the old concept of stations-as-machines, these are highly modern facilities which satisfy contemporary requirements for speed in travel, provide multi-functional spaces, and also challenge the resistance posed by the very nature of the materials used in their construction.

Separated from the airport by a freeway which cuts through this area, the Frankfurt station is designed as an autonomous structure with a footbridge linking the two facilities. The building occupies a site 700 meters long and 60 meters wide, and has been described as looking like "a glass and cement dragon" about to rise from beneath the earth (Meyhöfer 2000, p. 109). The wide concrete covering over the tracks and platforms has been

designed to serve in the future as a base of some 34,000 square meters on which it will be possible to raise a multi-story structure of approximately 180,000 square meters of floorspace. The entire weight of that new building will be borne by the concrete platform without the need for further structural intervention. Furthermore, in the later building phase that platform will also serve as a "horizontal barrier" between construction and the station between, so that rail traffic will not be interrupted at all.
The present station lies on two levels. The upper one, linked to the airport by the footbridge, houses the concourse for the direction of passenger flow; the lower level is that occupied by the high-speed rail tracks. The concrete roofing rests on some forty-three reticular steel girders of a span of 50 meters; placed at intervals of 15 meters, these define the entire space of the arrivals and departures zones. The decision to use lattice girders was dictated by the need for an intermediate space between the concourse above and the rails below, in which to house technical facilities and other service areas. Created in the gaps between the girders—whose thickness of 4.5 meters determines the height of the intermediate zone—these spaces are enclosed by glass partitions, thus establishing a visual link with the level of the platforms below.
A large elliptical shaft through the different levels carries light down to the platforms, thus creating the impression of a structure open to the air. The windows of the intermediate level look out into this shaft, across which run some of the reticular girders that bear the weight of the concourse level above. This idea exemplifies the BRT group's interest in exploiting the structural and technical details of the building as architectural features. At each end, the reticular girders are supported by three pillars inclined to form V shapes with each other; these rest on a single foundation bed that runs the entire length of the concrete roofing. Both the pillars and the foundation bed are designed to bear the entire weight of the structure that will in the future be raised above the station.
The side façades of the building are slightly-sloping glass surfaces held in place by a vertical metal framework. Of the three inclined pillars, the two on the inside of the façade are faced in bands of laminate steel which, due to the difference in their diameter, give the pillars the appearance of extended telescopes. The extrados structure of the glass cupola comprises lattice girders bound on the outside by a metal tube (diameter: 32 cm) which is destined to absorb all the transversal strain. Nine meters apart and slightly inclined towards the center, these girders support a secondary framework which holds the glass in place.
As Martha Thorne comments, the station has the appearance of "a UFO that has just landed at an airport" (Thorne 2001, p. 87). An "unlimited free-time object," within which are housed entertainment services and facilities, this space is designed not only to serve the immediate needs of travelers but also to permit extension in accordance with future needs. As such, the Frankfurt airport station is fully emblematic of a structure that combines two different spaces: an international traffic junction and a multi-functional facility.

Bibliography

"Reiseplattform. ICE-Fernbahnhof Flughafen Frankfurt a.M.," *DBZ*, 4, 1999, pp. 79–82.
D. Meyhöfer, "Bothe, Richter, Teherani... in acht Jahren von Null and Hundert," *DBZ*, 1, 2000, pp. 104–11.
M. Thorne, *Modern trains and splendid stations*, Merrel, London 2001.

Abfahrt Departure
Abfahrt Departure
Reisezentrum
DB
DB
Abfall
Für einen sauberen Bahnhof

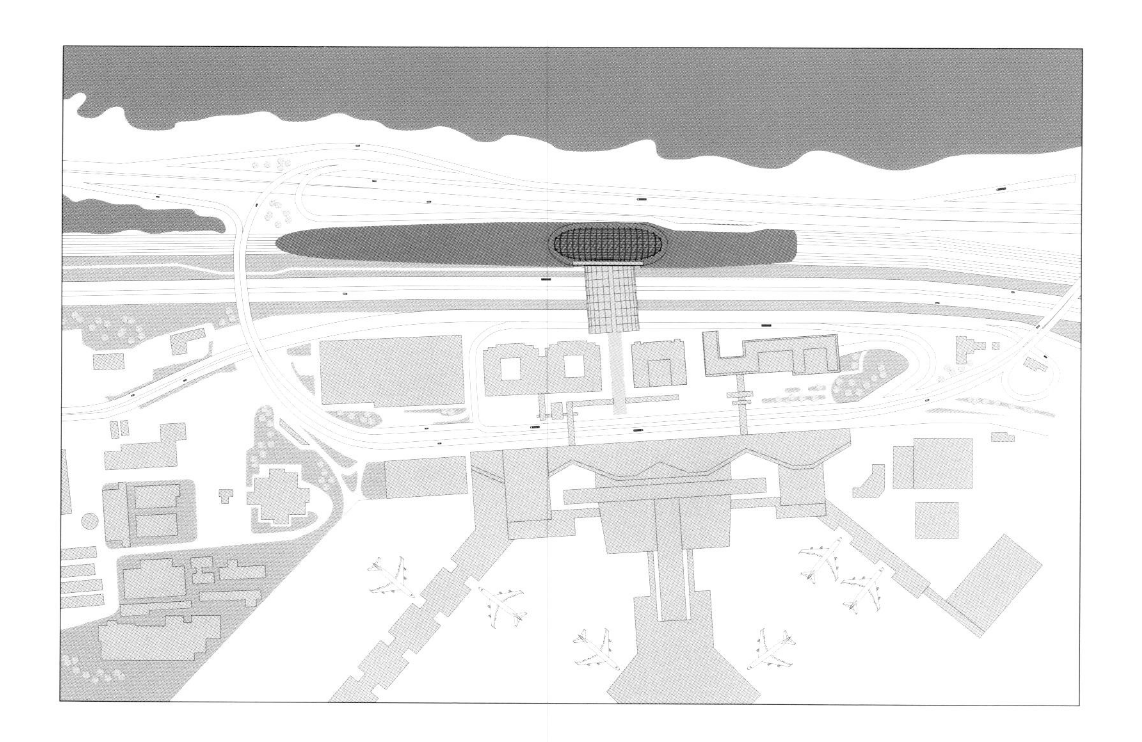

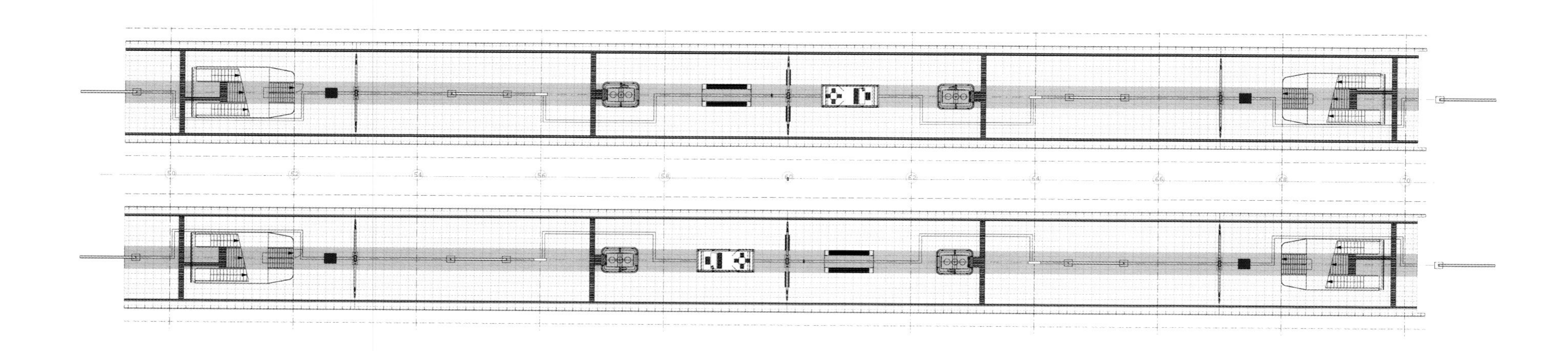

General plan of the platform level of the station.

Longitudinal section and plan of the atrium.

Previous page
The layout of the atrium satisfies contemporary requirements for speed in travel.

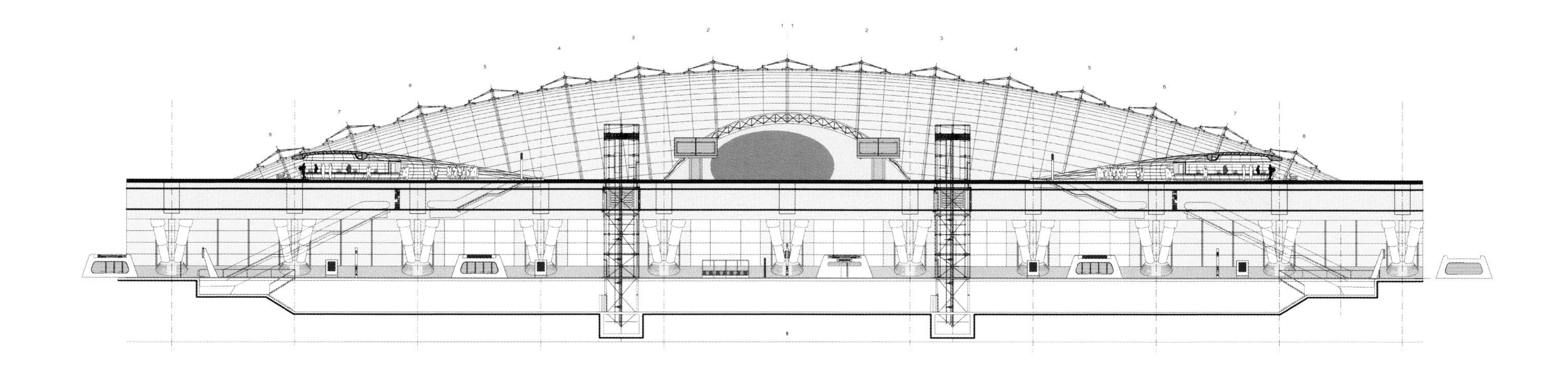

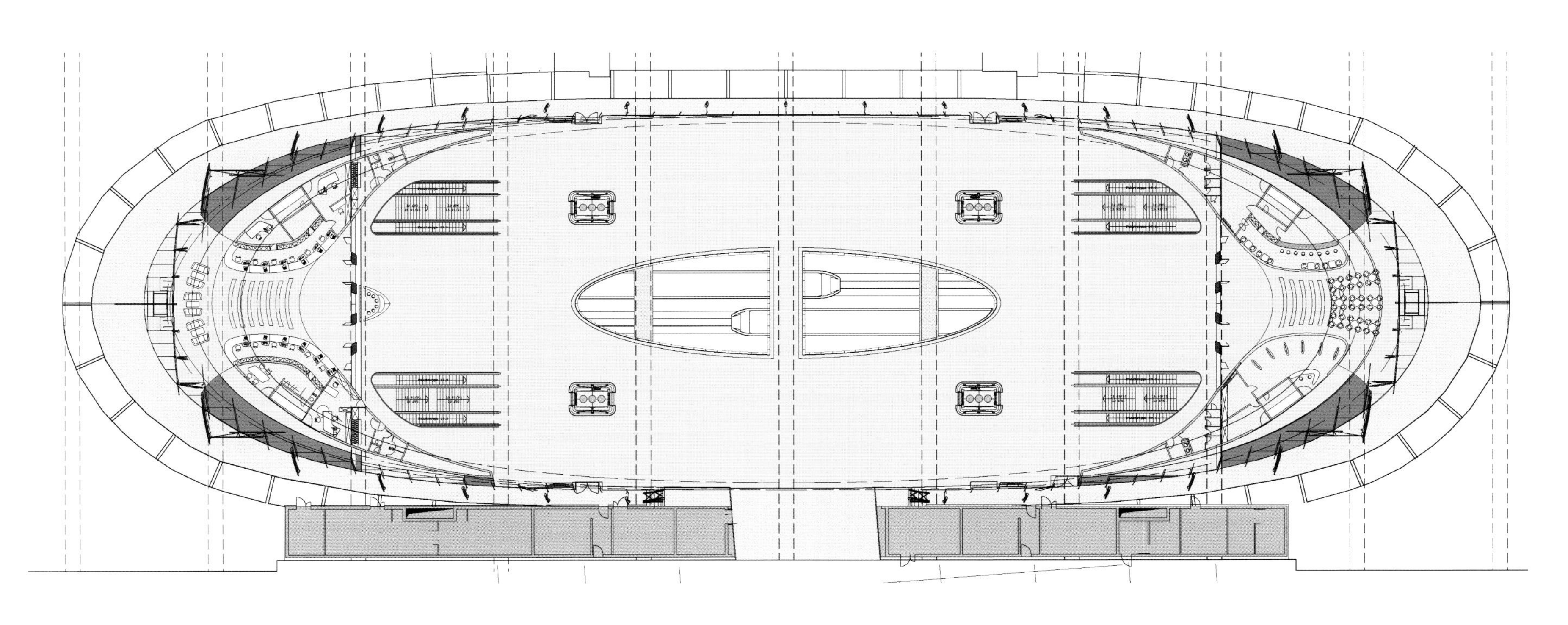

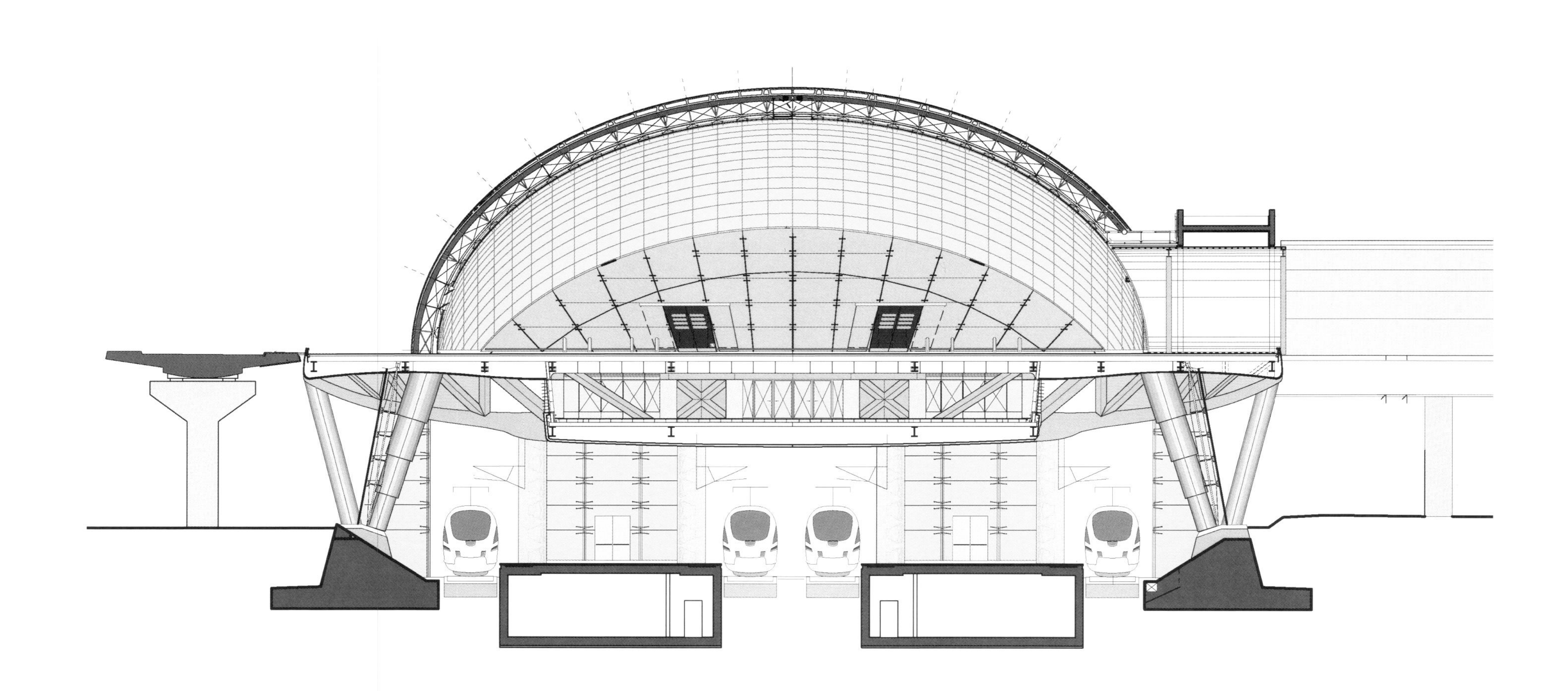

Cross section.

Sections of components of the large glass cupola.

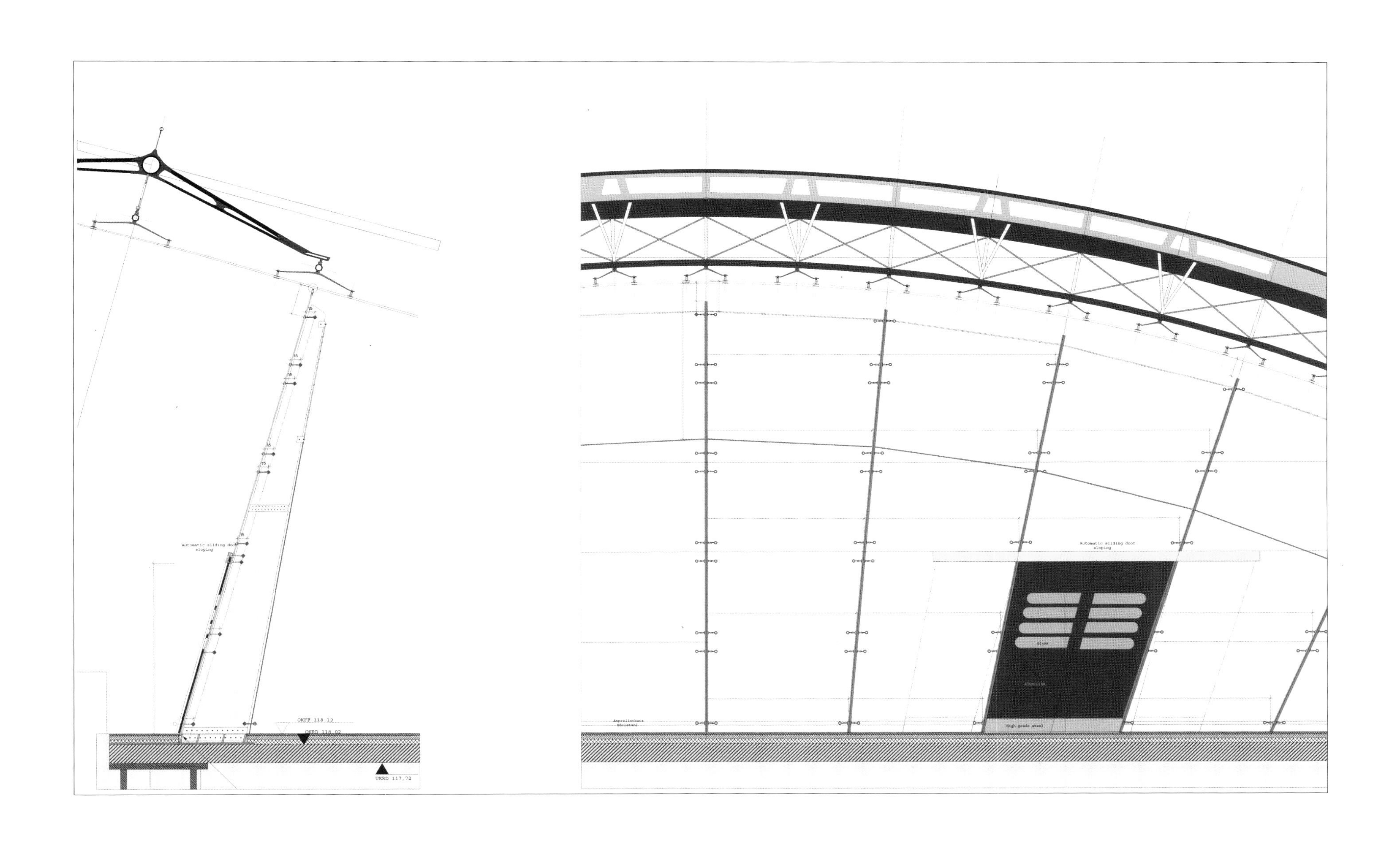
Automatic sliding door
sloping
OKFF 118.19
UKRD 117,72
Automatic sliding door
sloping
Glass
High-grade steel

The sole feature that arises from the vast slab of concrete covering tracks and platforms is a large elliptical cupola of steel and glass.

Above the building emerges the cupola; to the right is the footbridge giving access to the airport. Seen from outside, the structure has an aura of the indefinite and incomplete, which seems deliberately intended to negate its function.

Terminal 1
Terminal 2
Check in
Gleis 1-3
Track
Regionalbahnhof
Regional trains

Under the glass roofing, stairs and escalators link the platforms and the large atrium.

View of the space under the cupola and along the footbridge to the airport.

D
D
5
DATEV
Software
Service
Datenverarbeitung
Flughafen
Eine unserer Lieblingsbeschäftigungen: Aufrollen.
FrankfurterRundschau

A large elliptical shaft through the different levels carries light down to the platforms, thus creating the impression of a structure open to the air.

The windows of the intermediate level give onto the light shaft, which is crossed by some of the reticular girders that support the atrium above.
The differences in diameter of the bands of laminate steel around them mean that the two pillars on the inside of the façade have the appearance of extended telescopes.

10 ueli zbinden

bahnhof glanzenberg

dietikon, zurich, switzerland 1998–2000

project
Ueli Zbinden
structures
Sennhauser, Werner + Rauch AG,
Dietikon+Schlieren / Gutknecht AG, Urdorf
electrical installations
Herzog, Kull + Lüem AG, Schlieren
joinery
Steiner, Jucker + Blumer AG, Herisau
façade
Mebatech Ing., Baden
dimensions
28.000 sq.m: area of site
842 sq.m: area of building
7760 cu.m: volume of constructed space
location
Zürcherstrasse 181, Dietikon, Zurich,
Switzerland
chronology
1998–2000: construction

The Zurich urban rail network became operational in 1990, stimulating great development in the dormitory suburbs around the city. This in turn led to the planning of new SBB (Swiss Federal Railways) stations, one of which is the Bahnhof Glanzenberg, operational since May 2000.
The clients—the SBB, the Canton of Zurich and the four city councils concerned—commissioned the work from a team of architects, among whom was Ueli Zbinden. Responsible for the architectural, city-planning and landscaping aspects of the project, Zbinden had already worked at Dietikon in the early 90s, when he was commissioned to design a new bus station for the town center—complete with roofed bike stands—and draw up plans for the various surrounding areas left unused by the project. For that scheme he produced an "alphabet" of prefabricated components that were assembled to create a number of small structures, offering an autonomous reinterpretation of the few surviving remnants of the architecture of the historic town center. Here again, Zbinden had to work in a difficult context, in a situation where road and traffic links predominate and pose complex problems for the location of any architectural structure.
The Glanzenberg urban railway station is of particular interest because it proposes a new approach to the design of facilities for local public transport systems. Bideau has commented on the clear goal here of making a new type of railway station the key element in the project; Zbinden's designs, in fact, deliberately fly in the face of the usual tendency to make local public transport buildings rather anonymous structures which answer to purely functional criteria.
Situated in the Limmat river valley between Schlieren and Dietikon—at a site alongside a massive road overpass which cuts violently through the landscape—the new station is an architectural challenge to the context it occupies. Built in the early 1980s, the reinforced concrete structure of the overpass is undoubtedly the dominant feature in that context, even if it remains functionally isolated from its immediate surroundings: thanks to the acoustic paneling, the sight and sound of traffic is concealed, making the flyover a "mute" object which seems oddly out of place. Zbinden chose to emphasize this isolation by transforming the space under the overpass into part of the forecourt of the station. Poplars—the tree is very common in the Limmat valley—line the side of that forecourt and the Glanzenbergstrasse, forming a clear link between the buildings and the natural environment around them, while the clear and spare design of the streetlights reflect the principles that inspired the forms of the station itself.
As Zbinden has commented, in the creation of the station building and the facilities, the main criteria were safety, legibility, efficient use of space and ease of orientation within the structure. In effect, the project aims to establish a certain architectural and urban unity in a complex facility that extends for about half a kilometer along a site that is cut across by the pillars of the overpass. The minimalist solution adopted by the architect works upon the interplay between structure and form, technology and architecture.
In structural terms, the two levels of the station are antithetical: one, above ground, corresponds to the railway facility itself; the other, underground, houses underpasses

and the vertical and horizontal links between the various parts. The pavilion itself is a spare glass box some 35 meters long; the prefabricated steel components of the upright structure are positioned on a grid of 7-meter squares. The choice of prefabricated parts was made to reduce the time necessary for construction work in the immediate vicinity of the tracks and thus minimize interference with rail traffic (most of the work in this area was carried out at night).

Housing a waiting room, a general store, a newspaper kiosk, bathrooms and a covered stand for bikes, the pavilion stands on a cement base raised higher than the platform level, which are approached by a slightly sloping walkway which also leads down to the underpass.

The roofing of the station pavilion and the platforms is in steel and wood. The framework for the whole structure is made out of hollow rectangular-section components of folded and welded lamina. The pillars, fixed into the concrete base, are linked to the roofing by a semi-rigid joint.

The thickness of each girder's cross section was calculated according to its position and the stresses to which it would be exposed; this made it possible to reduce the quantity of steel used and eliminate the need for welding on site. From the outside the structure is finished with a framework of constant thickness, so the variations in the girders that go to make up the horizontal and vertical steel components of the bare skeleton of the building are not visible.

The roofing of the pavilion overhangs the entrance side that looks out onto the forecourt. On the opposite side of the building, towards the platforms, a jutting roof (lower than the roofing of the pavilion) rests on vertical supports and provides shelter for the passengers on platform 1. Above the structure in reticular girders are flat prefabricated multiple-cell components in wood (maximum length: 7 meters) that serve not only as roofing but also to reinforce the steel structure. The same type of roofing is used for the cantilever that runs down the middle of the platforms on the opposite side of the tracks. As with the channels within the rectangular-section girders, the hollow cells in these "Lignatur" components are used to house the wiring for the electrical installations and lighting.

The homogeneity of form and size in all the components—not only the pillars and girders, but also the roofing panels—give the pavilion the abstract appearance of an elementary geometrical form.

Comprising base platform, ramps and underpasses, the components in reinforced concrete are in clear contraposition with the reiterated form of the steel structure, serving not only as an anchor but also as the means by which the station establishes a relation with the freeway overpass above. All the underground areas are faced with bright yellow ceramic tiles that are easy to clean and create a uniform, warm and luminous environment. At the level of the platforms, between the tracks and the forecourt, there is a high concrete wall, in part faced with yellow tiles, which runs right up to the Limmat Brucke overpass, creating continuity between the underground areas of the infrastructure and its exterior. Inside the glass pavilion, a ramp leads down to the platforms and the underpass, marking the point where the two conceptually different systems of steel structure and underground space come into contact with each other.

The glass facing of the station is held in place on vertical steel mounts; double thickness, the panels are fixed to the structure by aluminum frames. The vertical mounts themselves are fixed to the top of the reinforced concrete base and attached to the flat roofing by a hinged metal structure.

By deciding not to differentiate between the different components of the structure, Zbinden moves beyond any sort of technological "rhetoric" to design a "silent" structure that appears almost extraneous to its context. But it is precisely this suggestion which is the basis for the relation established between the new facility and its setting, given that it underlines the key characteristic of the area itself. The orthogonal structure, which appears to have been assembled rather than built, creates a reticular space that can be extended to infinity; by the very nature of the technology employed in its design, the station enters into a dialectical relationship with both the lines of the train tracks and the overpass dominating the original site. Such transit space is typical of the linear city which extends between Zurich and Baden, with the Limmat valley now housing all those functions which Zurich has driven out from its own urban area over the last few decades: freeways, goods stations, shopping centers, etc. One might agree with Bideau when he wonders if it is still possible to draw up plans for such an area which reflect a clear conception of identity and context. However, this is precisely what the Glanzenberg station attempts to do in its use of constructivist idiom and anonymity of form within a junction of traffic infrastructures.

Bibliography

Hochparterre, October 1998.
Hochparterre, August 2000.
"Station Glanzenberg, Zürich-Dietikon," *Werk, Bauen + Wohnen*, 12, December 2000.

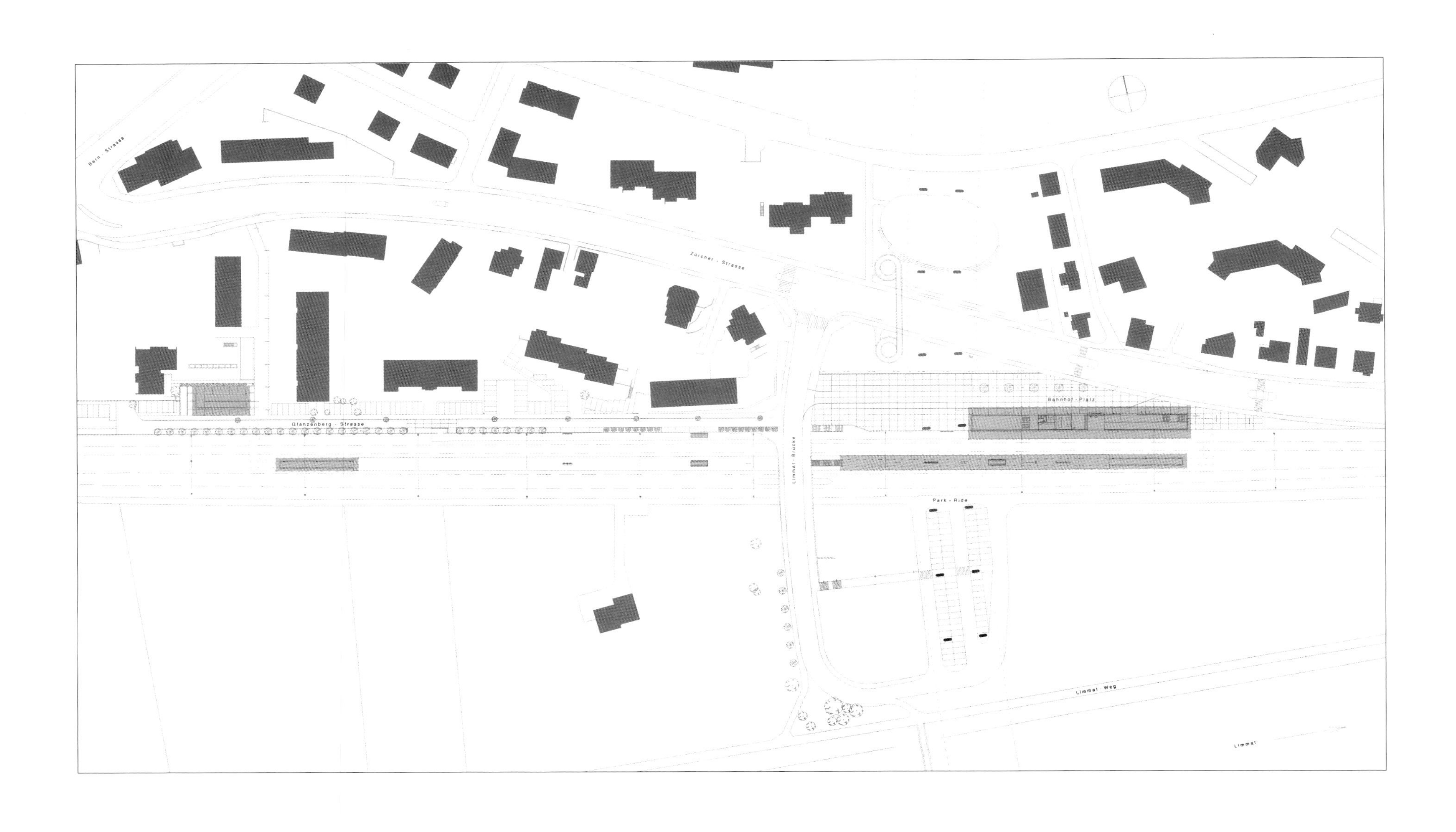
Bern - Strasse
Zürcher - Strasse
Glanzenberg - Strasse
Limmat - Brücke
Bahnhof - Platz
Park + Ride
Limmat - Weg
Limmat

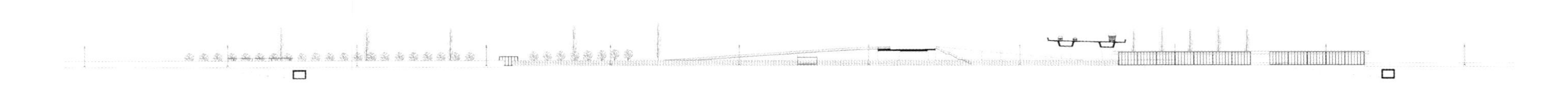

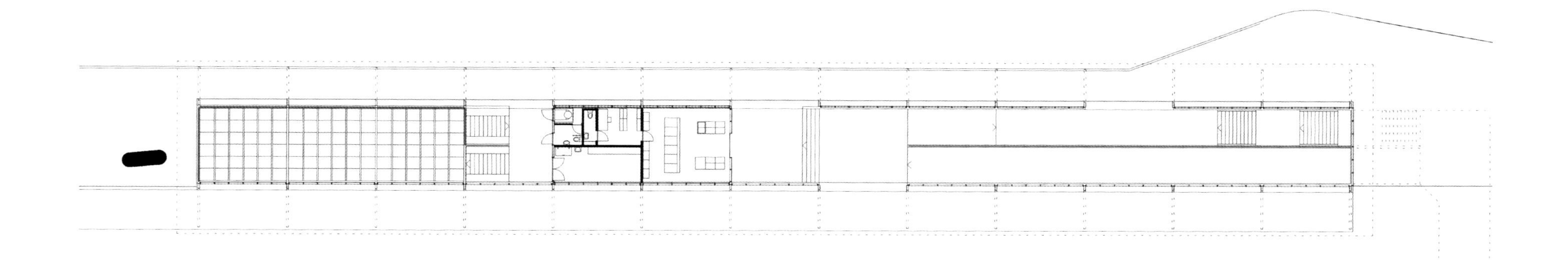

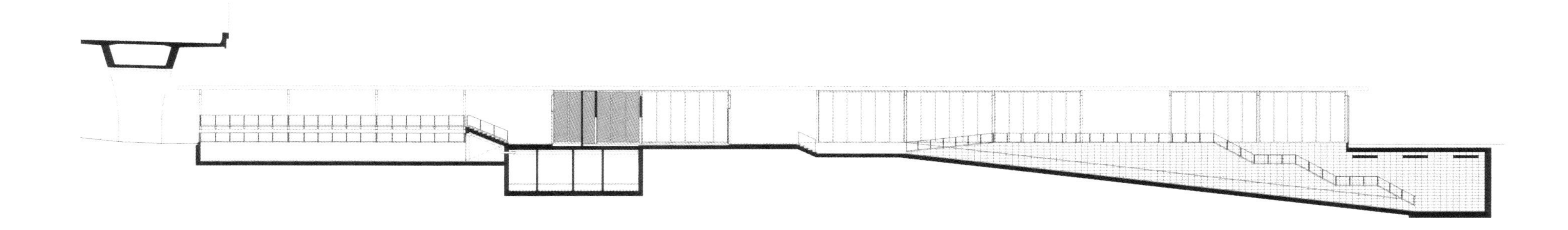

General ground plan and longitudinal elevation/cross section.

Plan and elevation/cross section of the station pavilion and platforms.

Previous page
The station pavilion is a spare glass box made up of prefabricated steel components positioned on a grid of 7-meter squares.

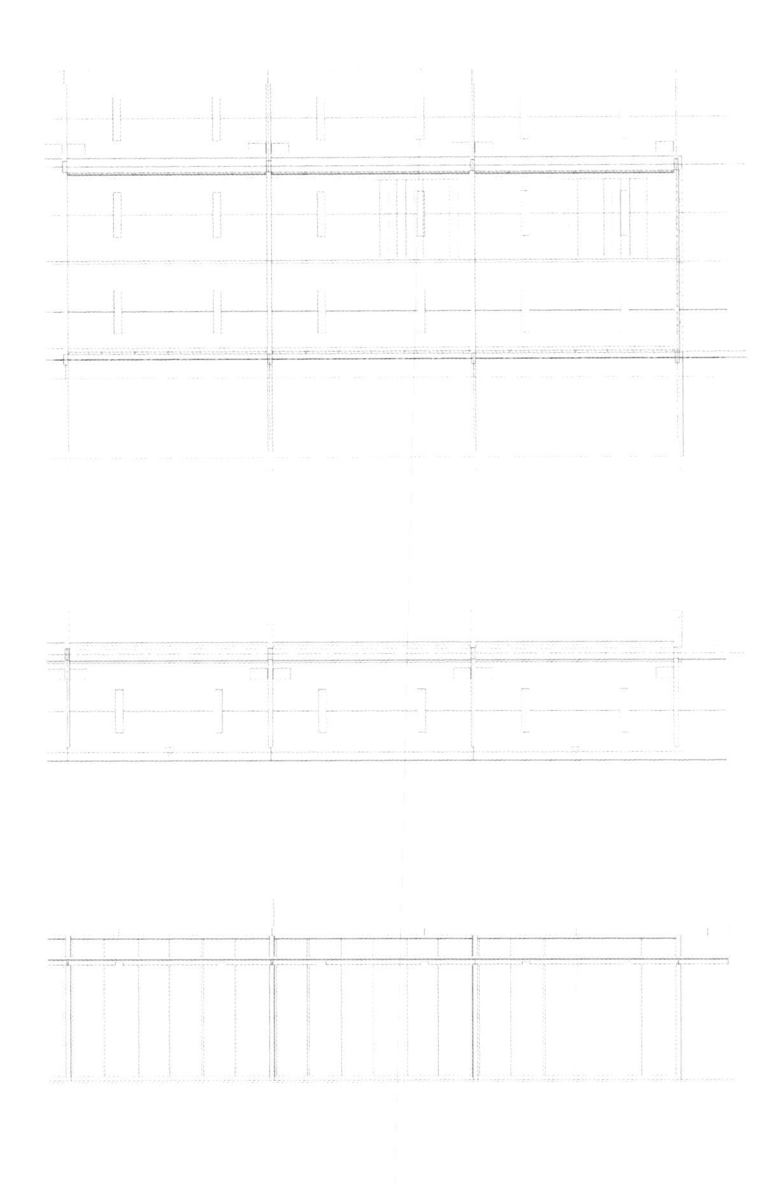

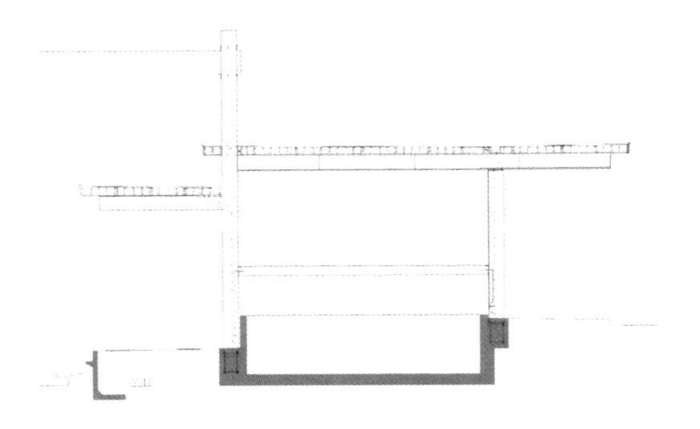

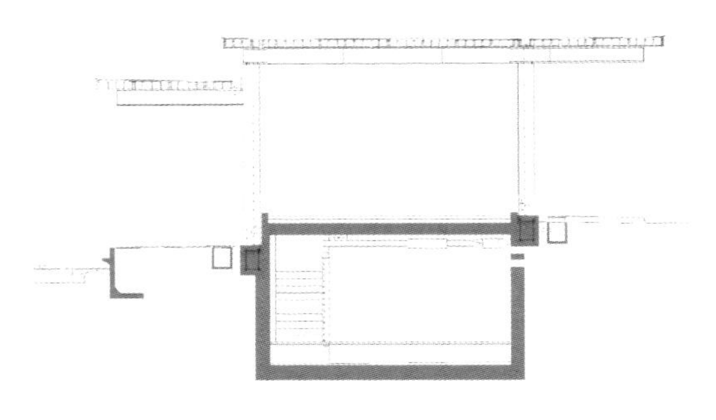

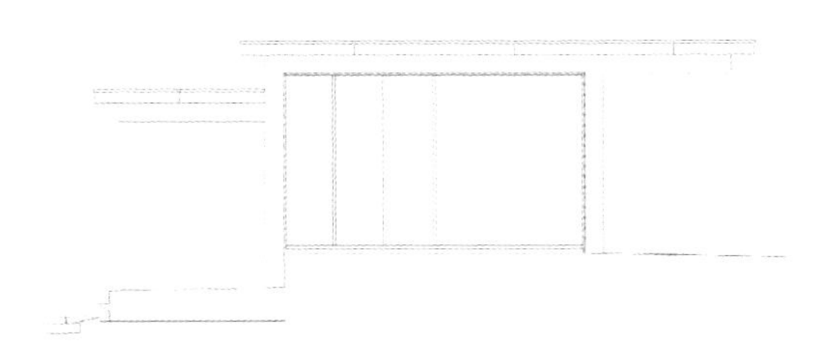

Plan and elevation of the base module used in creating the pavilion.
Cross section and side view.

The cantilever roof at the center of the platforms; the prefabricated "Lignatur" components not only serve as roofing but also reinforce the steel structure.
The pavilion stands on a cement base raised higher than the level of the platforms, which are approached by a sloping ramp that also leads down to the underpass.
All the underground walls are faced with bright yellow ceramic tiles, which not only create a warm and luminous environment but also unify the different areas.

11 sncf-arep

gare d'aix-en-provence tgv

aix-en-provence, france 1999–2001

project
SNCF-AREP
architects
Jean-Marie Duthilleul,
Étienne Tricaud, Daniel Claris
client
Société Nationale des Chemins de Fer
dimensions
10,200 sq.m: total built area
location
Plateau d'Arbois, Aix-en-Provence, France
chronology
1999: project
2001: construction

Opened in 2001, the Aix-en-Provence station was important because it marked not only a significant extension to France's high-speed rail network but also because it introduced conceptual and visual innovations in railway station architecture.
In 1980 the French government started work on an overall plan for its high-speed national rail services; approved in 1992, the scheme involved the modernization of existing track (to make it suitable for high-speed trains) and the creation of stations that could serve as architectural symbols of these new rail services.
The country had been the first in Europe to begin construction of such high-speed links (in 1981), with the Agence des Gares (the Technical Office of the Société Nationale des Chemins de Fer, SNCF) under Jean-Marie Duthilleul playing a key role in the reorganization of the entire national rail grid, the design of new stations and the redevelopment of existing station facilities. Responsible for both construction work and the urban layout of the areas around the stations, the Agence was thus involved in a multiple range of tasks: the reorganization of rail traffic, the design of large-scale structures, the study of terrain and local landscape, the creation of new fittings and installations.
In order to promote a systematic approach to the design of high-speed stations and the resolution of the problems they might pose at an urban level, Jean-Marie Duthilleul and Étienne Tricaud would in 1997 found AREP (Aménagement Recherche Pôle d'Echanges); an interdisciplinary studio, this would soon establish an international reputation for itself through its study and development of a railway-station architecture that strives to anticipate the characteristics of the city of the future.
AREP sees the TGV (Train Grande Vitesse) as "rehabilitating" train travel as such and transforming the very meaning of the term "rail line." With the opening of the TGV Atlantic service, this term took on a new significance: "The rail line becomes a structured and continuous system in which the stations are designed to emphasize train travel's reacquisition of its own identity. The gray-blue TGV implies a specific technical and architectural vocabulary, a precise approach to design and the use of specific colors and materials."
It was this approach—together with the acquired experience of the SNCF and AREP—which was to provide the starting point for work on the new TGV Mediterranée line that would link Paris to Marseille St. Charles, passing through Valence, Avignon and Aix-en-Provence. Further developing the studio's methods of architectural composition and design, this line and its stations would show AREP being ever more daring in the targets it set itself and ever more ingenious in achieving them. Opened at the beginning of the twenty-first century, the TGV Mediterranée line marks a turning point in the group's design work and forms an ideal bridgehead between past and future.
One constant feature of AREP's work is the clear desire to combine architectural design, technological standards and passenger comfort, choosing the forms that are most suited to individual context. In these three stations, therefore, location within a Mediterranean landscape played a key role in defining the architectural layout and the choice of materials.
Together with those at Valence and Avignon, the Aix-en-Provence station reveals just how the work of Jean-Marie

Duthilleul and Étienne Tricaud has developed to meet their goal of providing travel facilities which combine: transport services and urban fabric; architectural form and technology; the rigidity of infrastructures and the complexity of existing urban environments. For these two architects, the railway station is a hub of services on an urban and territorial scale; it is truly "part of a city."
This approach is clearly exemplified at Aix-en-Provence. Located on the as yet undeveloped Arboix plateau, which commands striking views in various directions (to the east is Mont Sainte-Victoire), the station becomes a magical space set within a vast Mediterranean garden, a center for future urban development in the area. In full respect of the landscape it occupies, the designers have produced an architectural structure that is an act of "homage" to the natural beauty of the site. Located at the intersection of the TGV line and the state highway linking Aix-en-Provence to Marignane, the new station takes on the form of a vast, slightly undulant, covering in panels of aluminum. Running at right angles to the train line, the highway splits into two separate lanes that pass under the station building, with access to the carparks provided by an ample oval ring road that embraces the entire station and runs over bridges to either side of it.
Fruit of the collaboration between AREP and the landscape architects Desvigne & Dalnoky, the green spaces around the station play on the juxtaposition of regularly planted trees and more random *maquis*, thus providing an area of mediation between the station and the surrounding natural landscape. Double rows of plane trees extend to the side of the tracks, thus underlining the axis on which they run, while the space between the platforms and the rows of trees is occupied by a garden of typically-Mediterranean oleanders. The mix continues in the parking lots (space for 633 cars, with the possibility of extension to take up to 1,100), where the landscape architects have brought together different types of trees and shrubs in two contraposed schema: the pines are laid out in orthogonal patterns, while the clumps of white oak and elms echo the asymmetry of the *maquis* that is typical of this zone (in particular, Thalweg).
The façades of the station building itself—entirely in glass—form two huge eyes looking out over the natural landscape towards Mont Sainte-Victoire. The architects have chosen to place the concourse and hall backing onto the tracks, with arrivals and departures located on opposite sides (west and east) of the building. The metal bridge over the tracks is designed to be a covered belvedere, giving views onto the surrounding landscape and the Mont Sainte-Victoire, whose outline was made so famous by Cézanne.
The ideal interchange between interior and exterior goes beyond this visual relation of landscape and internal space; the very architecture of the building enters into dialogue with natural forms. In effect a metaphor of the natural landscape, that architecture eschews emphatic design, favoring a predominantly naturalistic appearance which is the fruit of a clear-sighted decision: to raise a station that can be the center for the future urban development of this zone, an ideal link between natural context and rail tracks. The result of this is that the continuity between landscape and architecture is developed in the very details of the structure. The roofing rests on two lines of pillars (to the east and west of the tracks) which are rather like stylized trees in form: the "trunk" has glue-laminated wooden facing around a steel core, hinged at its base, and then opens out into sloping "branches" that support the roofing. The angle between the branches increases as one moves to either end of the station (where the down curve of the roofing flattens out), thus increasing the impression of depth as one looks through the building. The entire structure is reinforced longitudinally by transversal tie-bars between the columns.
Overhanging the façade, the roofing provides shelter for passengers leaving and entering the station as well as partial shade from the sun. As already mentioned, the station—like an airport—separates the arrivals and departures areas. Most of the service and shopping facilities are naturally located in the departures area, with only a few shops in the arrivals zone. On the inside of the station, the platforms and rails are overlooked by other façades entirely in glass. The external glass façade on the west side of the station is composed of double-layer modular components; red cedar-wood blinds fixed within an anthracite gray aluminum frame provide shade against the summer sun (this type of wood was chosen because it is lightweight and resistant to insects and mold). The glass walls and the red cedar blinds are held together in a steel structure.
Be it concerned with architectural details or territorial planning, the work of AREP has always been inspired by the principles of clarity and legibility of design—something which is so clearly illustrated by every aspect of the Aix-en-Provence station, from the materials chosen to the technology adopted.

Bibliography

Agence des Gares, AREP (ed.), *Parcours. 1988–1998*, Diagonale, Rome 1998.
"Le tre stazioni del TGV mediterraneo: Valence, Avignon, Aix-en-Provence," *L'industria delle costruzioni*, 367, 2001, pp. 54–59.
M. Thorne (ed.), *Modern Trains and Splendid Stations. Architecture, Design, and Travel for the Twenty-First Century*, Merrel, The Art Institute of Chicago, London 2001.

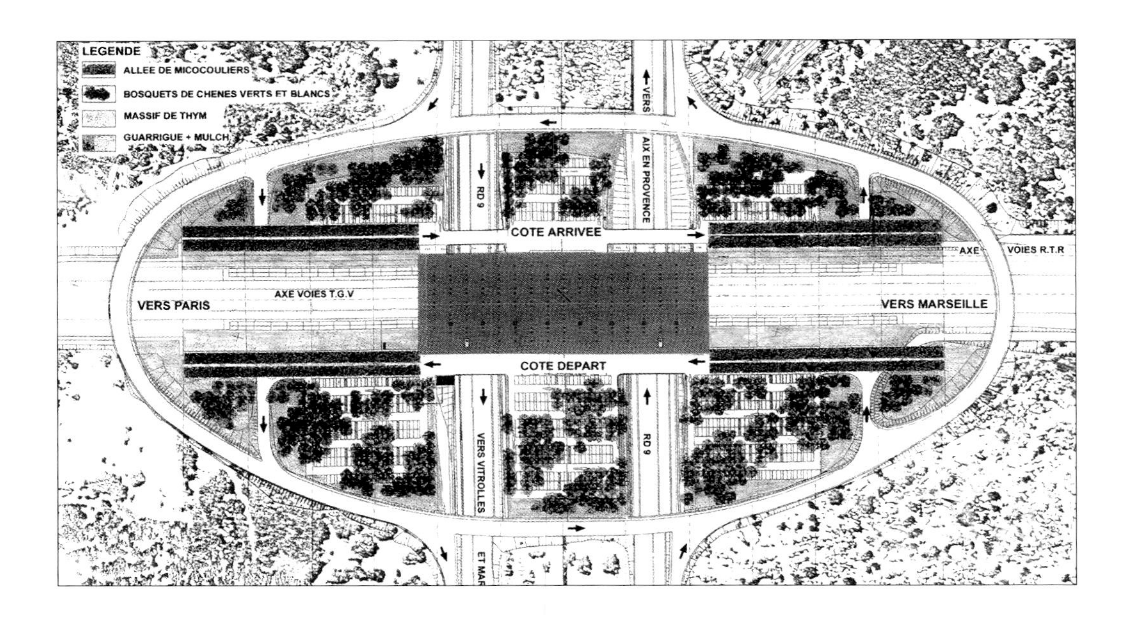

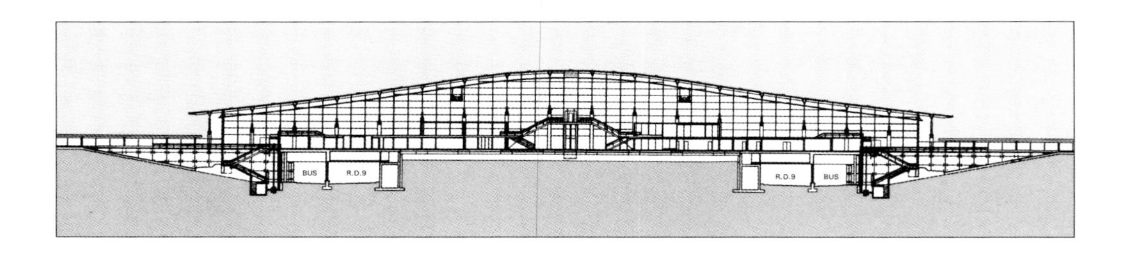

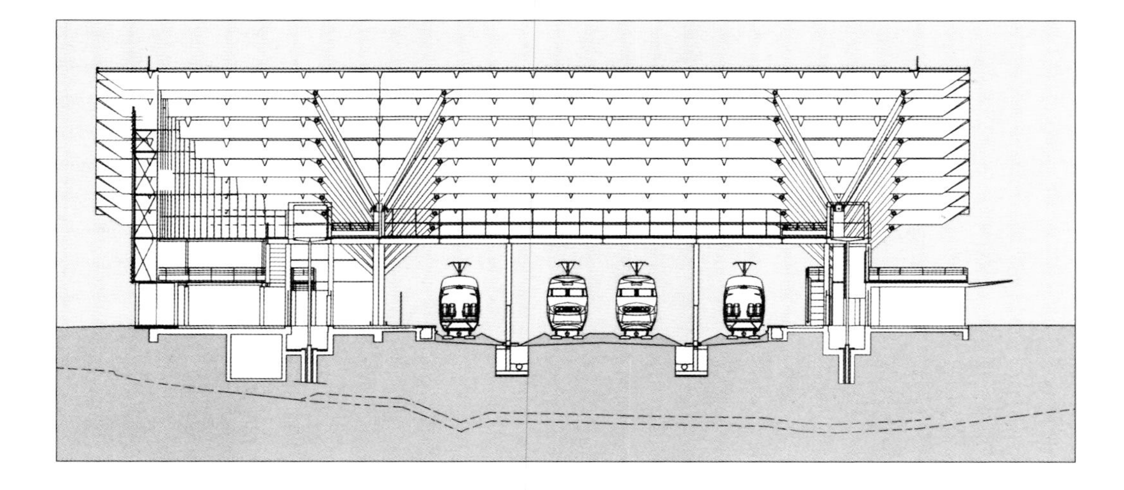

General ground plan, longitudinal section and cross section.

Plan of the mezzanine level, of the platforms and the footbridge (yellow: circulation areas; orange: operational facilities; red: passenger services; blue: shops; green: technical facilities; purple: platforms).

Previous page:
The hall backs onto the tracks; arrivals and departures are located opposite each other, on the west and east sides of the tracks respectively.

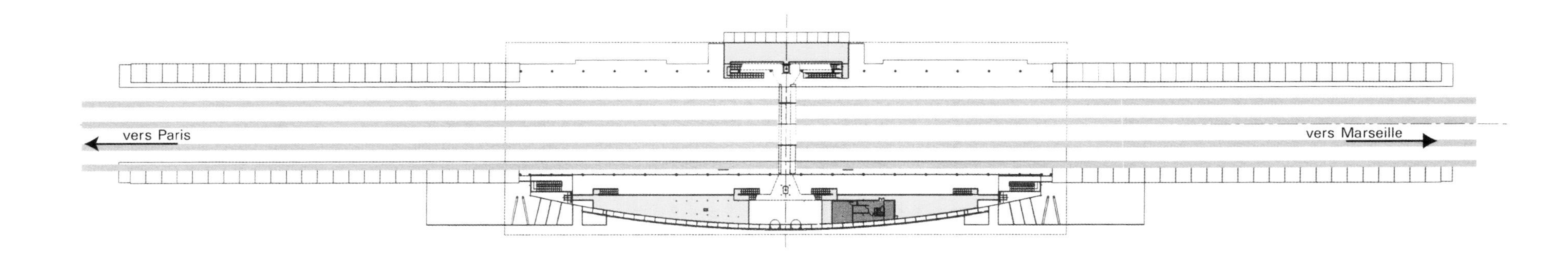
vers Paris
vers Marseille

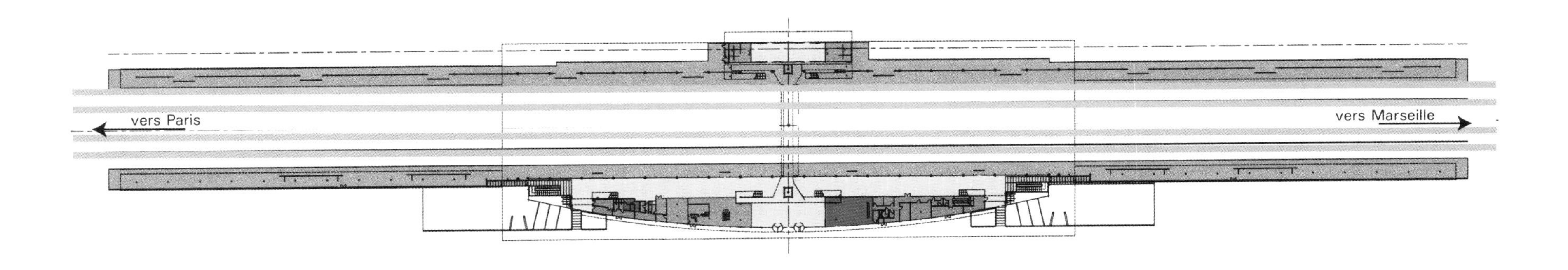
vers Paris
vers Marseille

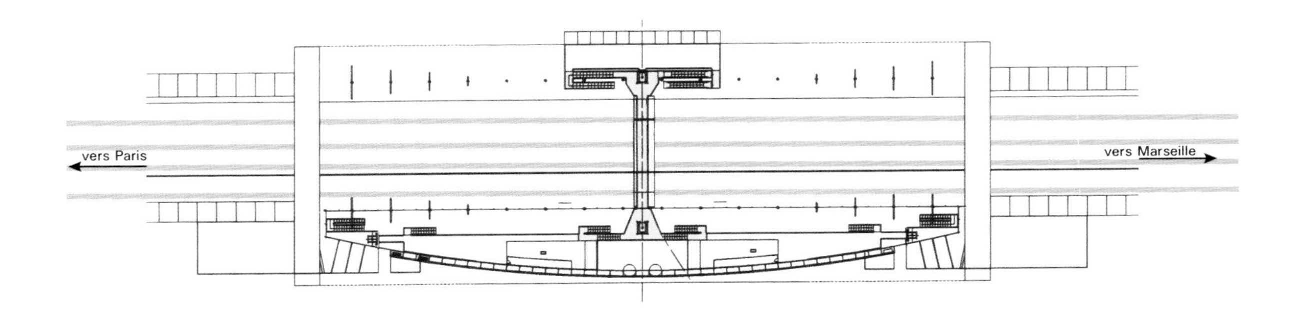
vers Paris
vers Marseille

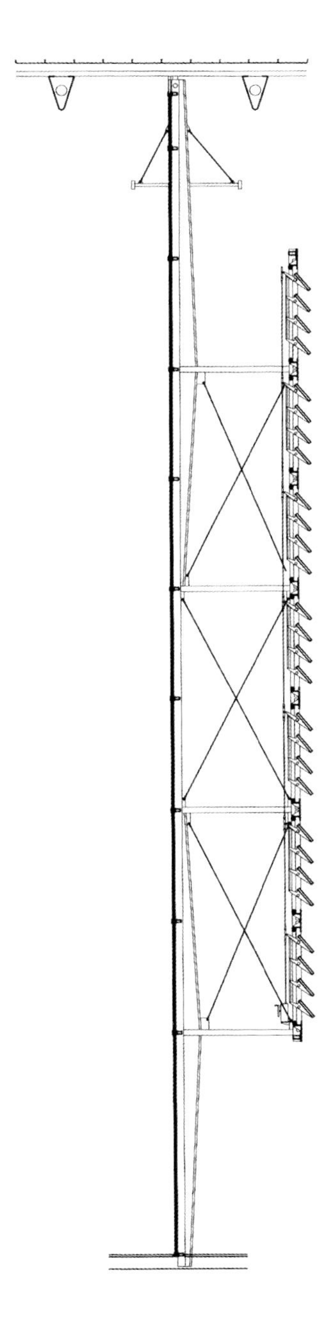

The new station takes on the form of a vast, slightly undulating covering in panels of aluminum.

Section of a detail of the west façade.
Red cedar-wood blinds fixed within an anthracite gray aluminum frame protect the west façade against the summer sun.

The platforms and tracks are overlooked by internal glass façades.
The metal bridge linking both sides of the station is designed as a covered belvedere.

A mezzanine level, designed to serve as a waiting room, links the platform level with the bridge over the tracks.

12 sncf-arep

gare du nord

paris, france 1997–2001

project
SNCF-AREP
architects
Jean-Marie Duthilleul,
Étienne Tricaud, Daniel Claris
consultants
OTH, Nicholas Green et Anthony
Hunt Associés (glass),
Observatoire 1 (lighting)
contractors
Eiffage TP (demolition, structures)
Cabrol (joinery, roofing, façades)
client
Société Nationale des Chemins de Fer,
Direction de Paris Nord
location
Paris, France
chronology
1997: project
2001: construction

Opened in September 2001, the Espace Transilien of the Gare du Nord had presented the SNCF-AREP group with an important new challenge: the design of a decidedly modern addition to a historical building. The structure they created has the form of a covered piazza, a transparent "luminous space" that serves to link together the various flows of traffic through the station.

One of the most important terminal stations in Europe, the Gare du Nord—like the nearby Gare de l'Est—had been a key model for such structures in the second half of the nineteenth century. Both stations reveal a development not only in architectural form but also in the internal distribution of space, intended to enable the station to house the various new structures and facilities required by the ever-increasing volume of rail traffic. Designed by Hittorff—working in collaboration with the engineer Léonce Reynaud—the Gare du Nord (1861–65) was soon being perceived as an important public monument to progress.

Caroll Meeks has been supported by various later scholars and historians in his claim that the innovations in the original Gare du Nord station were twofold, concerning not only the external features which enabled the new facility to be "absorbed" by the existing urban fabric, but also the structure and internal organization of the building. As in the Gare de l'Est, the façade echoes the form of the train shed behind it; but here, the thermal window is brought forward to form part of a single unbroken façade. The internal vestibule runs at right angles to the platforms; anticipating that transverse concourse which would become a feature of stations at the end of the century, it enables passengers to enter and exit the building without having to cross over or under the tracks. Above these spaces stretches the truss-structured roofing; a key component in establishing the logical coherence of the whole building, this takes up some of the pioneering ideas to be found in the designs of Polonceau. In the words of the designers of the new extension, Reynaud had recognized that the train station was beginning to pose new problems "as a result of the most admirable innovations of the day, which opened up new horizons and introduced new materials and innovative forms" (Agence des Gares, AREP 1998). The nineteenth-century engineer saw that the iron which was already used in the tracks should also feature in the architecture, as a celebration of the railway itself. The key area for such use was, of course, the train shed, which in France became an important opportunity for experimentation with daring and innovative structural ideas. In ideal terms, the train shed was an echo of the locomotive's power; it was the perfect transposition into solid material of the rising steam and smoke that were the visible signs of that power.

In designing their extension for the Gare du Nord, the AREP group were well aware that they had to take into account this historical and cultural significance in the original building.

A first renovation project (carried out 1990–93) had been commissioned by the SNCF when the Gare du Nord became the terminus for the Paris-London train link through the Channel Tunnel. The opening of this link and of the TGV Nord line resulted in the complete redesign of the area within the station, with the structure being adapted to the needs of high-speed rail traffic.

However, the new scheme was also predicated upon respect for the historic building; in effect, the area for the new high-speed line was found by clearing away the accretions of decades, thus restoring Hittorff's original conception of the interior. One addition was a 10-meter-wide raised walkway, destined for the various TGV passenger services; built backing onto the city façade of the station, this was a perfect viewing platform, looking out over the nineteenth-century atrium and concourse.
That first scheme was then followed by a new project which envisaged the creation of a space at the south-east corner of the station to serve as an interjunction for the pedestrian flow through the building; this would recompose the original elevation, which had been altered in 1971 by the demolition of two iron-and-glass structures to make way for a parking lot. The new atrium, linking together the mainline stations with suburban and subway lines, thus became the final stage in a project to "recover" the Gare du Nord. The Ile-de-France Nord interchange, in effect, forms a double hall that harmonizes in both scale and form with the roofing of Hittorff's station, using contemporary technology and materials to "restore" the original size of the existing hall. The two spaces thus become a perfectly natural extension of the monumental façade of the Gare du Nord. Celebrating the form and characteristics of the nineteenth-century train shed, the SNCF-AREP extension reiterates the cultural and historical importance of the station. Naturally, that original facility is here reinterpreted to answer to modern needs and functions, being transformed from a space reserved primarily for trains to one of public transit. The roofing is a double span of steel and glass, with the space beneath also enclosed in the same materials and well illuminated so as to be easily identified; it houses an entrance atrium (the area that mediates between the Gare du Nord and the underground levels) and the vertical and horizontal links between the various transport systems feeding into the station. The project focused particular attention on the development of links between these various transport networks: subway, RER (Réseau Express Régionale), TGV Nord Europe, Eurostar (to Britain) and Thalys (to Belgium and Holland).
Measuring approximately 50 × 100 meters, this interchange hall is a junction directing passenger traffic towards the various spaces that occupy the five underground levels. From the lowest level upwards, these are the Magenta station of the E line of the RER network; the mezzanine; the B and D lines of the RER; the subway lines; the historic core of the station and the street level. The different services are clearly signposted from the ground-floor hall, and can also be identified by the different treatment of the entrances to each: tiled walls for access to the subways; red-plastered beams and pillars for the RER mezzanine; acoustic isolation panels in wood for the area reserved to the E line of the RER. The stone floors and cement finish in the communal areas are in light-colored tones, with further light coming through the glass of the façade and roofing (the latter serigraphed to filter out excessive sunlight).
The internal walls of the hall are in concrete; the slabs in light-colored cement of smooth finish, the columns of the structure in high-resistance reinforced concrete and the floor paving in lightweight artificial stone. To prevent any hindrance to future changes in the layout of the public areas, all the technical services—fire hydrants, smoke ducts and electronic control stations—are, at each of the levels, located around the perimeter of the structure, leaving the central space free for passenger flow and the location of shopping facilities. The roofing itself echoes the truss roofing over the nineteenth-century train shed—a mixed structure of triple span with reticular girders, and straight girders for the side spans. Here, however, that structure is slightly simplified: the truss beams of the double-span roofing rest on metal columns and are composed of paired girders held rigid by tie-bars and struts.
Finished in 2002, the mezzanine is the space linking the platforms of the B and D lines of the RER (located above) to the Magenta station of the E line of the RER (below) and the interchange hall; it serves as part of the link between the long-distance train lines and the suburban and subway lines. Some 300 meters wide and 50 meters long, it is not only a passenger flow concourse, but also a shopping mall.
Among the priorities the AREP design team set itself were the requirements that the new structure should fit successfully within its context and that the interconnection of the various spaces and routes through it should be as rational as possible. From the outside, the extension looks like a covered piazza; inside, the juxtaposition of the horizontal and vertical links to the various levels emphasizes its role as a traffic junction. The pedestrian traffic flow is densest perhaps on the mezzanine, and here the layout of the shopping facilities becomes one of the keynotes of the project, which aims to "restore" this space a part of the urban fabric of the city.
As Duthilleul and Tricaud have observed, "for us at the Agence des Gares, the aim is not only to transform these legendary places of movement into highly-efficient train stations but also to make them into veritable public spaces, areas that are reacquired by the city around them." Such a goal naturally means combining the logic dictated by transport needs with that dictated by the needs of the city itself. So not only must the traffic flow for passengers be organized as efficiently as possible, the interchange through which they pass must also become a "public space of some significance," a statement of the station's role as a space mediating between city and the railway. In effect, the railway station is a paradoxical place that is "part of the city and part of a transport network; it is both mobile and immobile... a place when time is limited, but also one that can turn into an oasis for leisure activities." This project is predicated on this dual character of the station—as part of a system of flux and as a place in which one might pause, find oneself with time on one's hand.
The Gare du Nord extension is also interesting for another reason: illustrating further mutations in the form of the original train sheds, it offers us a compendium of the changes in railway architecture over the past one hundred and fifty years.

Bibliography

M. Canonico, "L'Agence d'Étude des Gares. I progetti per le stazioni del TGV," *ArQ 13*, monographic issue *La stazione ferroviaria. Verso un nuovo modello d'uso*, December 1994, pp. 110–32.
Agences des Gares, AREP (ed.), *Parcours. 1988–1998*, Diagonale, Rome 1998.
"Intermodale e 'cristallina.' Gare du Nord in Paris," *L'Arca*, 171, June 2002, pp. 60–63.
É. Tricaud, "La nouvelle gare du Nord," K. Bowie, S. Texier (eds.), *Paris et ses Chemins de Fer*, Action Artistique de la Ville de Paris, Paris 2003, pp. 242–45.

R DU NORD
SNCF
GARE DU NORD
P

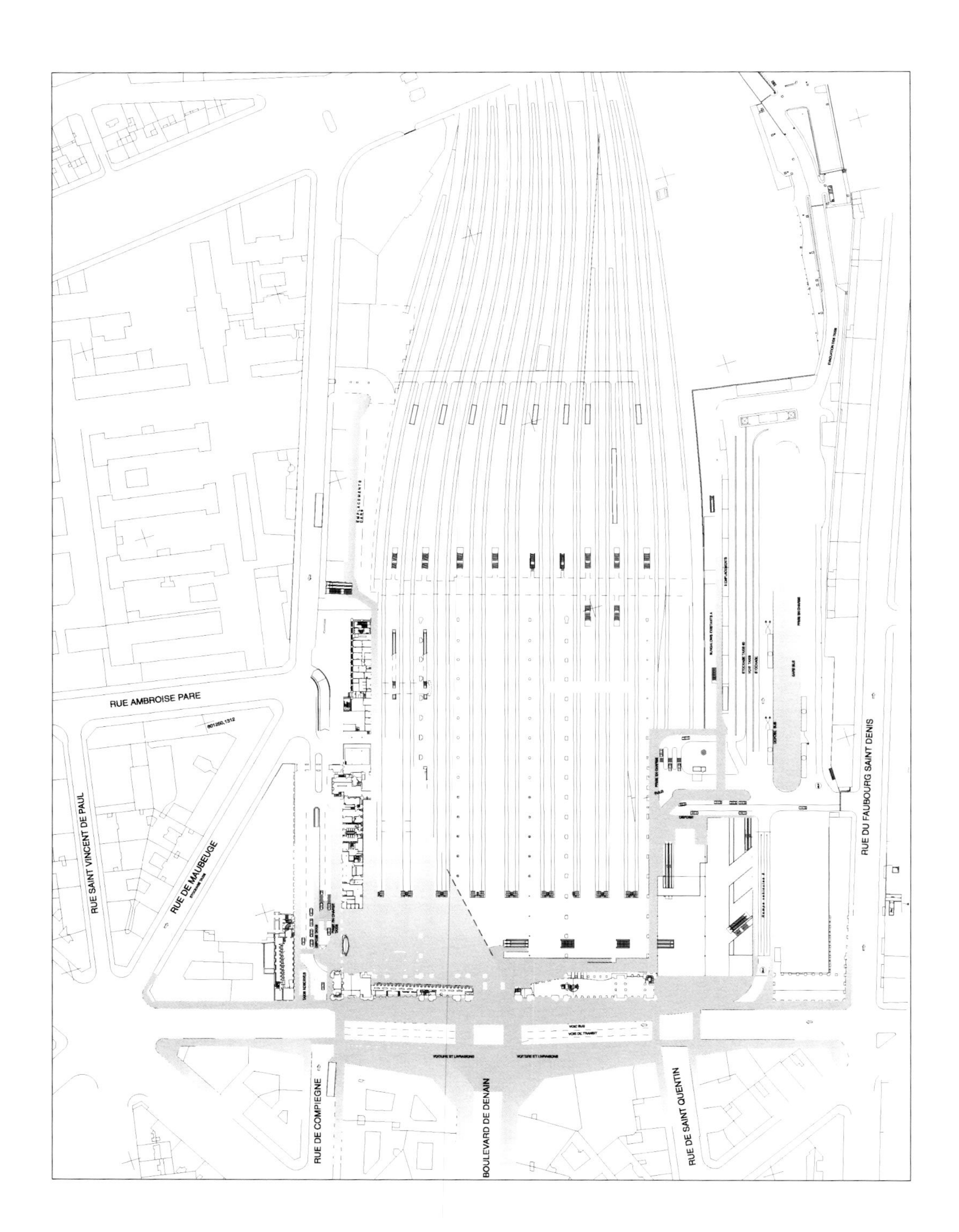

General ground plan.

Plan of ground level and second and first underground levels (orange: offices; red: passenger services; blue: shopping facilities; green: technical facilities).

Previous page:
The double-span pavilion of the new Espace Transilien harmonizes in both form and size with the outline of the nineteenth-century station.

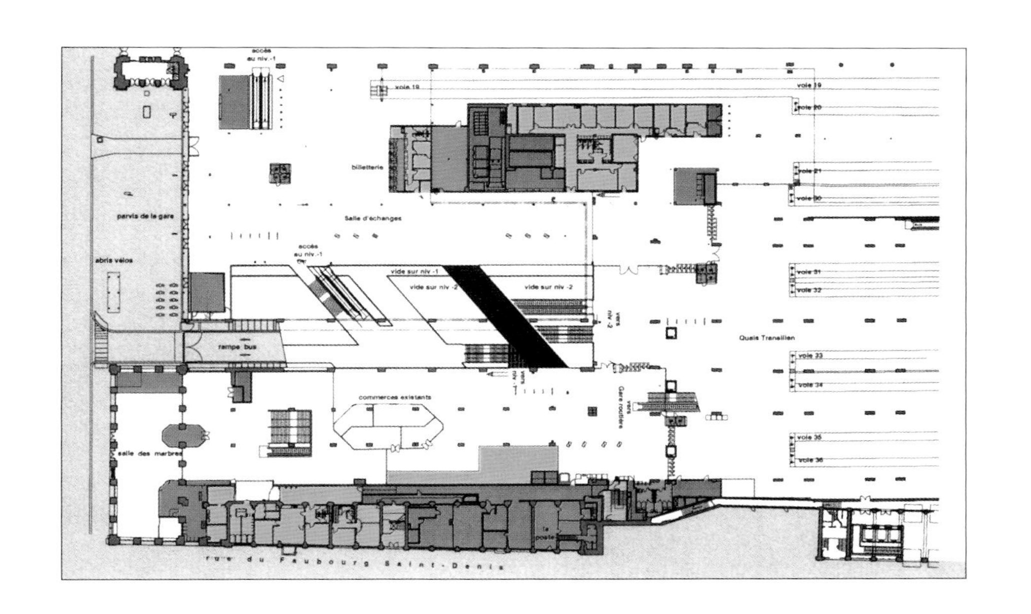
accès au niv.-1
voie 19
voie 20
billetterie
voie 21
parvis de la gare
Salle d'échanges
accès au niv.-1
abris vélos
vide sur niv -1
vide sur niv -2
vide sur niv -2
voie 31
voie 32
vers niv -2
rampe bus
Quais Transilien
voie 33
voie 34
vers niv -1
commerces existants
vers Gare routière
salle des marbres
voie 35
voie 36
la poste
rue du Faubourg Saint-Denis

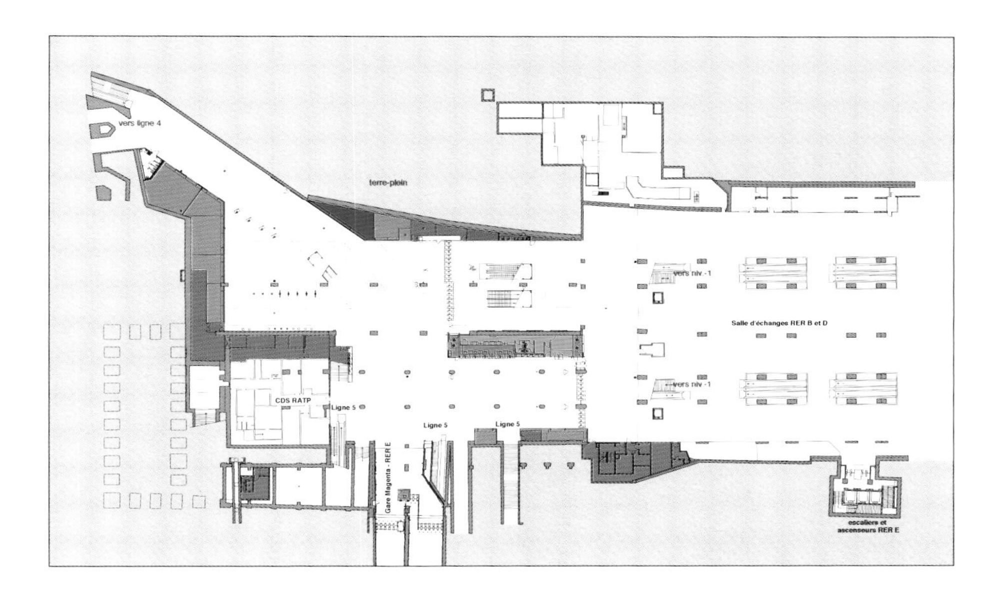
vers ligne 4
terre-plein
vers niv -1
Salle d'échanges RER B et D
vers niv -1
CDS RATP
Ligne 5
Ligne 5
Ligne 5
Gare Magenta - RER E
escaliers et ascenseurs RER E

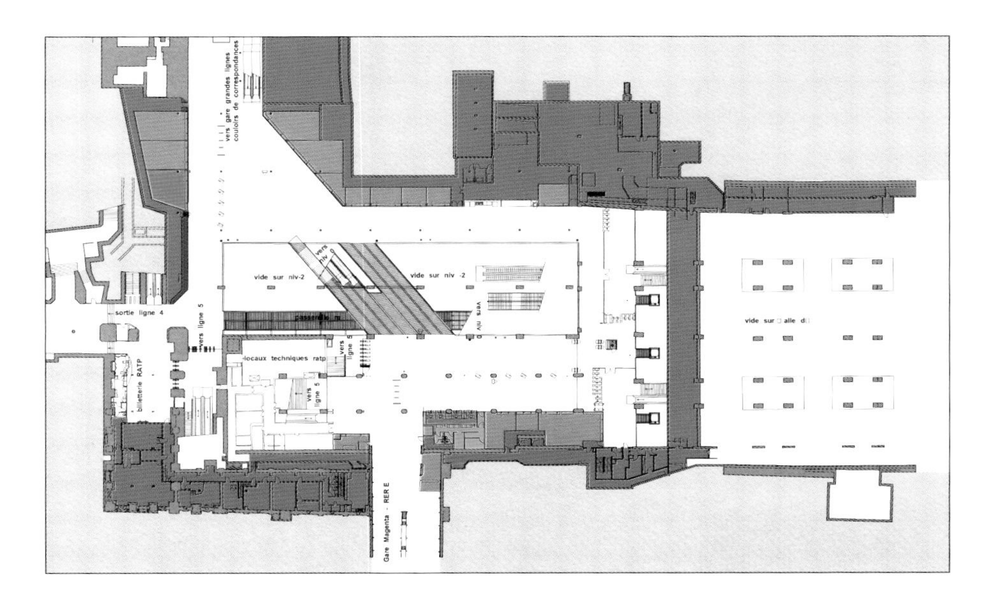
vers gare grandes lignes couloirs de correspondances
vide sur niv-2
vide sur niv -2
sortie ligne 4
vers ligne 5
locaux techniques ratp
vers ligne 5
billetterie RATP
vers ligne 5
Gare Magenta - RER E

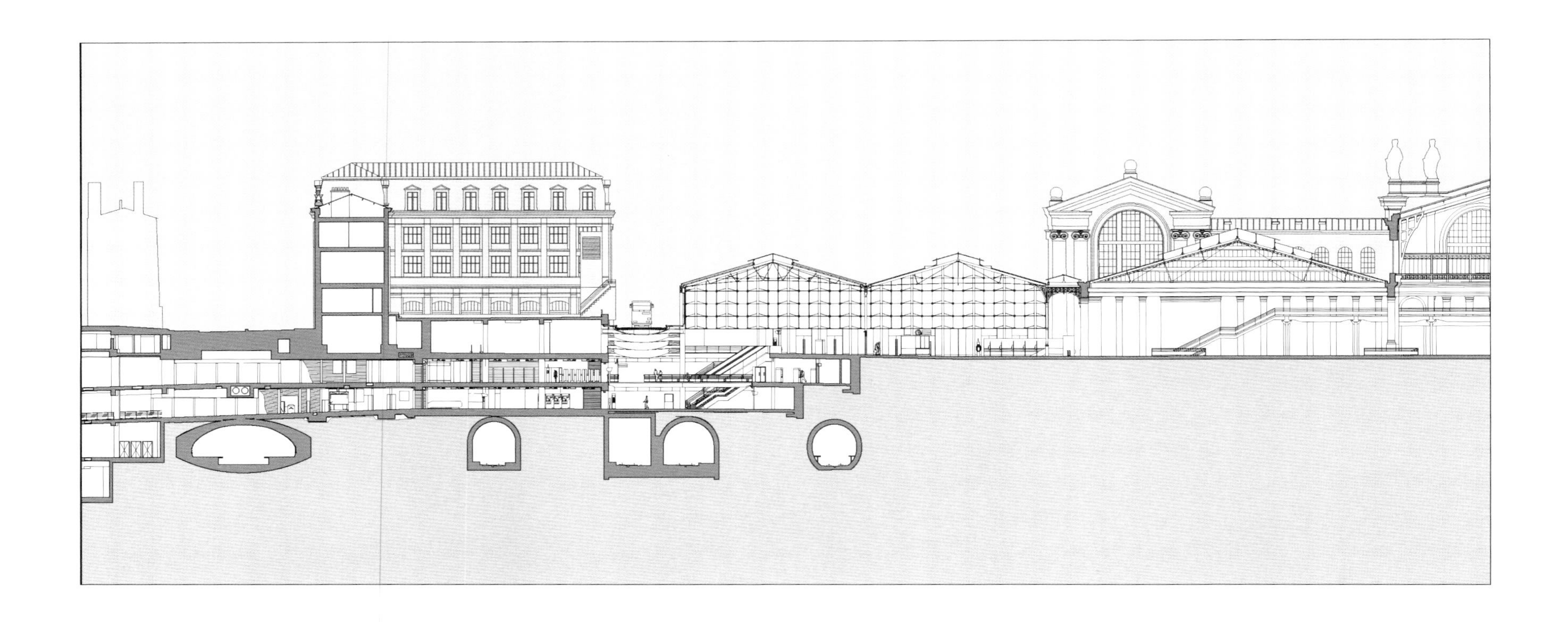

East-west section.

Longitudinal sections of the new hall and the ramp to the bus station.

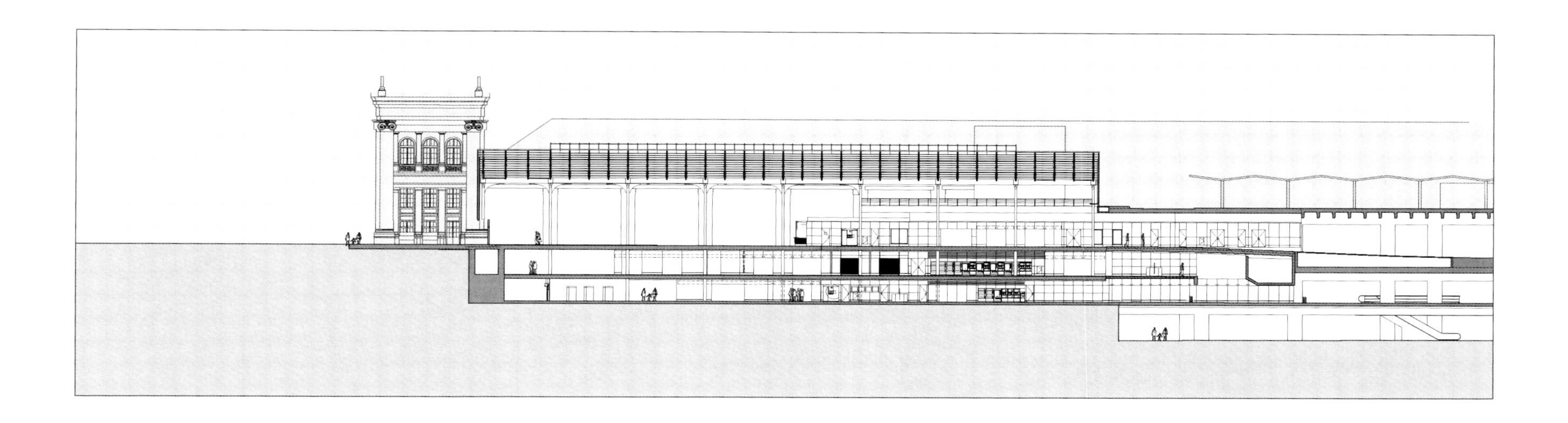

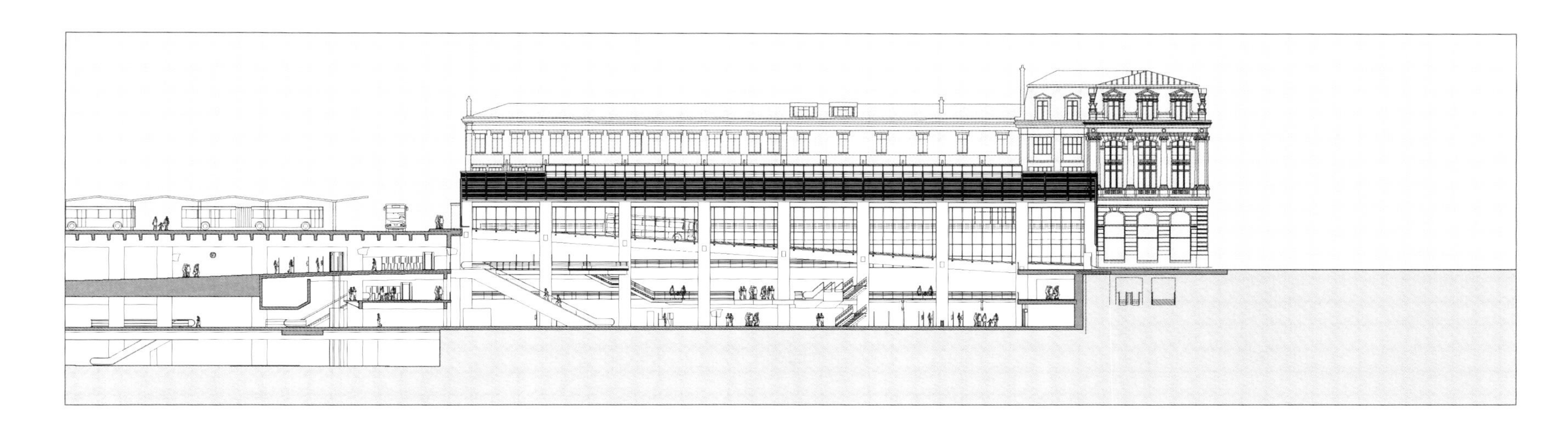

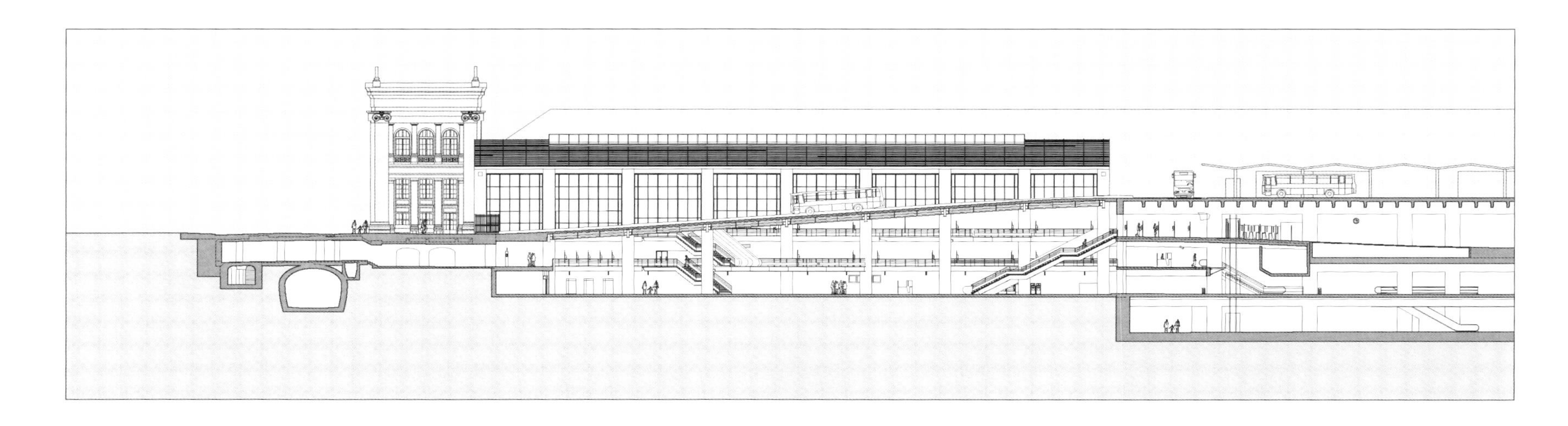

Sortie
Grandes lignes
l'été des festivals
l'été des festivals

From the interior of the new hall one can see the links to the various underground levels.

Natural light floods into the new atrium.

Accès aux trains
Grandes Lignes
RER
SPÉCIAL MODE
HOMME 2002
POUR HOMME

The hall is a junction directing pedestrian traffic to the various transport services located on the five underground levels.

Horizontal and vertical links run between the different levels. On the mezzanine, the layout of the shopping facilities becomes one of the key points of the project.

13 som

changi international railway station

singapore 1997–2002

project
SOM
architects
David Childs, Marilyn J. Taylor
collaborators
R. Smits, S. Ness, M. Fei, J. Del Fierro,
T. Ayoub, R. Galivanes, B. Lee,
J.-Y. Nakatsugawa, P. Papadapoulos
consultants
Ove Arup & Partners (structures), Susan Brady
Lighting Design Inc. (lighting), Cicada
(landscaping), Land Transport
Authority/Public Works Department
(structures and mechanical installations)
contractor
YKK, Japan
client
Land Transport Authority
dimensions
25,000 sq.m: total area
location
Singapore
chronology
1997–98: project
1998–2002: construction

Opened in March 2002, the station serving Changi Airport is in fact only part of a wider project commissioned from the SOM Studio by the Singapore Airport Authority in 1998.
Officially set up in 1936 by founder members Louis Skidmore and Nathaniel Owings, the studio had in fact been at work since 1930, the period in which Skidmore was architect for the 1933 Chicago World's Fair. In 1937 the two opened an office in New York—taking on John O. Merrill as the third "initial" of SOM in 1939—and the post-war period would see sizable expansion and internal changes within the studio. From its very early days, SOM has shown a marked interest in the technical aspects of architectural plans, proposing designs that are based on spare geometrical forms. It is this core element which provides continuity and coherence within a constantly developing approach to architectural design that has spread from America to all areas of the world (nowadays it is particularly evident in the architecture of the Middle East). As early as the 50s and 60s, in Europe and Asia one could already see "design adapting to the needs of large-scale demand. The architectural profession was restructured and there was a passive acceptance of the need for rapid turnover from drawing-board to construction work, and an adoption of the standardization that was required by industrialized building projects" (M. Tafuri, F. Dal Co, *Architettura Contemporanea*, Milan 1992, p. 329). Tafuri sees SOM as one of the architectural "companies" capable of "meeting this intense rhythm of output and the ever-increasing demand for work to high technological standards." Rapidity in the design phase, a marked interest in technological research and the development of innovative solutions are characteristics that distinguish the work of the studio, which has shown itself capable of adapting to the specific needs of the different contexts in which it has been called upon to operate. One of the most distinctive features of the group is its openness to experimentation, relying on flexibility of organization and close collaboration between architects and engineers; and the importance of the architectural repertoire resulting from this has been underlined by Henry-Russell Hitchcock, who sees SOM projects as reflecting "some of the most important and useful components of the city of the future, which one hopes will become a reality in the next few decades (*Architektur von Skidmore, Owings & Merrill, 1950–1962*, edited by H.-R. Hitchcock, Verlag Gerd Htje, Stuttgart 1962, p. 13). Throughout the work produced by the studio one can see certain leitmotifs: not only this interest in technology and experimentation, but also an interest in understanding the very experience and perception of spaces and structures—features which are certainly clear in the designs for the station of Changi Airport.
The competition won by SOM envisaged not only the building of a station for the rail link between city and airport, but also the creation of a new third terminal—extending the airport area by a third—and the renovation of the existing terminal 2; the first terminal of Changi Airport had been built in 1981, across the head of a tree-lined boulevard, with the second (1991) built alongside that avenue. The airport authority's specifications for the new terminal laid down that it should harmonize with the existing structures and be suitable to the tropical climate of the location; it was for this reason

that the designers proposed a structure of around the same size and shape as terminal 2, occupying a site on the opposite side of the boulevard. The rich vegetation of this avenue was to be preserved by locating the train tracks and main body of the station underground, with two atria opposite each other, on the terminal 2 and terminal 3 sides of the boulevard.

Linking the airport to the metropolitan system of Singapore, the station serves as a direct interface between a global system of transport and a local one; as such, it is designed to be an imposing gateway to the city for air passengers arriving there.

The first problem to resolve was the positioning of the vertical structures linking the airport and the underground station. Two glass rectangular volumes (60 meters wide, by 20 deep by 36 high) were located at each end of the station, housing not only the escalator links but also providing a visual link between the train platforms and terminals 2 and 3. There were two main reasons for the choice of glass here: to allow natural light down onto the platforms and to establish a direct and atmospheric interplay between the interior and the lush tropical vegetation of the boulevard. The main structure of these two high "atria" consists of a long girder serving as a central "spine," the northern end of which rests on a concrete block, placed asymmetrically to the building, and the southern end on an A-form support in steel. The girder tapers from a maximum width of 4.5 meters at this latter end to 1.5 meters where it rests on the concrete block. At three-meter intervals along its length is a secondary structure of reticular girders, the form of which is gradually modified as it adapts to the tapering form of the main structure. It is these secondary girders that support the covering of the atrium and the components that bear up the façade; the latter comprise a series of high-resistance pre-tensed steel cables fixed to horizontal supports and reinforced by diagonal tie-bars. This entire structure is located in the space between the two glass walls of the façade. That space also contains horizontal "baffles" that serve not only as support platforms for maintenance work but also as the blinds that regulate the flow of sunlight into the buildings.

A parallelepiped faced in granite, the underground station measures about 200 meters in length, 25 in width and 11 in height. It comprises two levels: that for the train tracks themselves and a mezzanine that serves as a link between atrium and platforms. This intermediate level is designed as a low-arch triple-span bridge (the central span is 140 meters wide, the two side ones 30 meters). As well as providing a physical link between the different parts of the structure, the bridge provides an ideal link between the "unlimited" dimension of Singapore Airport and the more contained space of the urban fabric itself. This double significance makes it the most powerful single component of the entire project. Made up of a framework in tubular steel that is entirely faced with translucid glass, the bridge is lit from within in such a way that it appears like a blade of light cutting across the station.

The walkway across the bridge has three points of access for the escalators down to the platforms: in line with the central axis of the structure is a diamond-shaped floor opening, with two trapezoidal openings placed in conjunction with the support "piers."

Encased within the granite block of the station, this glass bridge is not only a form of remarkable elegance and refinement, it is also a significant work of technological design. In effect, it is a fitting symbol of that research for innovative technical solutions that has been the hallmark of the work of the SOM studio over the decades.

Bibliography

Skidmore, Owings & Merrill. Selected and Current Works, Images Publishing, Mulgrave 1995.

"Changi International Railway Station," *Architecture and Urbanism*, 386, November 2002, pp. 76–89.

Skidmore, Owings & Merrill. Architecture and Urbanism, 1995–2000, Images Publishing, Mulgrave 2000.

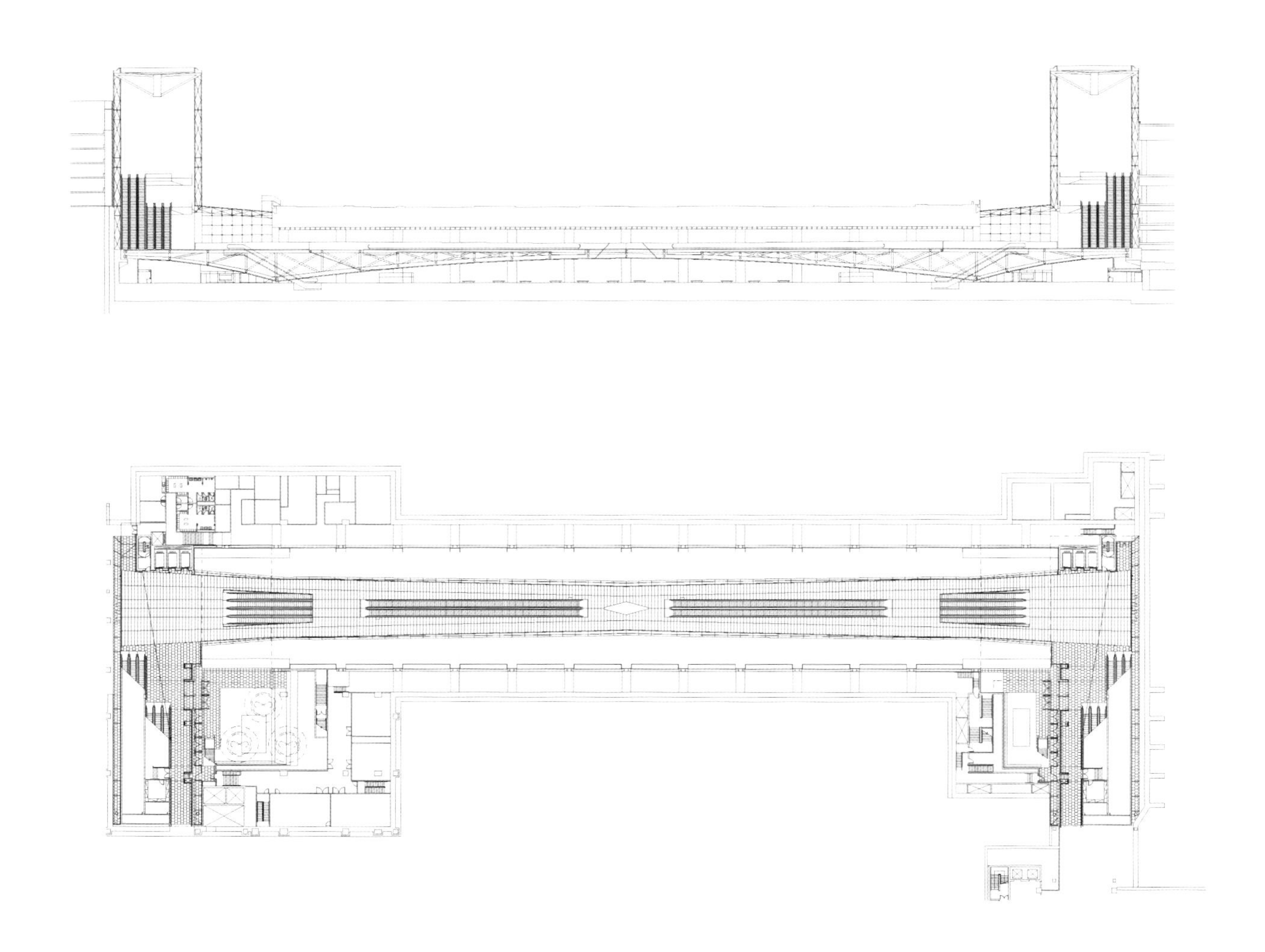

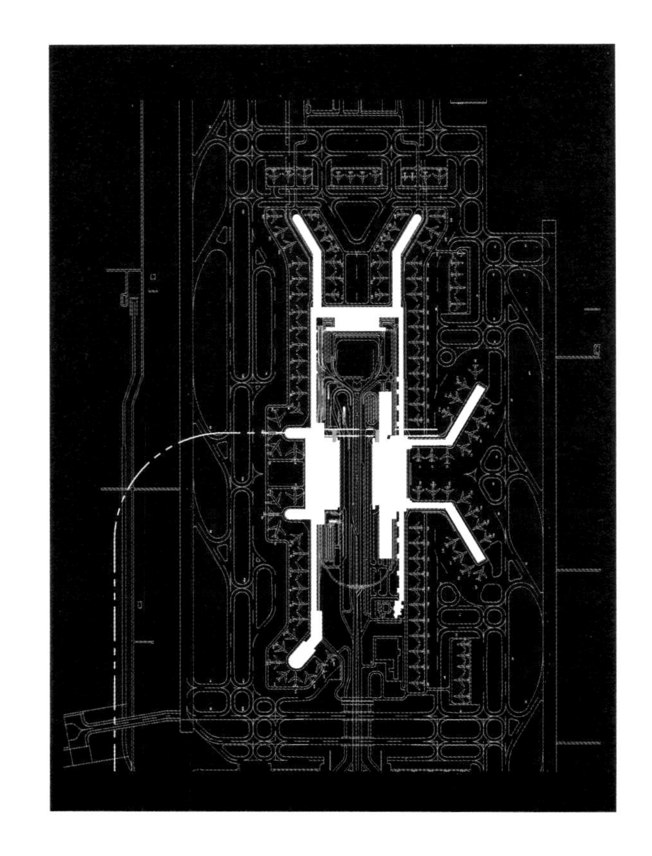

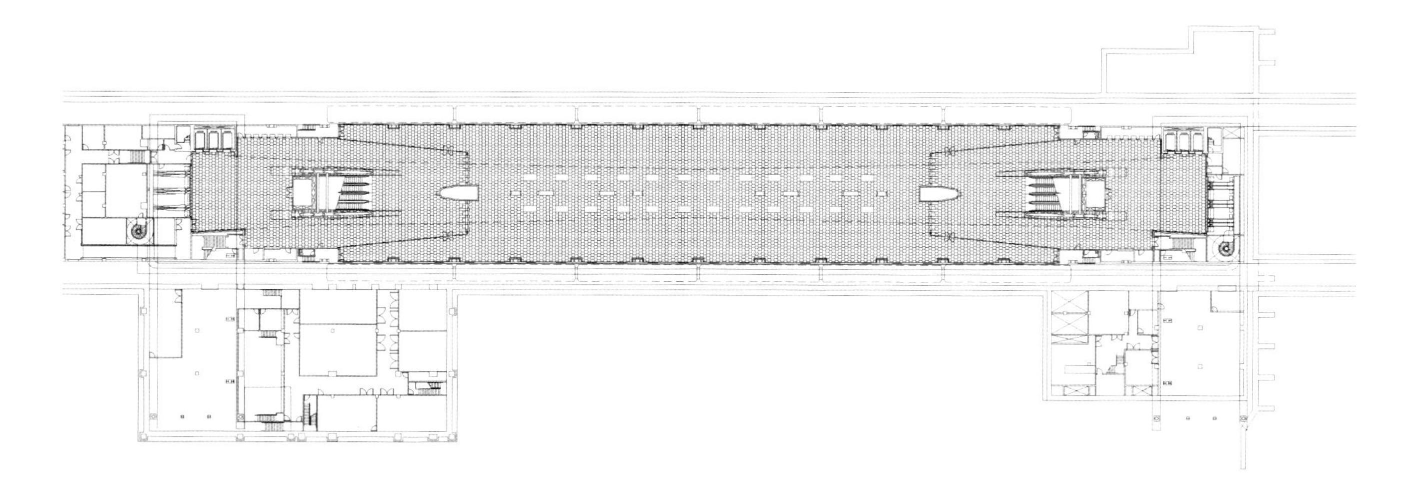

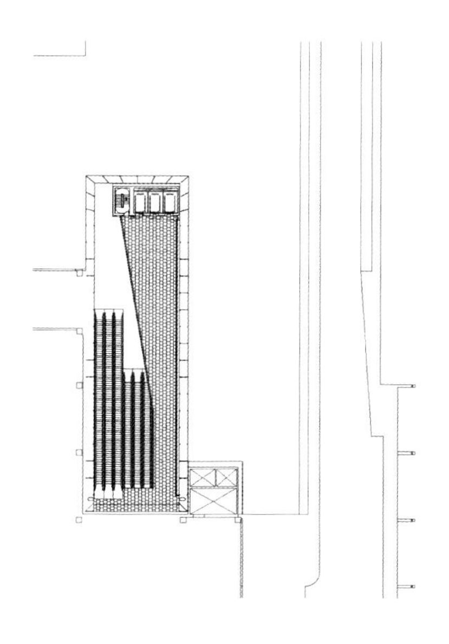

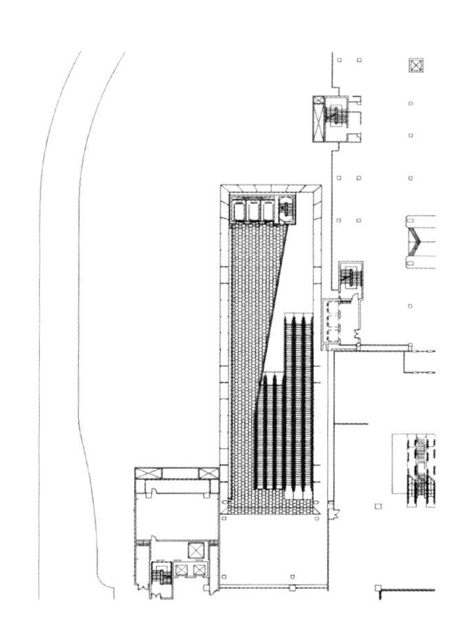

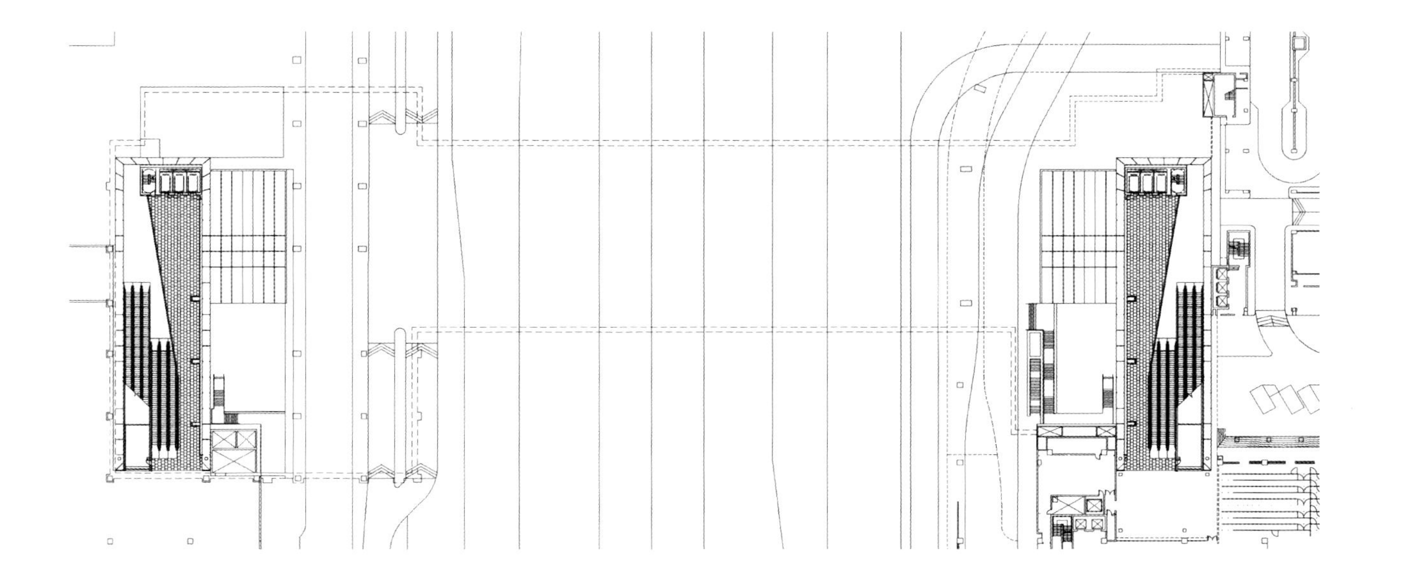

Section across the central boulevard; ground plan of the mezzanine level and plan of the platform level; general ground plan.

Plans of the upper and ground levels of the two glass atria.

Previous page:
A rendering of the view looking down onto the wide central boulevard, across which the two glass atria face each other.

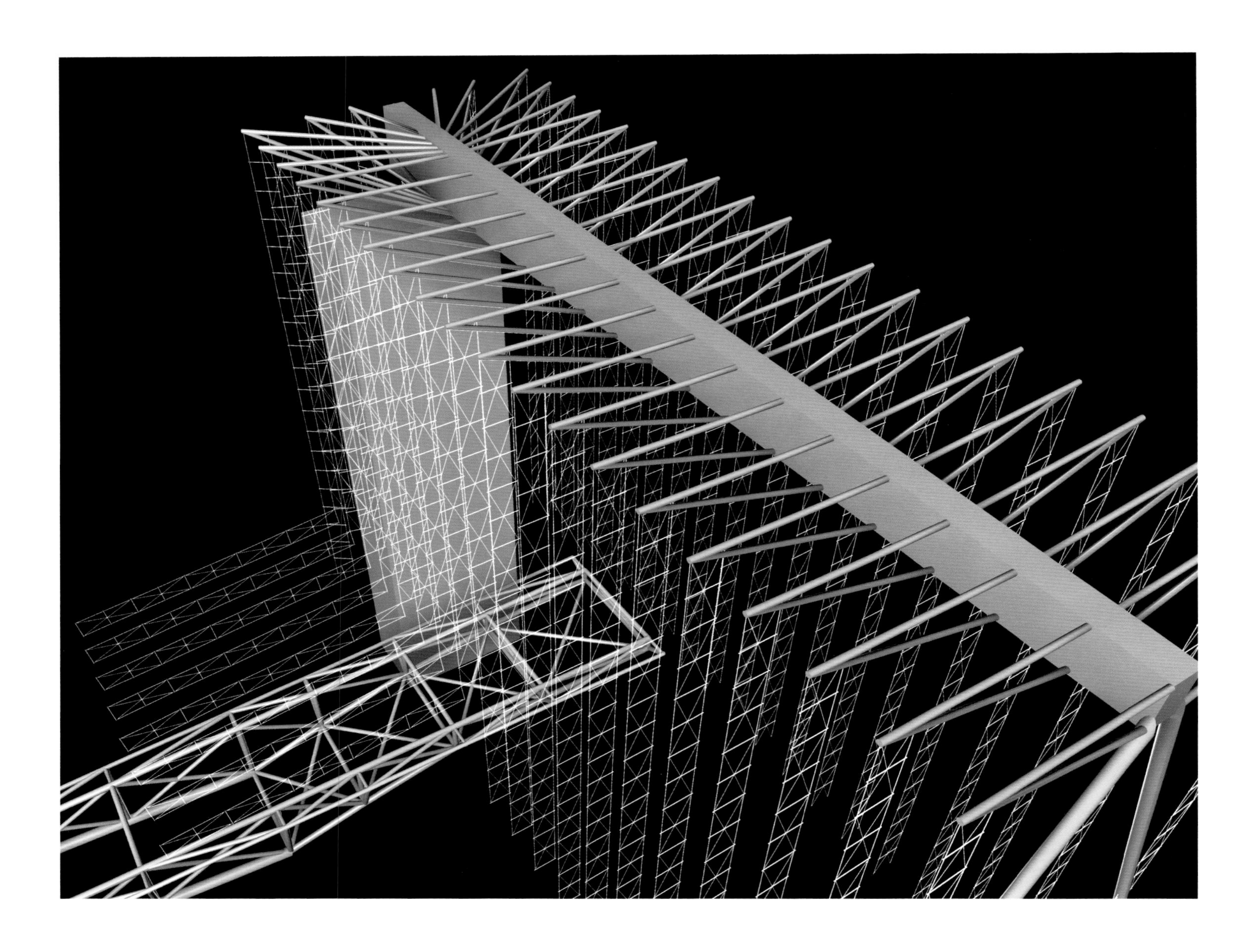

Rendering of the structure of the glass atrium (on the right), into which feeds
the underground bridge (on the left).

Two rectangular glass volumes, at either end of the station, form a visual and physical
link between the platforms and terminals 2 and 3.
The components of the structure for the façade consist of a series of high-resistance
pre-tensed steel cables, held in place by horizontal fixtures and reinforced
by a network of diagonal tie-bars.

The interior of the rectangular volumes is in glass: to allow light down to the platform levels and to establish a direct atmospheric interplay between the interior and the lush tropical vegetation of the boulevard.

2 Boon Lay
4 mins

Designed as a low-arch, triple-span bridge, the intermediate level is the most striking feature of the entire project.

The underground bridge, which links the two atria, is made up of a framework of tubular steel that is entirely faced with translucent glass; the lighting within it is even and homogeneous.
The walkway across the bridge has three points of access for the escalators down to the platforms: in line with the central axis of the structure is a diamond-shaped floor opening, with two trapezoidal openings placed in conjunction with the support "piers."

14 gmp

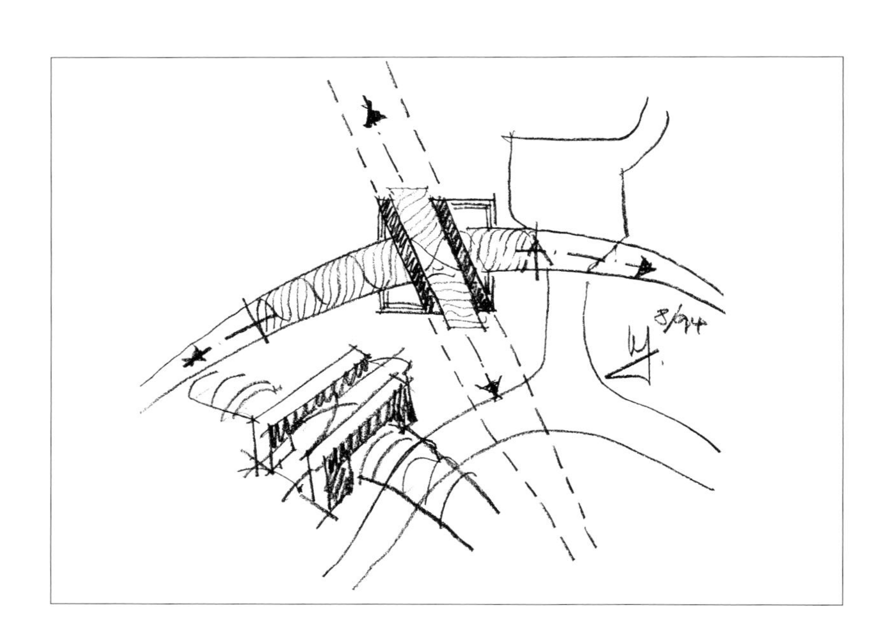

lehrter bahnhof

berlin, germany 1993–

project
GMP (Von Gerkan, Marg und Partner)
project architect
Meinhard von Gerkan
structures
Schlaich Bergermann und Partner,
IVZ/Emsch + Berger
client
Deutsche Bahn AG
dimensions
100,000 sq.m: area of site
175,000 sq.m: area of different levels
location
Berlin, Germany
chronology
1993: open competition for designs
1993–96: project
1996: start of construction
2006: expected date of completion

Still under construction—completion is expected in 2006—the Lehrter Bahnhof is one of the most imposing projects undertaken in recent years by the Von Gerkan, Marg und Partner studio; it is challenging not only because of the technical and structural qualities of the building itself but also because of the urban-planning issues raised by the location of the station. Sited in the Zoological Garden district of the city—to the west of the Humboldt River port—the new facility will occupy the position of the nineteenth-century station that was destroyed long ago. To the south of the bend in the Spree lies the area of the Reichstag and government ministries, to the north the district of Moabit; such a location required that this station—intended to become of the most important rail traffic hubs of Germany—be given suitably significant architectural form.
Founded in 1965 by Meinhard von Gerkan and Volkwin Marg, the studio which was awarded the contract is considered one of the most important in Germany and has extensive experience not only in the design of transport facilities but also in the redevelopment of vast urban areas. The Lehrter Bahnhof may be seen as the most mature expression of the structural and architectural languages that Von Gerkan, Marg und Partner have developed over the course of the past few decades.
Volkwin Marg himself (2003) has stated that the continuity in the studio's work is to be looked for in its constant experimentation with innovative systems of construction and its development of structures which offer the most ingenious and suitable solutions to the problems posed by a particular context. In other words, the studio's objective is to design buildings whose powerful presence as structure serves to define the territory within which they stand.
The idea at the heart of the Lehrter Bahnhof design was twofold: emphasis of the existing east-west train tracks within the surrounding urban context and, at the same time, the creation of a structure in which the new north-south train lines would be a clearly legible feature (they pass through a tunnel running some 15 meters below the Spree and the Zoological Garden). These latter lines will be served by an eight-platform underground station for high-speed and regional trains; parallel to the easternmost platform there will also be a new station for the U5 line of the city subway. Above ground, a new rail bridge—some 10 meters above road level—will follow the curving line of the old east-west tracks.
Thus the station is a great traffic junction, into which flow high-speed lines, regional train lines and the various city subways—all at different levels and aligned along the two east-west and north-south axes. The second underground level (-15 meters) will house the regional lines, the high-speed lines running north-south and the U5 subway line; at ground level will be local road transport facilities, bus bays and parking for private vehicles; and at the curved upper level (+10) there will be the ICE long-distance train services, and various regional and metropolitan overground lines (S3, S5, S6, S7 and S9).
At the junction of the two rail axes stands the entrance atrium, ending east and west in two structures (entirely finished in glass) which will house offices; extending over the overground tracks these will underline the north-south flow of train traffic below ground. The two aligned buildings are divided by the curved

roofing over the raised rail bridge. All the structures are faced in filigrane glass.
The precursor of the Lehrter Bahhof project was the GMP Studio's Berlin-Spandau Station (1993–99), the glass roofing of which might be taken as a prototype for the structure being used at Lehrter. The raised "rail shed," the structure of which takes up the schema first developed for the platform roofing at Spandau, is enclosed for 321 of its 430 meters by an imposing filigrane glass covering held in place by a metal structure of daring design. Forty-five meters wide and 159 long, the atrium too is covered by filigrane glass roofing which projects north-south; this space is conceived not only as the entrance to the station but also as a "bridge" between the Moabit district and the ministry district beyond the Spree. The structure supporting the roofing over the raised tracks comprises an arched metal framework with trusses about 13 meters apart supporting a square-grid reticular metal structure which is strengthened by diagonal tie-bars. The trusses and curved girders are aligned perpendicularly to the curve of the tracks, thus fanning out as these bend east-west; this means the distance between the supports is lesser on the south side of the bridge—that is, on the inside of the curve.
During the planning stage, the architects and engineers developed a special geometrical stressed truss and a reinforcing system for the structure which could be adapted to the varying span of the roofing. The thrust within the arch is counteracted by a special metal tie-bar arrangement; partly internal and partly external, this is adjusted in size according to the strain to which it is to be subjected.
The glass plates on the top of the vault were fixed in place with a 60-millimeter-wide layer of silicon on the upper jack rafter of each of the rods in the network frame. The thickness of the glass plates varies according to the static stress it will bear. To avoid interruptions in the glass roofing, a special silicone frame was developed that could be adapted to the changes in size throughout the curving structure. The glass is also held in place by circular disks and screw-thread cylinders which are fixed at the corners of the plates; the joints are made water-tight using silicone, with no need for overlapping strips to protect them. Given the longitudinal and transversal variations in the grid of the support framework, the size of the actual glass plates varies from a maximum of 1.7 × 1.7 meters to 1.5 × 1.4 meters.
Air renewal within the station relies on a system of natural ventilation, through openings that can be adjusted for the admission or expulsion of air and the extraction of smoke. Heated by direct sunlight through the glass, the air—in part, thanks also to the curved section of the covering—rises to the top of the roofing; the ventilators that admit fresh air are located in conjunction with the line of the rainwater drains, while those that expel stale, hot air and smoke are located at the very top of the glass vault.
The vault further exemplifies the idea of a "ventilated shell" because it comprises a simple system of a double layer of tempered glass between which are photovoltaic cells incorporated in a layer of high-transparency resin; the opacity of these cells helps to create shade for the platforms below.
To improve conditions in the east-west gallery and the north-south atriums during winter, a system of windbreaks has been erected towards either end of the tunnel (at the sixth arch westwards and eastwards from the central axis).
Rainwater is drained off the covering by an external system of water spouts aligned, north and south, with the main supports for the structure; prefabricated reinforced-concrete components, these spouts rest on the bridges for the urban railways, which have a layer of heat insulation and PVC waterproofing.
The design also provided for the future cleaning of the higher and more inaccessible parts of the glass gallery: there are vertical-movement fixtures—one located near the top of the vault, the other in correspondence with the line of the eaves—as well as a completely automated mechanism for the cleaning of the intrados of the glass vault.
The central core of the station rests on a structure that serves not only as the base but also as the link between the two perpendicular wings of the building. A rectangle measuring 132 meters (east-west) by 144 meters (north-south), this space has access stairs on all sides. Large open spaces (piazza and waiting areas) that are clearly distinguished from the flow routes through the station are situated 4.43 meters above road level.
The parts of the building incorporated within the base not only link the perpendicular galleries with the surrounding urban area but also house other facilities, making the station a stimulus for development in the entire area.
The ground and first underground level of the western building will mainly house shopping facilities, while the mezzanine will be reserved for the technical facilities of the station itself. Where the two galleries intersect, aligned openings in the floor levels mean that natural light reaches the platforms far underground; these also serve to establish a visual link between the various parts of the structure and thus facilitate orientation within it. Further vertical links are provided by in six steel-and-glass elevators.
To simplify use of the building, the staircases are all aligned along the longest side of the various floors and levels. This means that all of the stairs linking the underground long-distance train station with the upper levels run parallel to the tracks, while direct access to the tracks on the raised gallery is by a series of stairs aligned east-west.
Four platforms for regional and long-distance traffic will occupy the second underground level (15 meters underground); each 11.4 meters wide, these are aligned north-south and covered by a vault which rests on columns located either in the center of the platforms themselves or in the space between the pairs of tracks. The south and north ends of the platforms narrow slightly towards the train tunnel openings.
Lying across the central part of the underground rail station like a bridge, the first underground level serves to distribute passenger flow through the building; as it occupies only the central part above the platform level, to the south and north ends the underground space is double in height. Maintaining the same system of cross vaulting as the platforms beneath, this mezzanine level is surrounded by spaces used to house the various service and technical facilities of the station: the projecting cantilever floor in the area of the shopping facilities creates sufficient space for the location of various plant installations (air extractor, lighting, etc.). Here too are located the 3.5-meter-high girders that support the spans of the overhead station.
The two buildings over the east-west train lines occupy a total area of around 183 × 22 meters. Reticular modular structures (base unit: 8.7 × 10.7 meters), their glass façades have the same filigrane appearance as the vaulting over the station. The steel exoskeleton of these structures is visible from the outside and also influences the appearance of the north-south entrance atrium. Just like the base structure, the external front of these buildings forms a unified visual whole with the atrium of the station, as well as serving to mark the limit of the atrium from ground level up to the fourth floor. Based on an almost square module, the reticular exoskeleton of uprights and transverses extends over the entire surface of the building.
The four towers (two at either end of these bridge structures) rest on the outer walls of the long-distance rail station underground as well as on a system of girders that is incorporated in the roofing of the first underground level. The reticular structure means that the weight of the buildings can be distributed over the columns at the various levels of the underground station. In fact, one side of the base unit for the module used in the construction of that station is 17.4 meters, exactly double that of one side of the base module in the upper buildings.

Views of the site.

Above the urban rail bridges runs a cantilever roof over 87 meters in length, which leaves the levels at +7 and +10 meters open. Here again, the design exploits the idea of an exoskeletal structure. The weight of the roofing is borne by a steel framework of the exact same height as the sections of the bridges, which forms an integrated whole with the external uprights and cross braces of the exoskeleton of the buildings that arch over the tracks.
The access approaches to the station and the buildings are determined by the immediate urban context. Like those to the station atrium, the main entrance points for the glass towers are at street level, with the fronts of the buildings being approached by forecourts lying to the north and south of the station.
The space within these structures is divided into two clearly distinct functional sections. As in the first underground level of the station, the ground level and the mezzanine level house facilities for passengers, shopping, catering and other services. Accessible from the glass-faced atrium of the station, these are situated to the sides of their respective malls and form a homogeneous functional whole (the distinctive feature of the atrium itself is the alternation of walkways and open shafts).
The shopping and other services extend as far as the base structure and the space under the bridges of the urban railtracks (at the mezzanine above ground level).
Nine of the ten floors in the towers on either side of the station will provide flexible office space; the two central sections over the tracks will be entirely given over to open plan and mixed office space. The areas near the vertical and horizontal points of access will house service facilities such as storage archives, cooking areas, bathrooms and technical equipment.
Once completed, the Lehrter Bahnhof will handle more interconnected rail traffic (subway, local, regional, long-distance, international) than any other station in Europe. What is more, due to the presence of extensive shopping and office space within the structure, the station will not only interact with the area of government offices and ministries immediately around it, but it will also become a complex with an inherent vitality of its own, a hub that links urban areas of widely different character.

Bibliography

Renaissance of Railway Stations. The City in the 21st Century, BDA-AG-DAZ in collaboration with Meinhard von Gerkan, Hamburg, 1996.
Von Gerkan, Marg und Partner, *Architekture fur den Verkehr*, Birkhäuser, Basel 1997.
P. Wolff, "170.000 Kubikmeter Gerüst. Montage des Hallendachs am Lehrter Bahnhof," *Bauwelt*, 26, 2000, pp. 10–14.
H. van Dijk, "Lehrter Bahnhof. Ein Holländer wirft einen kritischen Blick auf die Baustelle," *Bauwelt*, 24, 2002, pp. 94–100.
Meinhard von Gerkan, von Gerkan, Marg und Partner, *Architecture 2000–2001*, Birkhäuser, Basel 2003.

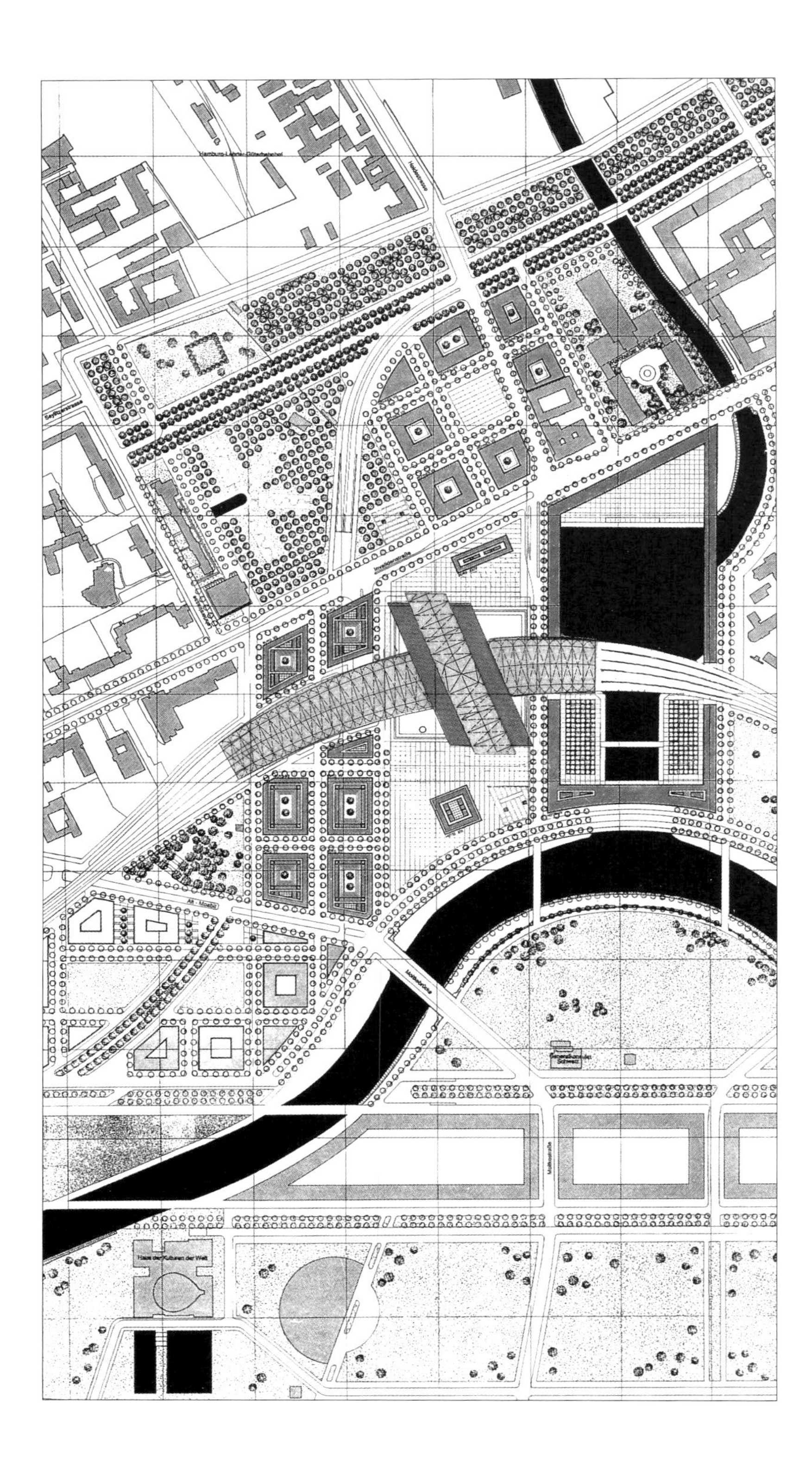

General ground plan.

Plans of the underground level, of the raised level and the ground level.

Previous page
The rendering shows all the complexity of the project, from the underground and raised tracks, which run in different directions, to the large vault covering the overground tracks and the two buildings which bridge over that vaulting.

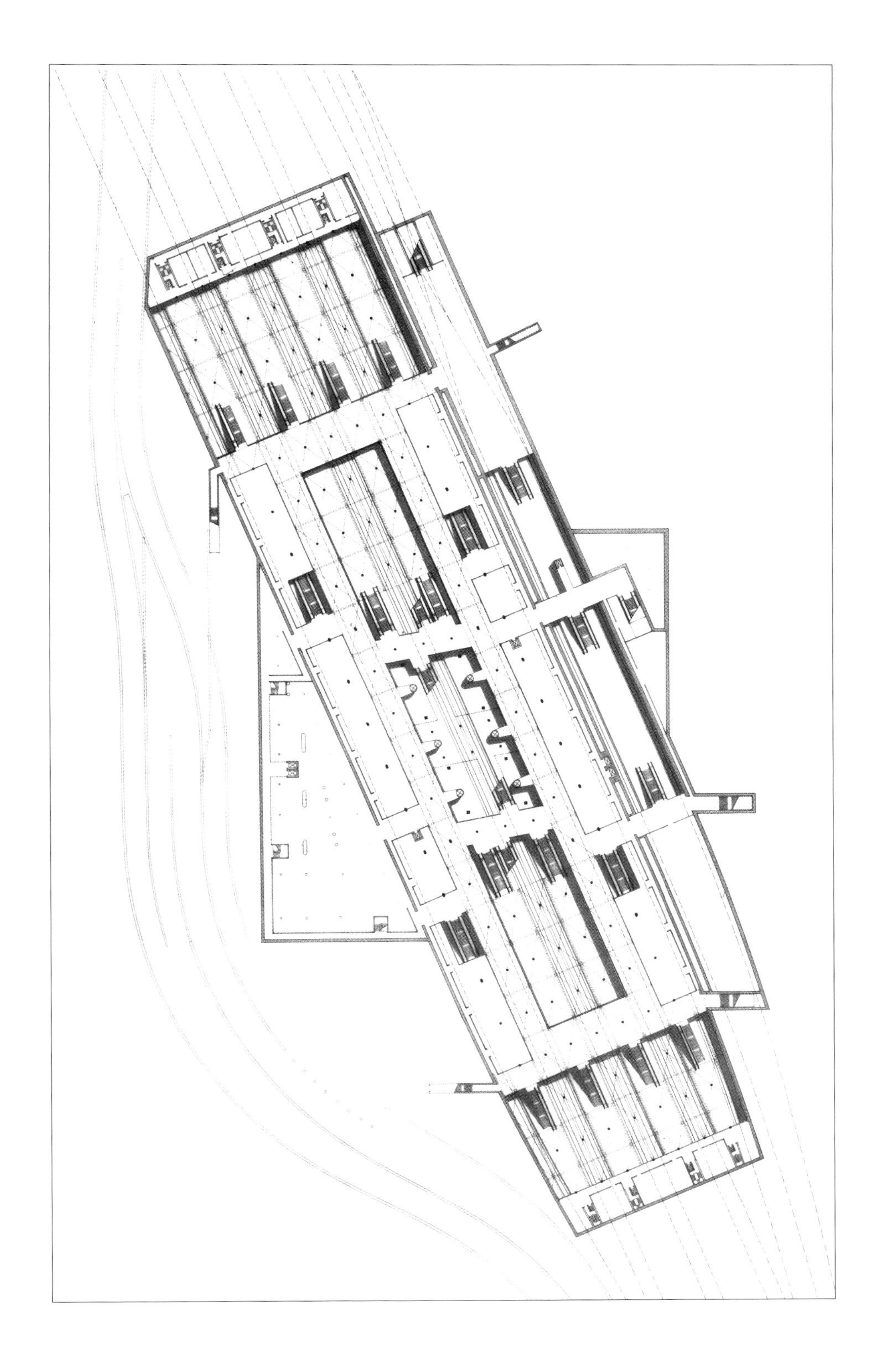

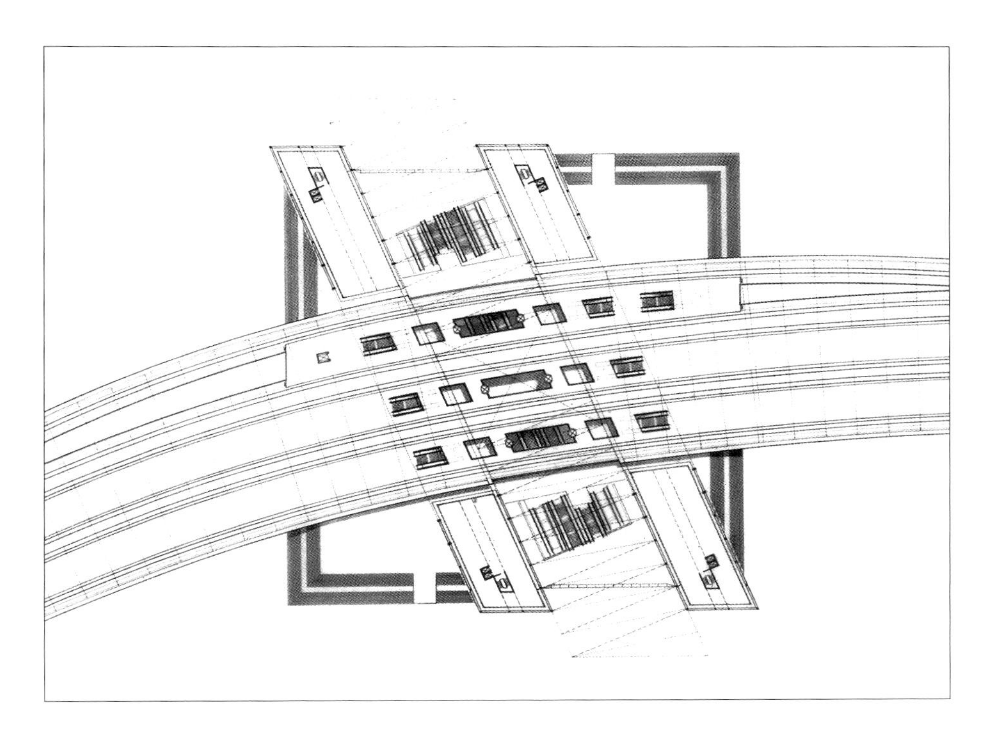

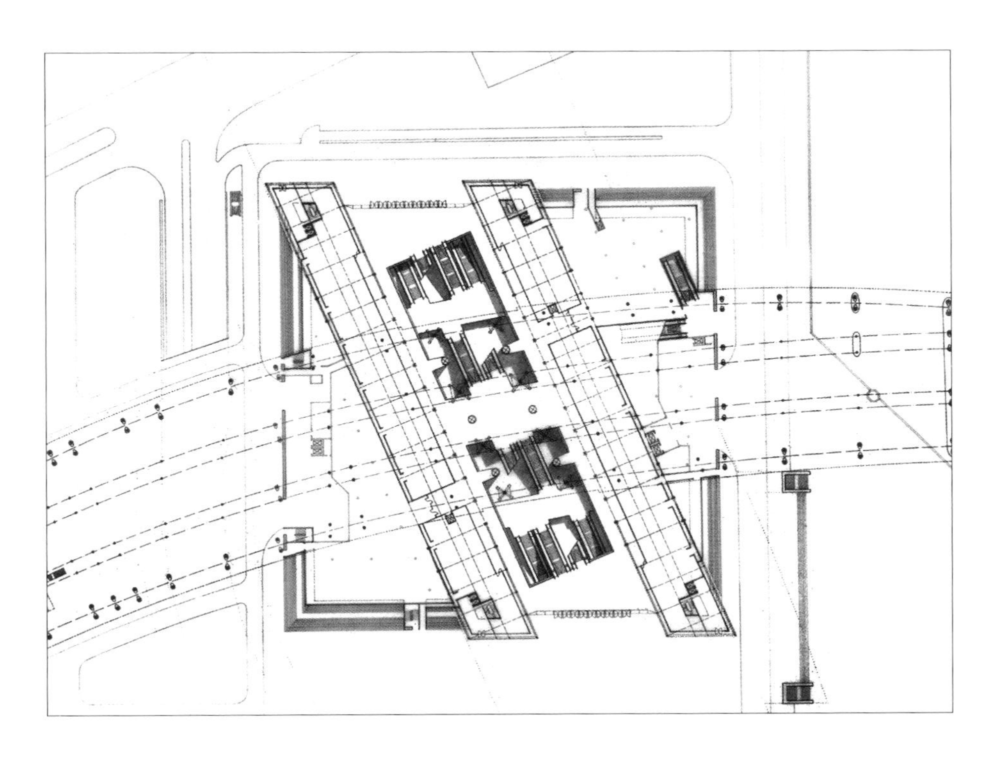

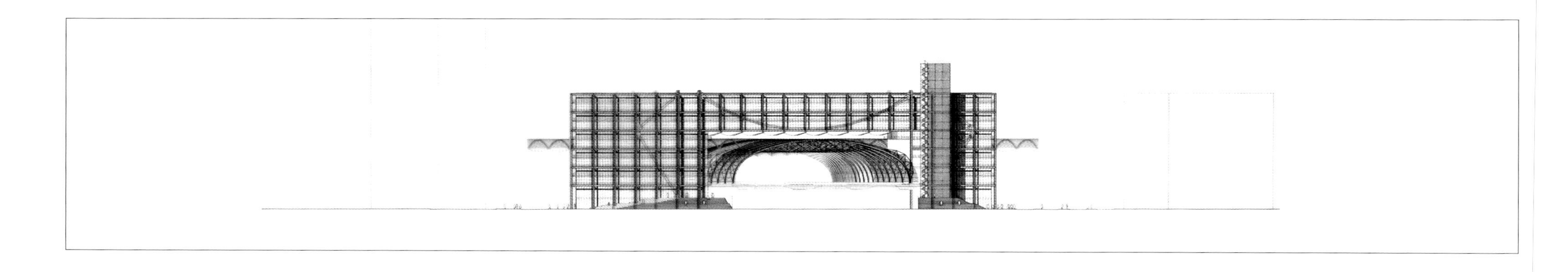

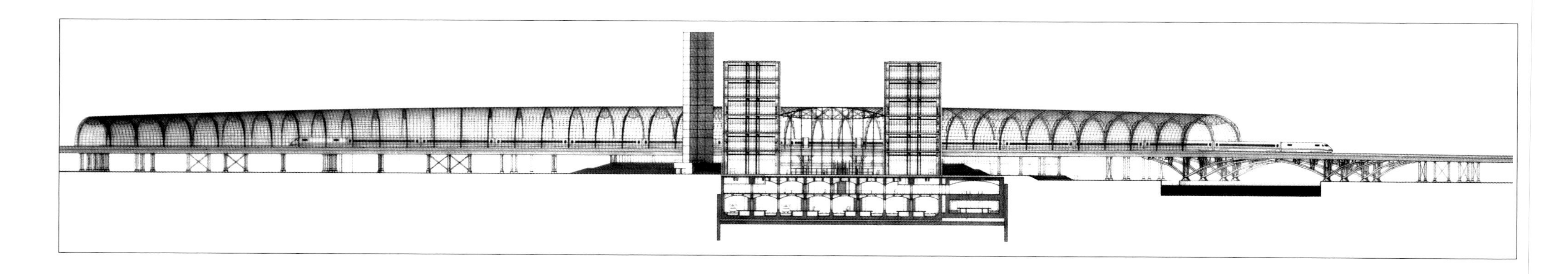

Longitudinal section/elevation and cross section.

Section showing details of the interior.

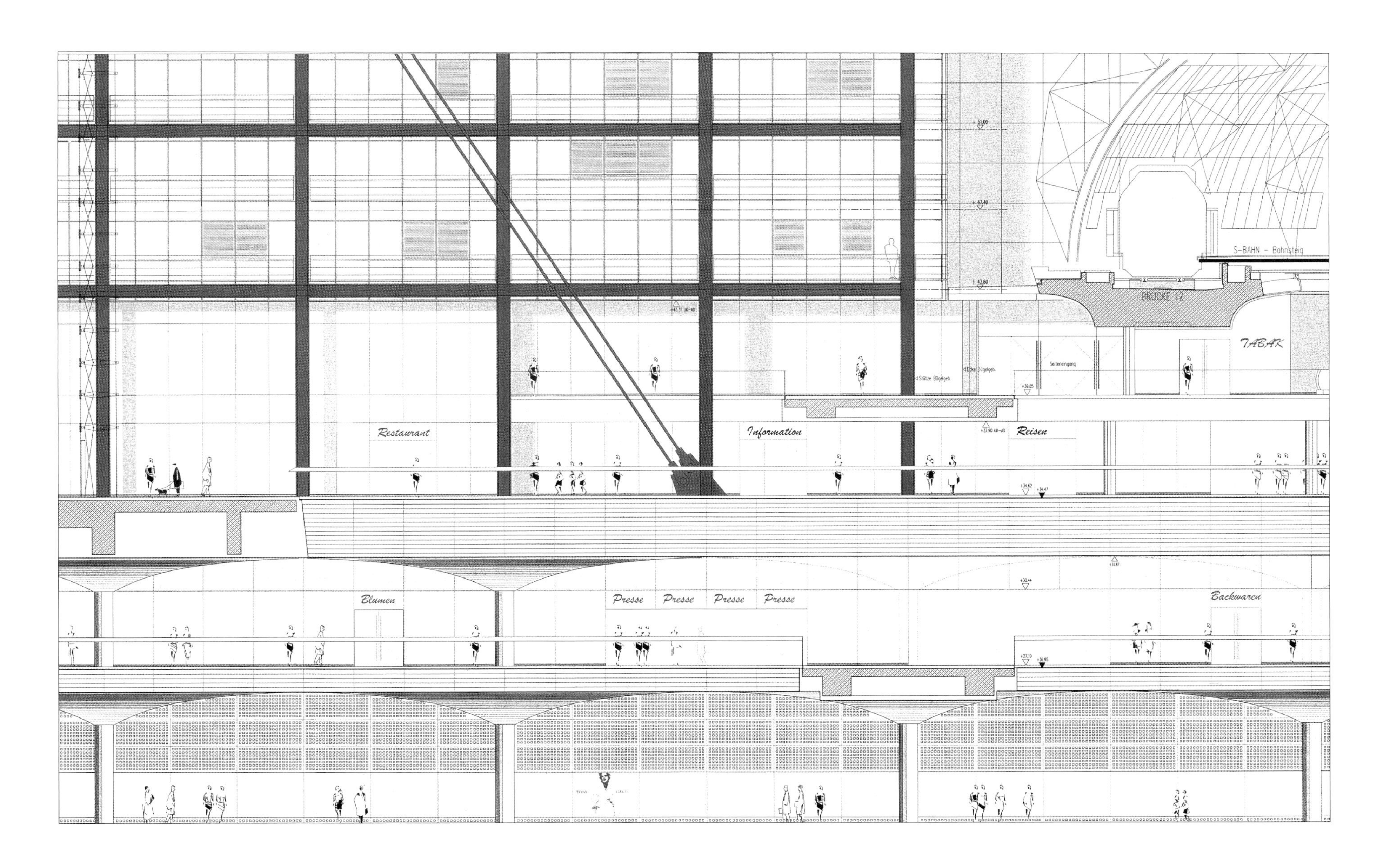
S-BAHN - Bahnsteig
BRÜCKE 12
TABAK
Seiteneingang
Restaurant
Information
Reisen
Blumen
Presse
Presse
Presse
Presse
Backwaren

The raised "rail shed" is enclosed by an imposing filigrane glass covering held in place by a metal structure of daring design.

The present gap in the vaulting will be occupied by the station atrium, delimited on either side by two buildings entirely in glass.
The structure supporting the roofing over the raised tracks comprises an arched metal framework with trusses about 13 meters apart.

15 un studio

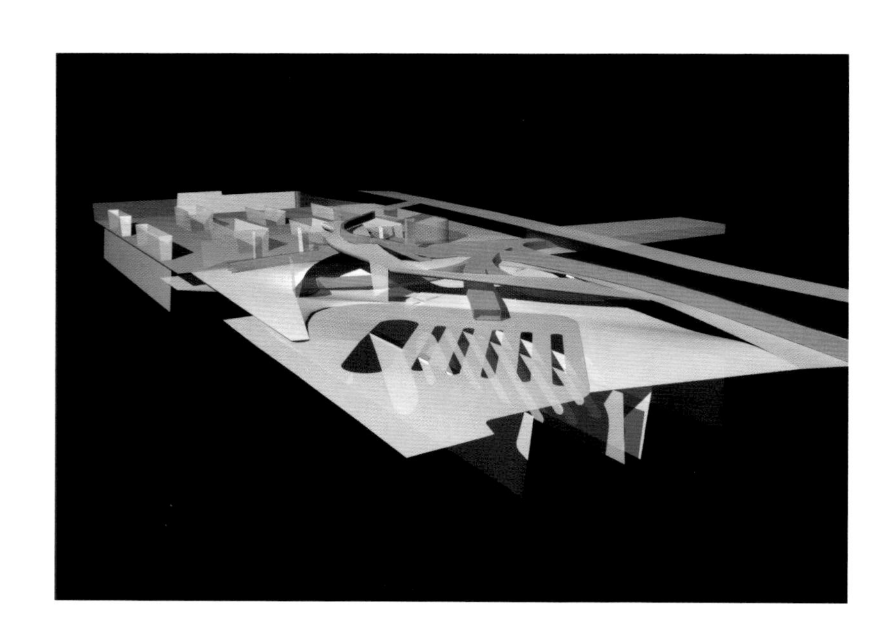

arnhem central station

arnhem, the netherlands 1996–

project
UN Studio
architects
Ben van Berkel, Caroline Bos
with
Ove Arup & Partners
dimensions
6,000 sq.m: transfer hall
8,000 sq.m: shops
8,000 sq.m: offices
11,000 sq.m: apartments
location
Arnhem, The Netherlands
chronology
1996–98: project
1997: start of construction
2007: expected date of completion

"... In the dream she passed through a large space shedding all sorts of things, until she was left totally naked. The space was like a large tunnel, with sloping walls faced in stone. At the end there was no light, but the floor and ceiling ran into each other in a thin black line. Walking slowly towards that horizon, she left behind a swathe of objects in her wake. Together with her clothes, everything fell away from her body—a happy tinkling cascade of fruit, chocolate bars, postcards, magazines, kitchen utensils and articles of clothing. Suddenly she heard a rustle at her back and turned to look. From very high up a group of people was watching her and applauding. The sound of that applause was transformed into the splashing noise that water makes against the shower curtain, and then Diouma got out of bed. Today, she was going to encounter the spirit who was stealing things from her.

She drove to her new place of work by car, finding a parking lot in an abandoned building site behind the station. She was late and hurriedly gathered her things. Dashing across the building site, she stumbled against the stones that were scattered here and there. Suddenly she stopped and began to sort out the mass of objects she was clutching in her arms: her handbag, her scarf, her keys, her walkman... Everything was there. No, her leather jacket was missing. In the end, she had finally managed to do it, to lose the most precious thing of all. She ran back to the car park. It was too late. The area was deserted; there was only a dirty red car pulling away into the distance. Without thinking about it, Diouma found herself back in her car. With a screech of tires, she pulled out of the parking lot and set off in pursuit of the phantom that had taken possession of her soft, black kidskin jacket. She followed the car through the hectic morning traffic, ignoring the other cars which tried to get between herself and the red vehicle that was ahead of her. Through furious looks and irate blasts of horns, she followed the car into the garage near the station, on the other side of the tracks. The two vehicles drove down into the underground levels, past brightly colored walls in yellow, orange and red. At each turn, the tires screeched on the smooth cement; passing under a bridge encased in glass, Diouma recognized the immense empty space of her dream.

She got to the lowest level of the garage but the red car was not there. She moved slowly across the large open space where there were no columns but only long sloping walls to divide the three lanes: however, there was absolutely nothing there. She parked her car in a free space in Section 45 and then got out. Slipping into the first exit she came to, she found herself in an enormous room flooded with light. Again, there was no one there. She took the elevator to the floor above. With her heart in her mouth, she went over the entire floor. But that, too, was deserted. She ran to the other part of the building, along the walls of unfinished stone that she had seen in her dream. Those surfaces of friable stone appeared absurd in this landscape of clay and sand.

There was still no trace of the car. Breathing heavily, Diuoma pushed open a heavy glass door and went into a second space, which cut the garage in half. Ahead of her was a very long flight of stairs. She just glimpsed a fleeing figure at the very top and then set off in pursuit. The walls of smooth cement and the steel and galvanized-metal stairs glowed brilliant white under the fluorescent lighting.

She managed to reach the top. Almost totally out of breath, she opened the door to the top floor and turned quickly. A few meters away she saw a woman with short blonde hair who was busy slipping a parking lot ticket into the front part

of her handbag. Nonchalantly hanging from her forearm was the leather jacket. In a few steps Diouma had caught up with her and snatched the jacket away; the startled woman opposed no resistance. Falling to her knees, Diouma buried her face in the smooth black leather, inhaling the smell of talcum powder and the pungent odor of leather. 'Thank you,' she said breathlessly. 'Thank you for finding my jacket.' 'I had lost it,' she explained. 'I have lost a lot of things.' She then stood up and walked quickly away. Once she was back in her car she burst out laughing, and was still laughing out loud when she drove over the glass bridge. Looking down, she saw the immense space beneath, which was so bare and empty, so beatifically free of objects and their images."
In this short tale, Caroline Bos—who, together with Ben van Berkel, is the head of the UN Studio of architects—describes the sensations that inspired the design for the Arnhem Central Station. Architecture here is presented as the most personal of experiences; it reflects an oneiric world of wide spaces and fluid channels of movement, a place where the disorder and confusion of the city is temporarily transmuted into order.
The UN Studio views architecture as "existing in a locus that is without imposed order, which is continually undergoing change; it is a place where mutual interference between the various components is not an incidental feature but something to be valued" (Negrini 2001). In the preliminary design stage of any project, the studio gathers together information and stimuli from the surrounding environment, in order to identify those features "that suggest an overall approach to the complexity of the scheme, a logic that might be followed." The two architects are well aware of the uncertain and shifting nature of contemporary reality; hence, in their projects they strive to take that very feature as the inspiration for the development of their own original ideas. "The space in which we move," says Ben van Berkel, "is defined by the superimposition of orders, by the juxtaposition of sources which emit at varying frequencies. Borders tend to evaporate; outlines become mobile; reality is governed by flux, interpenetration, accumulation." The contemporary world is solely the starting point; architecture is to function as a series of "snapshots" of an ever-changing and shifting reality. To produce these "stills," the architects rely a lot on diagrams, which make it possible to fix things for a moment and yet "leave room for different possible interpretations and new organizations of order." The diagram can offer a summary of functions and identify directions of experimentation; hence, it is "the best possible means for working within an open system." Van Berkel describes himself as interested in "the 'open-system' quality of diagrams, in the fact that they can generate and reproduce ideas." In effect, while the process of reflection and information gathering continues, the diagram becomes an instrument for the proliferation of notions and concepts.
Aaron Betsky has described the architecture of the UN Studio as relying on systems that seem to fold back on themselves, like a Möbius strip or, to take the three-dimensional equivalent, the Klein bottle (the basic inspiration for the Arnhem Station project); over time, the flow backwards and forwards through the spaces they create can generate new uses and new experiences. Computer graphics are fundamental to the work of the two architects, given that it makes it possible for them to turn abstraction into a key strategy in project design. In line with the theoretical approaches expounded by the likes of Jeffrey Kipnis, Sanford Kwinter and Greg Lynn, van Berkel sees forms as forces which act upon the urban landscape, consolidating organization within the chaos of the city and creating points of cohesion. Betsky himself has referred to these points as "blobs," that flow from one space to another, from ceiling to wall to floor. The characteristics of a specific environment and setting are absorbed by a vortex of forms that transform the external into the internal, creating a space of continuous transformation.
The most powerful expression of these ideas is to be found in the new Arnhem railway station complex. Still under construction, this station—intended as a junction of local, private and long-distance transport—comprises a series of interconnected halls ending in two identical towers that will serve as office space. The structure is, in fact, so fluid in conception that it is difficult to establish where the routes of flow through the building end and the enclosed spaces of the halls begin.
Key considerations in the UN Studio project were so-called "mobile forces," those changing circumstances (political imperatives, economic pressures, conditions of infrastructures, building requirements, etc.) which can over time lead to changes in the use of the structures. This is why one might define the projects of Ben van Berkel and Caroline Bes as exemplifying "flexible" systems, which can respond to variations in the surrounding conditions. As in their Erasmus Bridge project, the architects here develop upon the theme of a nodal infrastructure, which they see as one of the most significant notions in contemporary architecture: it reflects all the indeterminacy and unforeseen developments that are integral to the modern urban world.
The new Central Station is a stratified structure of various layers, comprising areas of common interest and shared space. The railway station proper and the large terminal for provincial and regional bus services converge in a large air-conditioned space from which one can make one's way to the various forms of public transport, to the parking lots, to the office space in the two tower blocks and to the shopping areas. This nodal infrastructure is, in effect, a sort of "social condenser," within which various aspects of the metropolitan environment interpenetrate and intensify each other.
Pedestrian flow through the facility is the core consideration that brings all the different uses together; it is this which determines the physical location of the junctions between the parts. Part of the initial project stage, therefore, involved extensive observation and statistical analysis of the logics that determine orientation and intensity of pedestrian flow within new spaces.
The station is an open system of integrated parts between which no division can be drawn. The ideal inspiration here is the diagram of the Klein bottle, with its notion of uninterrupted transformation: the floors of the entrance hall become empty spaces, air shafts that open up into the external air without negating the fluidity of the space.
Given the complexity of the project, the building work is being carried out in phases, each dedicated to autonomous sections. First came the underground levels for car parking; these are designed in such a way that they do not comprise future possibilities for variations in the upper levels, which house the covered piazza and the entrance hall, the shopping mall and the office tower blocks. The weight-bearing structure, the plant installations and vertical links within the building all exploit a system of spaces created using V-shaped components in cement, which serve to funnel light and provide natural ventilation. These rigid components constitute the points of reference within the flexible and variable system of the nodal infrastructure. As Laura Negrini points out, "the existence of such resistant forms is the necessary condition for the creation of an open system; it means that freedom in the organization of space is not reduced to the mere abstract identification of some sort of empty neutrality" (Negrini 2001, p. 31).

Bibliography

G. Lynn, "Conversaciòn vìa modern con Ben van Berkel," *El Croquis*, 72, 1995.
B. van Berkel, C. Bos, *Move*, UN Studio & Goose Press, Amsterdam 1999.
L. Negrini, *Ben van Berkel. UN Studio – van Berkel & Bos*, Edilstampa, Rome 2001.
VV.AA., *UN Studio Un-Fold*, NAI Publishers, Rotterdam 2002.

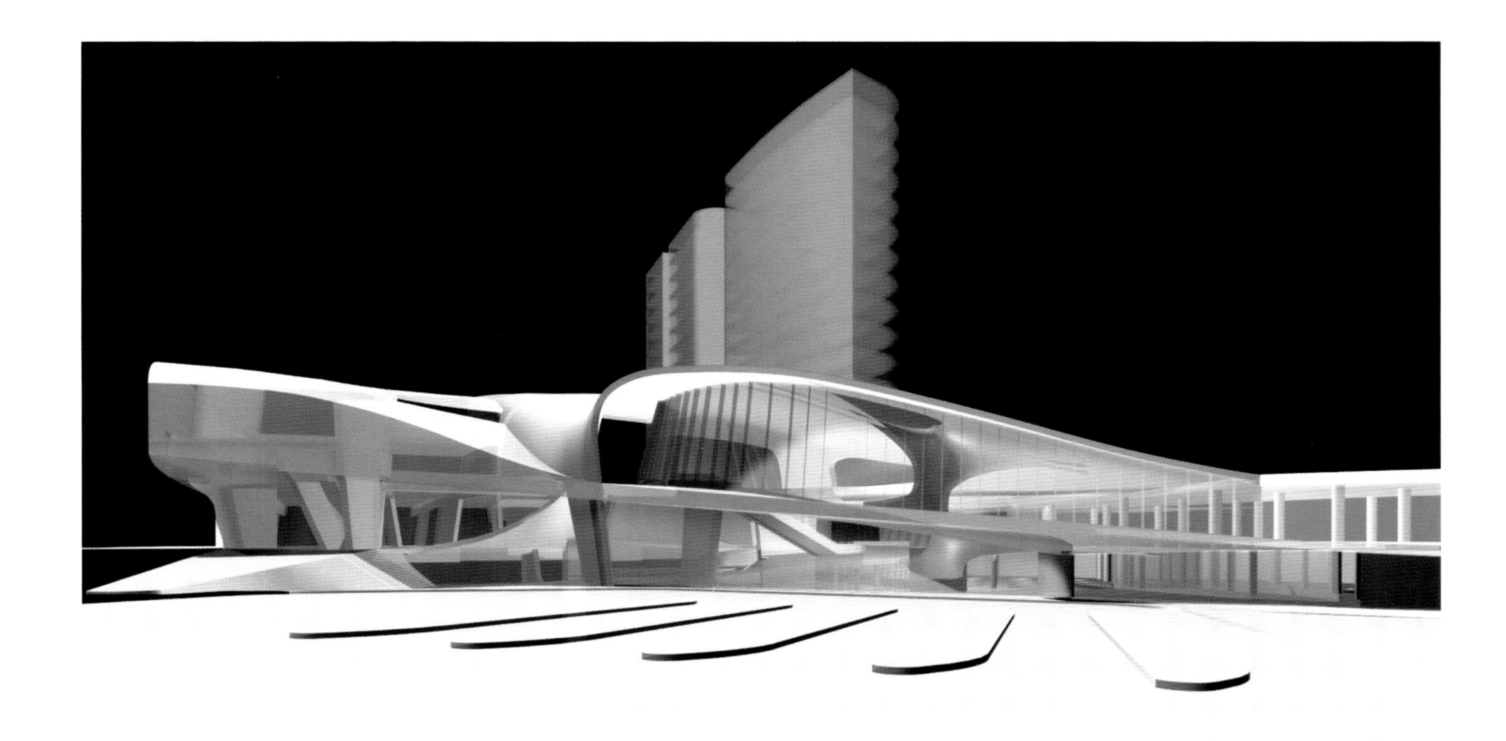

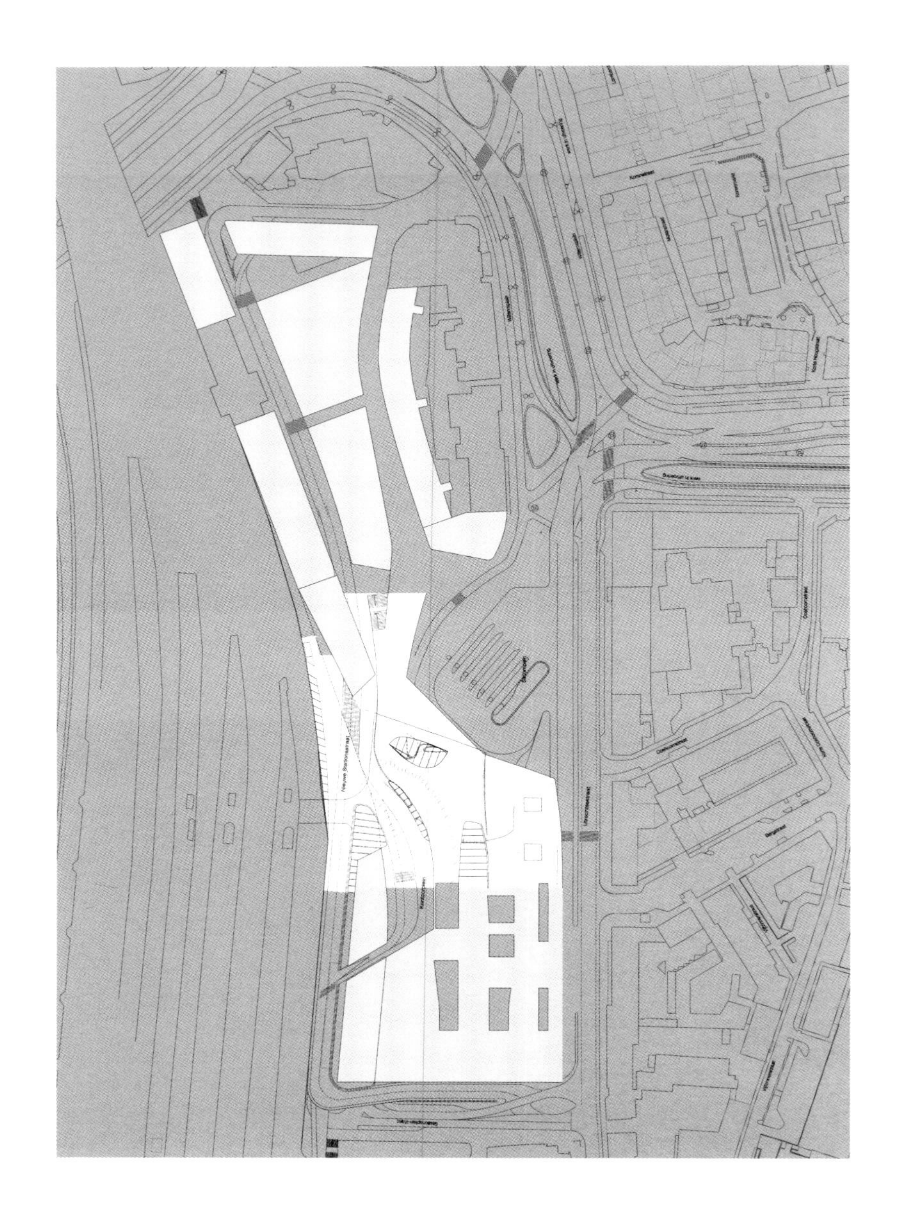

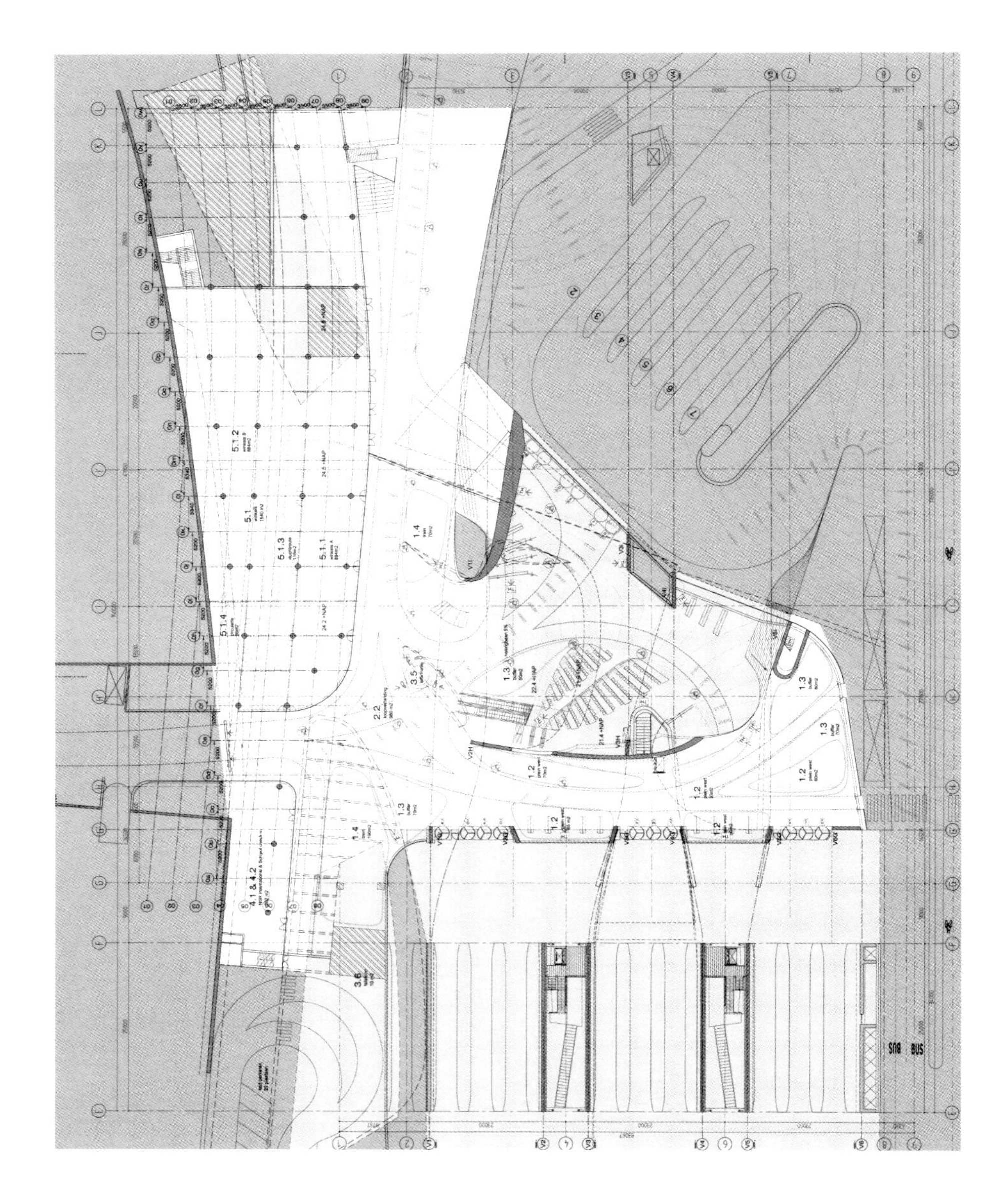

General ground plan and plan of the second level above ground.

Elevations east and south.

Previous page
The station comprises a series of interconnected halls ending in two identical towers that will serve as office space.

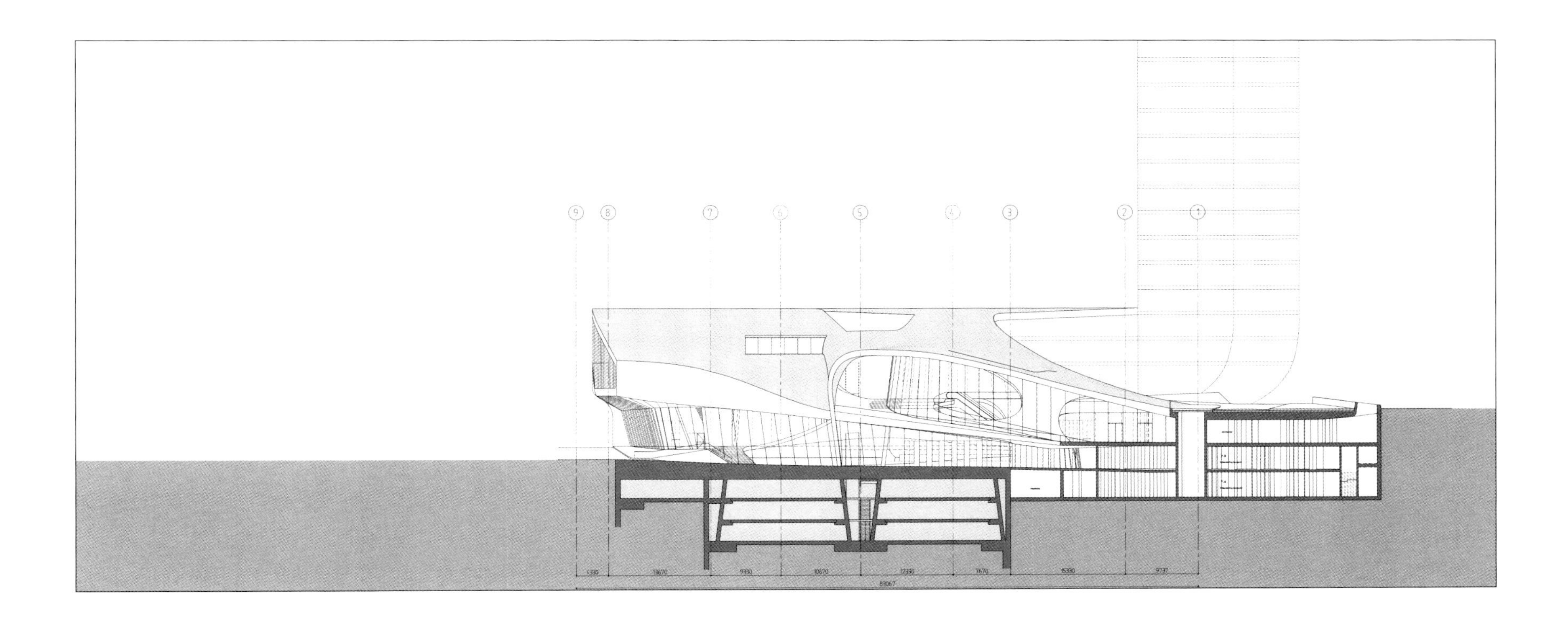

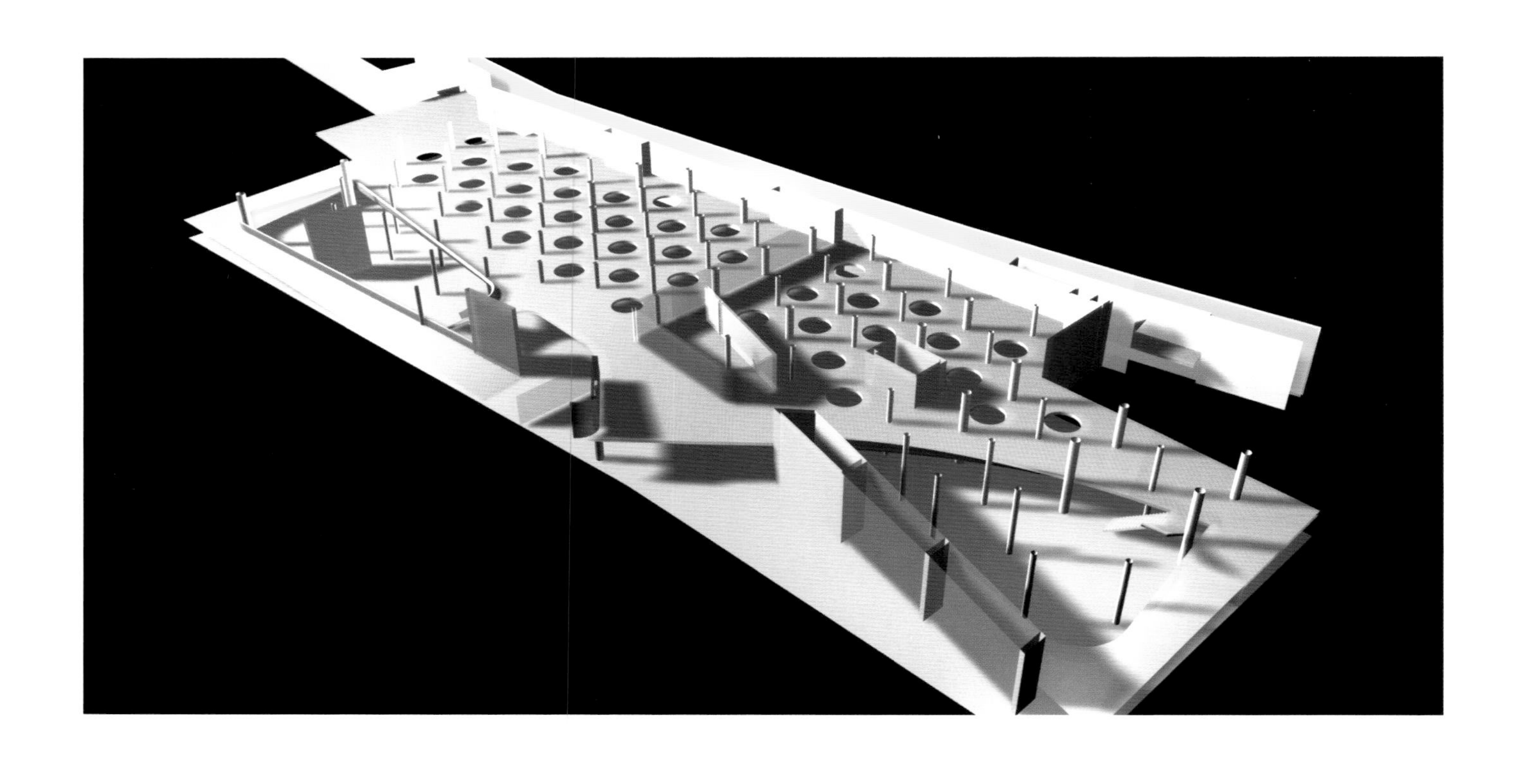

The bicycle area.
The new Central Station is a stratified structure of various layers, comprising areas of common interest and shared space.

From the large air-conditioned space one can gain access to the different means of public and private transport, to the parking lots and to the offices.

The tunnel leading down to the underground parking lot.

The underground parking lot.
The weight-bearing structure, the plant installations and the vertical links within the building all exploit a system of spaces created using V-shaped components in cement, which serve to funnel light and provide natural ventilation.

16 som

pennsylvania station

new york, united states 1998–

project
SOM
architects
David Childs, Marilyn J. Taylor
collaborators
C. Bemis, S. Duncan, M. Fei, M.-Y. Kim,
V. Pajkic, A. Pascocello, T. Vinh
consulents
Ove Arup & Partners, Parsons Brinckerhoff
Quade & Douglas (structures)
clients
Pennsylvania Station Redevelopment
Corporation (PSRC),
United States Postal Service (USPS)
location
New York, United States
chronology
1998: open competition for designs
1998-2001: project
2004: start of construction
2008: expected date of completion

Used every day by half-a-million passengers—more than twice those using Grand Central Station, and equivalent to the sum daily total of the travelers passing through the three New York airports of Kennedy, La Guardia and Newark—Pennsylvania Station is the busiest rail junction in the US. However, at present, the various facilities within the building are distributed through a network of corridors that date back to the historic Penn Station designed at the beginning of the twentieth century by McKim, Mead & White.
Along with the Grand Central, Penn Station was one of the most important illustrations of how the function and layout of railway stations changed during the end of the nineteenth–beginning of the twentieth century; one cannot but agree with Steven Parissien when he observes that the demolition of that building—between October 1963 and summer 1966—robbed the United States of "one of its most significant modern monuments" (*Pennsylvania Station, McKim, Mead and White*, Phaidon, London 1996). With its underground rail tunnels running east-west into a large multi-story building, the original project drawn up by McKim, Mead & White reflected how the replacement of steam engines by electric locomotives deprived the old train sheds of their reason for existence. As we have already seen, this technological development meant that tracks and platforms could be moved underground and that large surface areas were now free for redevelopment. These were the key factors in the transformation of railway station design, with the great stations of America—for example, Grand Central Terminal and Penn Station—becoming multi-story buildings incorporating tracks that were only visible to those within.
After the train shed had disappeared, it was the entrance atrium-ticket office concourse which became the most innovative feature of train stations; envisaged as an urban "promenade," a public space with its own attractions, this area was the very symbol of the new railway architecture. However, as the station became a more interior space, the concourse adapted the formal characteristics of those large glass-and-iron train sheds of the nineteenth century, becoming a permeable space through which flowed the pedestrian traffic moving from the city towards the waiting trains. This naturally meant that the station and the city thus began to find themselves reflected in each other.
In the old Penn Station, the platforms were approached through a series of monumental spaces (waiting rooms and concourse), each of which had its own distinct character: the massive masonry of the waiting room called to mind monumental Roman ruins (Parissien describes the travertine facing as making the place "cavern-like"), while the concourse, with its reticular girder columns and its roofing in steel and glass, recalled the appearance of nineteenth-century train sheds, thus functioning as the physical and visual link between the station building and the tracks below. In effect, the heterogeneous architectural languages used in the various service areas (waiting room, ticket offices, arrivals and departures atrium) were—along with the underground location of the tracks and platforms (45 feet below street level) and the care taken to guarantee fluidity of movement through the building—the most striking features of the design.
Occupying a site bound east-west by 7th and 8th Avenue and south-north by 31st and 33rd Street, this station was

from the start intended to be the major traffic junction of New York. The main entrance was in the center of the 7th Avenue façade and opened into a wide shopping mall, from which a monumental staircase led down to the large underground waiting room. Secondary entrances on 31st and 33rd Street took passengers directly onto the train concourse.

The historical and symbolic significance of the old Penn Station survived the destruction of the actual building, and the full force of it reemerges in the redevelopment project drawn up by the SOM Group; inspired by the characteristics of the old building, this sophisticated design aims to use a contemporary architectural language to restore the structure to its public role in the city around it. In the words of Ross Wimer, senior designer with the SOM Group, the reconstruction of Penn Station shows how the studio can overcome budget limits to produce "spectacular" architecture. Backed by an "enlightened client," SOM aspires "to make the new Penn Station the New York equivalent of the Grands Projets undertaken in Paris. The spatial geometry of the shell over the station atrium seems to extend beyond the limits of the Farely Post Office to embrace an entire area of urban space" (Bussel 2000).

The general aims of the project are to create a large public space at street level and also extend the area given over to station facilities. The new structure will be raised within the enormous site of the Farely Post Office immediately to the west of the Station—again between 8th and 9th Avenue and 31st and 33rd Street; built over the underground tracks, the original 1913 post office was by McKim, Mead & White, but in 1935 it was extended to its present 1,400,000 square feet, creating a massive facility that is largely closed to the public (most of it is used as a postal sorting office). As a result of the SOM project, the building will undergo substantial modification in order to house not only the postal facilities but also the extension to the station. The loading and unloading areas will be reorganized; the postal services and facilities modernized; and the areas given over to the railway station (the ticket office, the commuter concourse, the high-speed train concourse and the shopping malls) will be redefined. The basic layout for the redevelopment, therefore, started from the ground plan of the Farely Post Office, which now occupies a site between a previously existing roadway and the postal loading/unloading area (situated between the historic core of the post office to the east and the 1935 extension to the west). The new Penn Station will ultimately stand at the center of the site, leaving the original façade of the post office unaltered. The very symbol of the new building will be a steel-and-glass structure that rises some 80 feet above the springer level of the roof and marks the position of the main entrances and the ground floor ticket office. The extension of the station to occupy some 30 percent of the non-public space of the Farely Post Office also requires some modification of the exteriors: the forty-foot-wide "moats" around the building—originally designed for the ventilation of the platforms and tracks—have been reduced to 30 feet in width, in order to make the building accessible from both 31st and 33rd Street; in the forecourts that open out at the corner of 8th Avenue, secondary entrances have been created, under roofing structures of ultra-light steel and glass (though immediately identifiable, these do not interfere with the imposing form of the stairs up to the post office). Located in the central part of the building, between 31st and 33rd Street, the main entrances have projecting cantilever roofs that provide shelter for waiting passengers and those lined up at the taxi stand. Above the main entrances rises the 150-foot-high shell of steel and glass that identifies the station from a distance. This new structure circumscribes a half-moon-shaped area measuring 350 by 100 feet, which will house the hall/concourse and ticket offices. The actual form of the shell—a rather flattened spherical section—is determined by the need to adapt it to the existing structure. If it were extrapolated and completed, the shell would cover the whole of the Farely Post Office; as it is, the fragmentary segment extends eastwards, visible to the pedestrians in the surrounding streets and providing a point of orientation for those within the station who are making their way to the arrivals-departures area.

Designed to direct passenger flow from the central entrance through the waiting areas to the platforms, the geometrical concourse is contained under "roofing" that comprises two different sections: to the west, the double structure that delimits the area of the ticket office is made up of a reticular girder framework in thick metal; to the east, the glass—mounted on a wind-resistant steel structure of vertical curved tubular components—sweeps down towards the entrance, over which it extends as a protective roofing in the lower, cuneiform, section of the structure. On the western side, the reflecting stratified glass provides protection from direct sunlight, while the glass on the eastern façade is clear. Natural lighting also plays an important part in the area for arrivals and departures: the floor slabs of the base and the first floor of the existing courtyard (originally designed as the area for postal distribution) have been demolished, making the platforms visible and physically accessible. A glass covering, reinforced with tie-rods, strengthens the reticular girder structure of the courtyard.

In the new station, the various concourses—for commuter and high-speed traffic—become areas of conjunction between the ticket office, located in the soaring space of the atrium, and the platforms, located at four different underground levels. Also accessible from 8th Avenue, this occupies a space of 35,000 square feet under massive bare girders which have been stripped of their old decorative masking. The floor space beneath the overhead skylight has been removed to create a wide staircase down to the trains. The eastern wall of this area is given over to monitors providing passengers with timetables, travel updates and entertainment features; beneath that wall, a transparent area reveals the platforms below, which thus receive natural light from outside.

The Pennsylvania Station Redevelopment Corporation have produced a building which is not only large enough to met functional requirements but also reveals careful consideration of the local and overall impact of the new structure—for example, the extension of the public areas and the improvements in road and pedestrian access to the station mean that those buildings that previously languished in the shadow of the Farely Post Office now enjoy enhanced commercial value. Long a junction between national and regional rail traffic and urban transport systems (subway, bus, taxi), the extended station will also provide links to the city's airports, thus becoming a truly "global" hub.

Bibliography

Skidmore, Owings & Merrill. Selected and Current Works, Images Publishing, Mulgrave 1995.

A. Bussel, *SOM Evolutions*, Birkhäuser, Basel 2000.

Skidmore, Owings & Merrill. Architecture and Urbanism, 1995–2000, Images Publishing, Mulgrave 2000.

"Train Station Renovation and Addition. Pennsylvania Station," *Architecture and Urbanism*, 386, November 2002, pp. 122–26.

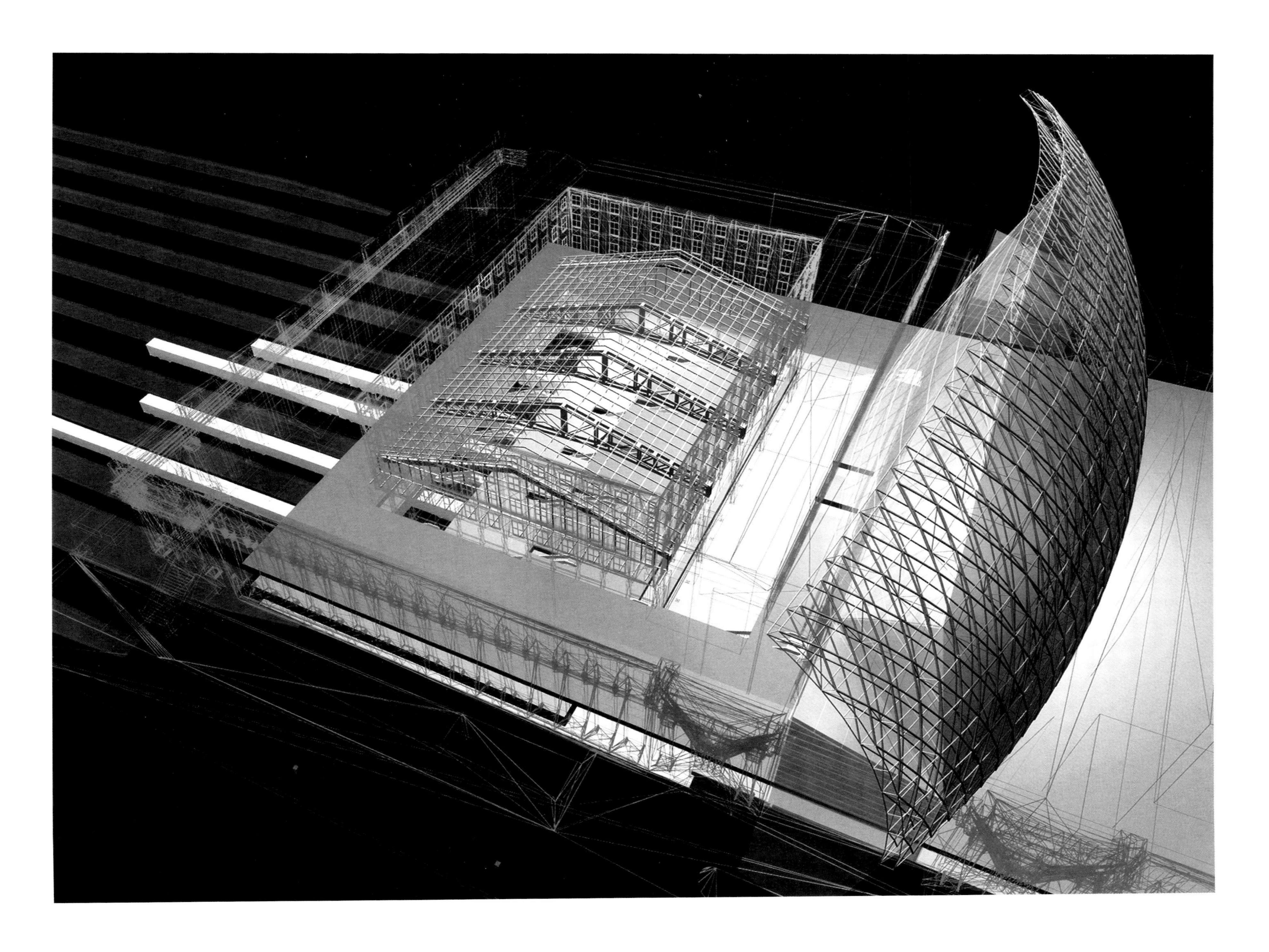

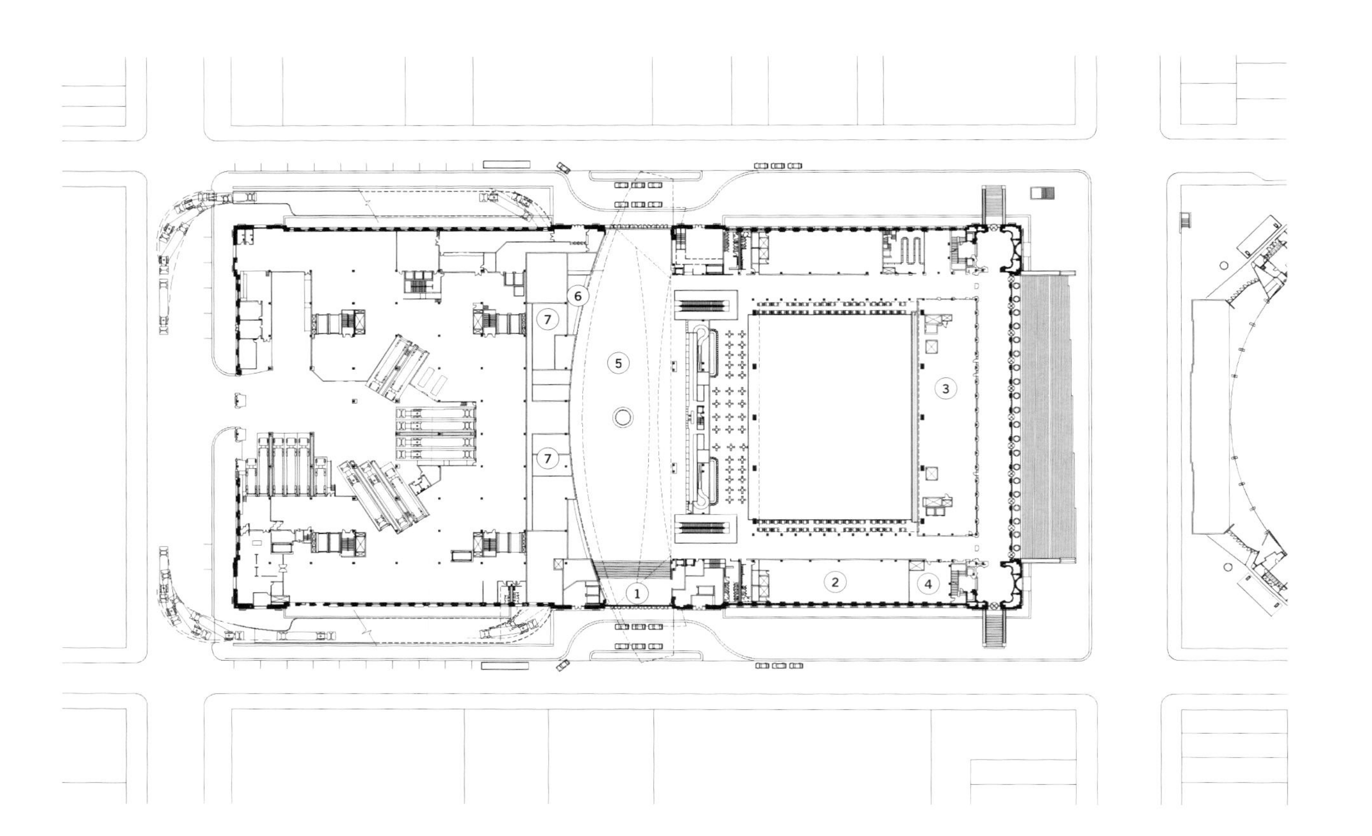

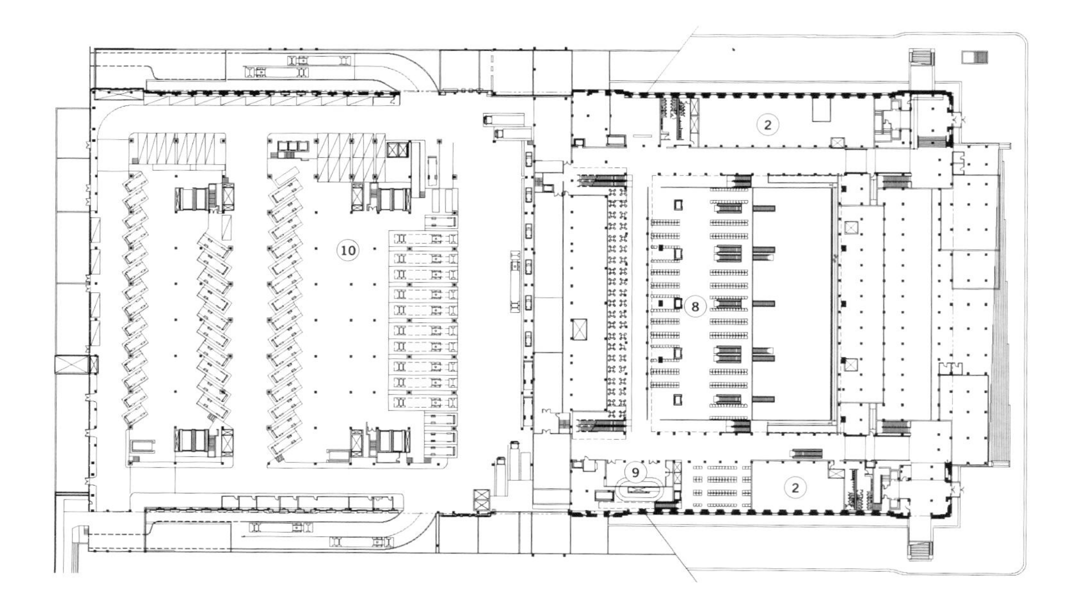

Plan of second and ground floors.
Key: **1** entrance **2** shops **3** post office **4** postal museum **5** concourse **6** airport check-in **7** offices **8** waiting room **9** baggage deposit **10** post-office storeroom.

Previous page
Study rendering.

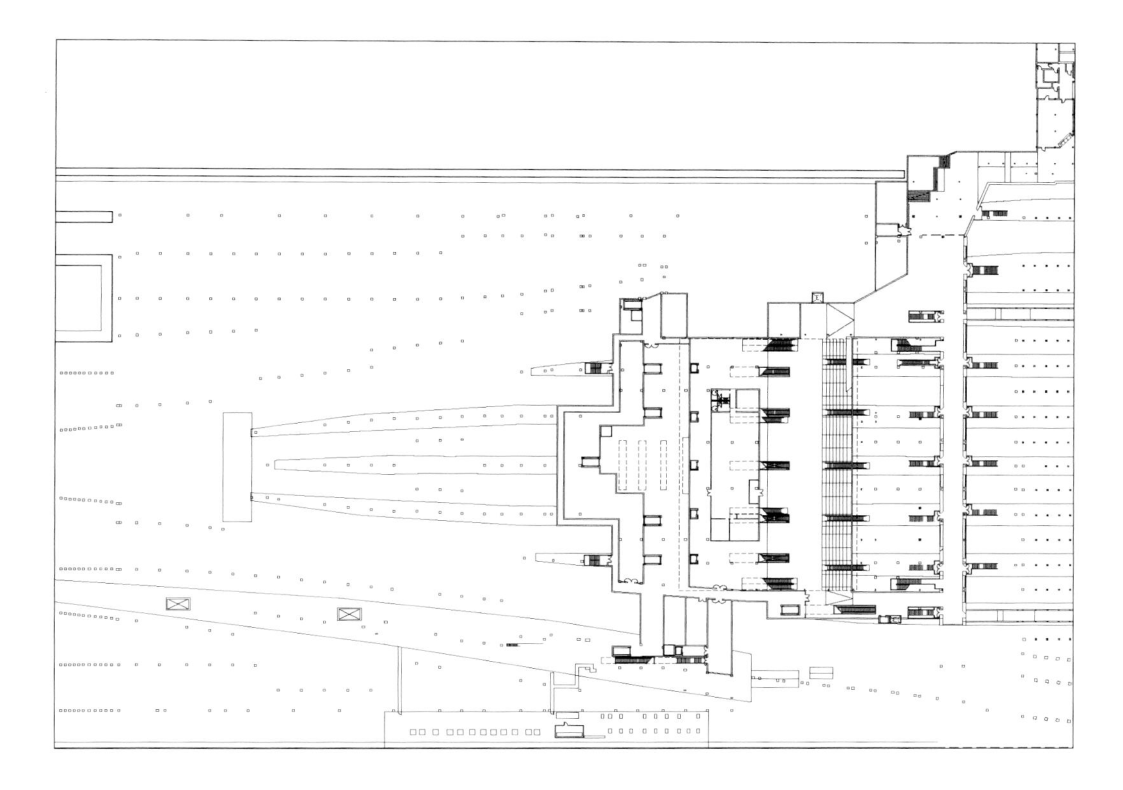

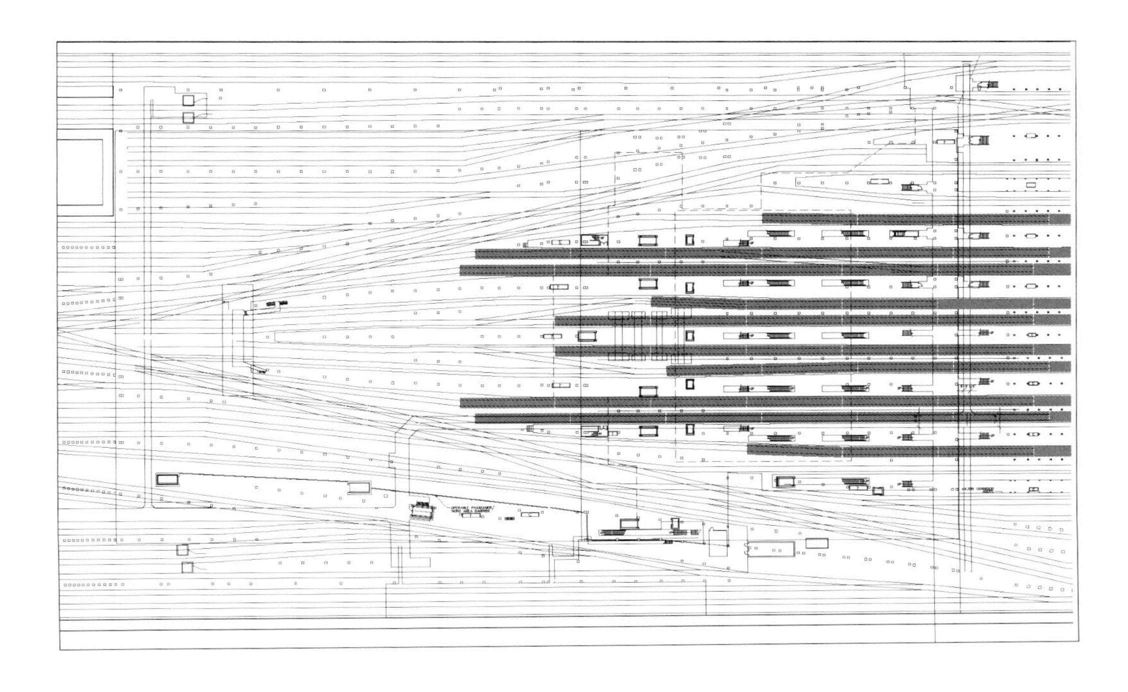

Plans of the underground levels.

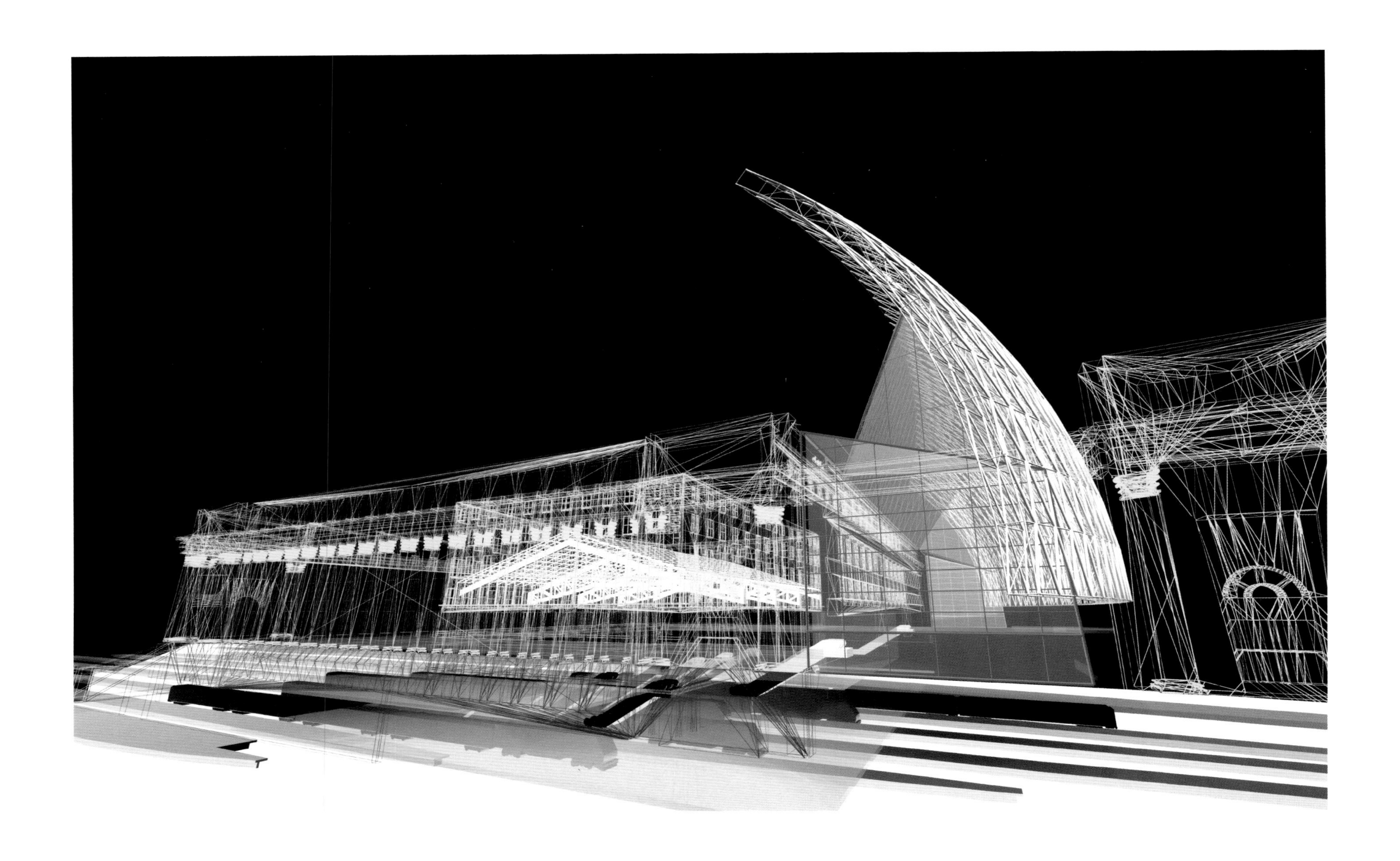

The train room is the first in a series of spaces through which one passes from the main concourse to the platforms. The floor space beneath the overhead skylight has been removed to create a wide staircase down to the trains.

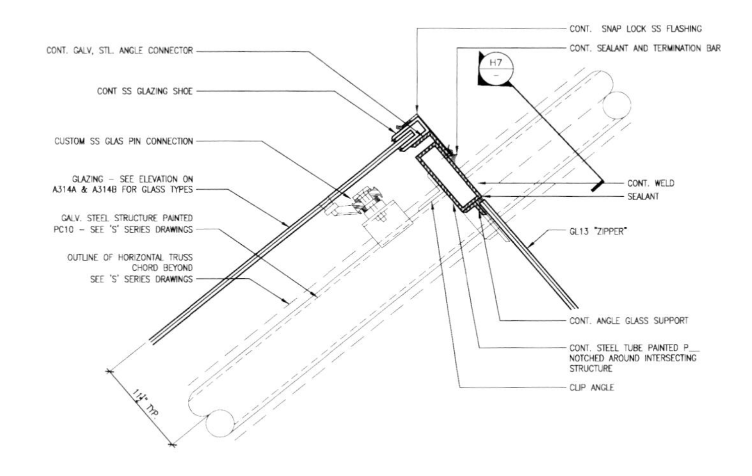

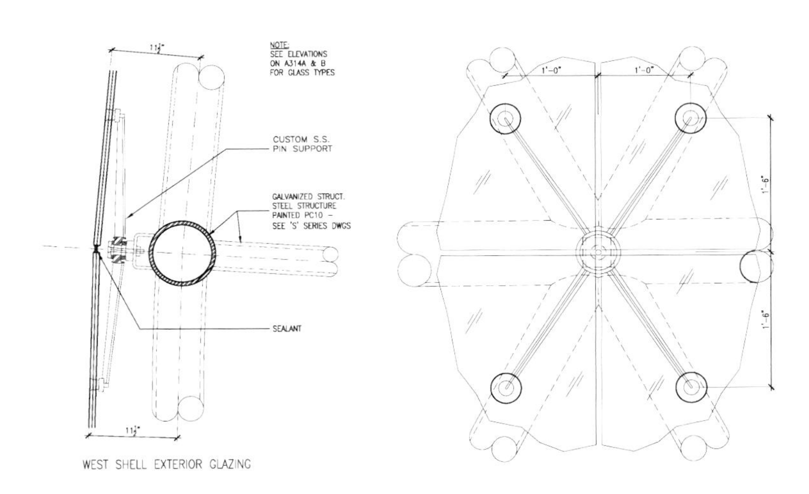

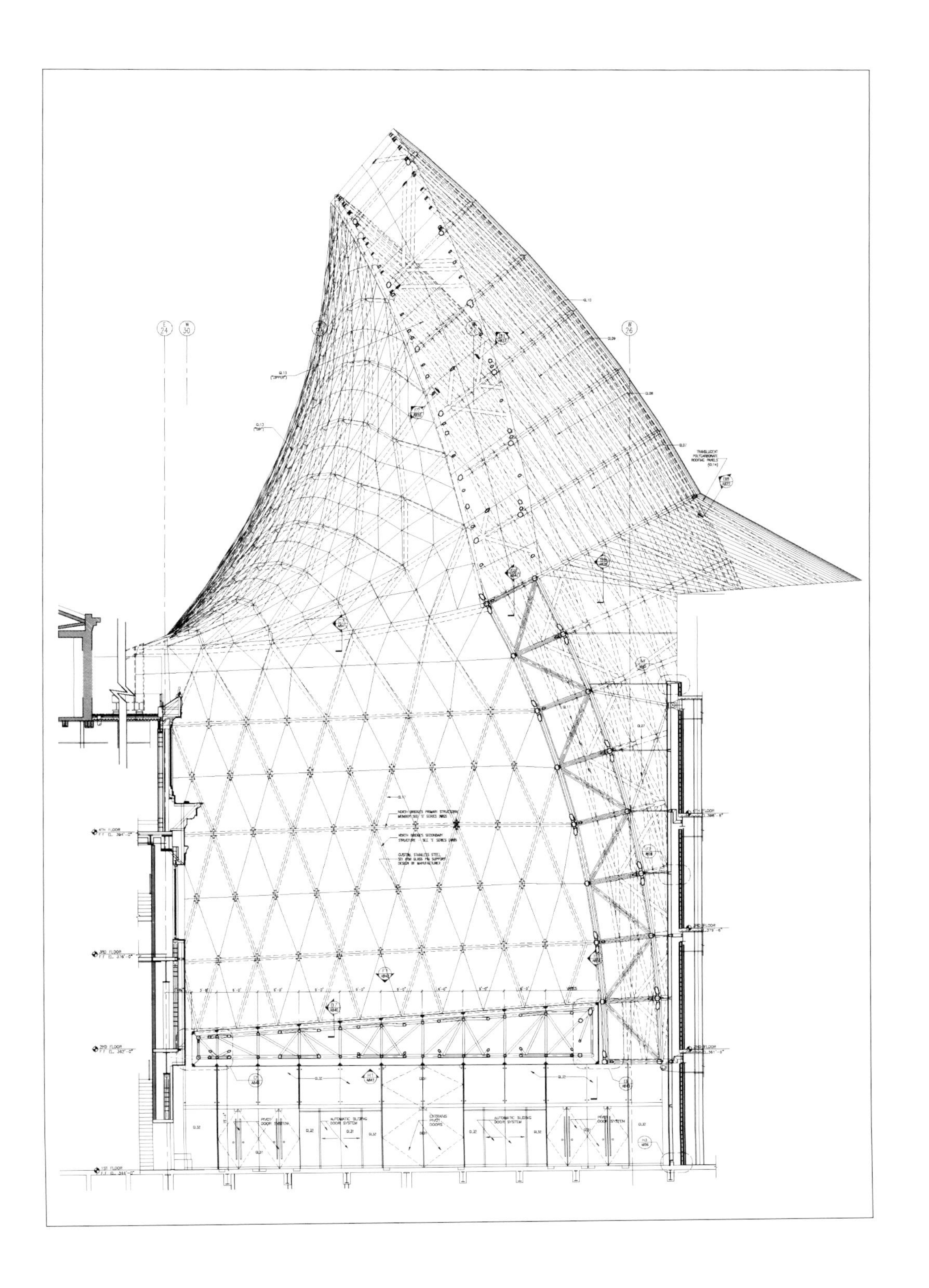

Details of the roofing structure for the concourse.

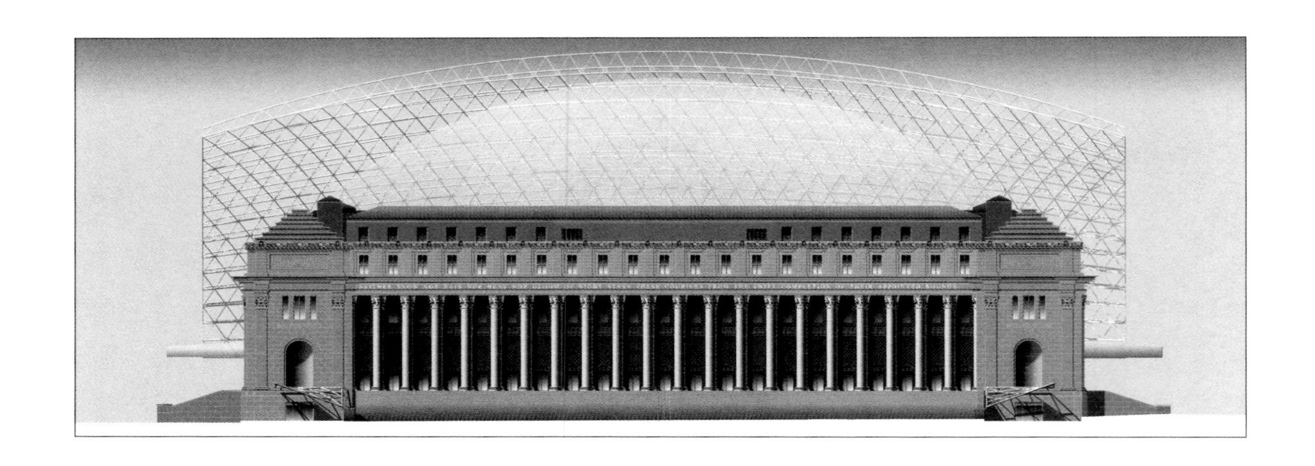

Elevation on 8th Avenue and cross sections.

The main entrances on 31st and 33rd Street are marked by projecting cantilever roofs. A shell in glass and steel rises over the main entrances, making the station visible from a distance.

The concourse is in the form of a half-moon.
Its geometrical layout is designed to direct passenger flow from the entrance
to the waiting areas and the platforms beyond.

The east wall of the train room is given over to monitors providing passengers with
timetables, travel updates, news and entertainment features.
Wide bands of natural light fall onto the platforms areas in the underground levels.

photograph credits

We wish to thank the architectural studios for having provided the photographic material for this volume and authorized its publication, including, among others, those listed below:

Archivio servizio lavori e costruzioni FF.SS., Rome (photo Giuseppe Schiavinotto), pp. 48–53
Artur, Cologne (photo Felix Borkenau), pp. 114 (top), 116 (right), 117
Artur, Cologne (photo Jochen Helle), pp. 128, 140, 141
Artur, Cologne (photo Jörg Hempel), pp. 131, 136–39
Atelier 5, pp. 104, 107, 114 (bottom), 115, 116 (left)
Avery Library, New York, pp. 39, 40 (left)
Bibliothèque Nationale de France, Paris, pp. 22–23
Andrew Bordwin, p. 40 (right)
Chris Caulfield-Dollard, p. 126
Fototeca FF.SS., Rome, pp. 42, 44, 45, 47, 54, 55
Tim Griffith, pp. 172, 179–83
Roland Halbe, p. 188
Andrea Helbling, pp. 142, 145, 149
Susan Kay, pp. 125, 127
Duccio Malagamba, pp. 74, 77, 83-87
FA. Mero, pp. 194, 195 (bottom)
Metro North Railroad, New York, p. 38
New York Public Library, pp. 26, 29-37
Photorail / Diaporama, pp. 16, 18–20, 24, 25
Alessandra Pizzochero, p. 195 (right)
Oltmann Reuter, p. 187
James Rudnick, p. 41
SNCF AP-AREP, pp. 154, 155, 157 (left), 164-167
SNCF AP-AREP (photo D. Boy de la Tour), pp. 153, 156,
SNCF AP-AREP (photo M. Denance), pp. 150, 157 (right), 158
SNCF AP-AREP (photo S. Lucas), pp. 160, 163, 168-171
SNCF AP-AREP (photo C. Michel), p. 159
Christian Richters, pp. 204, 205
Timothy Soar, p. 121
Morley von Sternberg, p. 118

contents